Red, White, and True

D0651113

# Red, White, and True

Stories from
Veterans
and Families,
World War II
to Present

*Edited and with an
introduction by*
TRACY CROW

Potomac Books
*An imprint of the
University of Nebraska Press*

© 2014 by the Board of Regents of the University of Nebraska

Acknowledgments for the use of copyrighted material appear on page 275, which constitutes an extension of the copyright page.

All rights reserved. Potomac Books is an imprint of the University of Nebraska Press.
Manufactured in the United States of America.

♾

Library of Congress Cataloging-in-Publication Data
Red, white, and true: stories from veterans and families, World War II to present / edited and with an introduction by Tracy Crow.
pages   cm
ISBN 978-1-61234-701-1 (pbk.: alk. paper)
ISBN 978-1-61234-707-3 (pdf).
1. Veterans—United States—Anecdotes. 2. Veterans—United States—Family relationships. 3. Veterans' families—United States—Anecdotes. 4. Soldiers—United States—Anecdotes. 5. United States—Armed Forces—Military life—Anecdotes. 6. United States—Military history—Anecdotes. I. Crow, Tracy, editor of compilation. II. Title: Stories from veterans and families, World War II to present.
UB357.R42 2014
305.9'06970973—dc23
2014007438

Set in Minion Pro by L. Auten.

In memory of you who have gone before us.
You will not be forgotten.

The world breaks every one and afterward many are strong at the broken places.

—ERNEST HEMINGWAY, *A Farewell to Arms*

# Contents

# Acknowledgments

Truth is, the idea for this anthology was not even a thought creeping in and out of consciousness until my dear friend Jeffery Hess, who is himself the editor of two military fiction anthologies—*Home of the Brave: Stories in Uniform* (2009) and *Home of the Brave: Somewhere in the Sand* (2013)—and now a contributor here, suggested nearly two years ago that I compile an anthology of *nonfiction*.

Jeff warned against all the hard work, namely, the difficult selection process that befalls an editor when too much good work continues to find its way into your in-box, even long after your deadline. And he was right. He was also right about the rewards. I have never enjoyed a writing project more, for I believe I can speak for all of us when I state that *Red, White, and True* has become a labor of love. Thank you, Jeff, for your unwavering encouragement and support of this project and of everything I do with my writing life.

After my conversation with Jeff, I contacted the one person with whom I most wanted and needed at the helm: Bridget Barry, my editor at the University of Nebraska Press. Bridget immediately responded with Jeff's level of enthusiasm, and within twenty-four hours of that discussion with Jeff, the first call for submissions was relayed to the world.

I would like to thank the Military Writers Society of America for helping with calls for submissions. Thanks, too, to MFA writing faculty around the country and to those folks closely associated with the Veterans Administration (VA) for encouraging veterans to submit their stories and for everything you are doing in your writing programs for veterans and their families.

For their personal recommendations of talented writers whose voices had not yet been discovered, a special thanks to Dinty W. Moore, Michael Steinberg, Ron Capps, and Jessica Handler.

I am enormously appreciative to everyone who contributed to this book. Thank you for trusting me with such intimate material. Thanks, especially, for your service to our country. Reading your work—whether your work appears between these two covers or not—profoundly affected me and helped to guide and shape the overall tone. And to the thirty-two contributors within, I owe a debt of gratitude that I will never be able to adequately repay.

Many thanks to Sabrina Ehmke Sergeant, Annette Wenda, and the entire University of Nebraska Press and Potomac Books team. Thanks to my former colleagues and students at the University of Tampa who continue to support my writing projects. A special thanks to my incredibly loyal Queens University of Charlotte MFA and Eckerd College families for their emotional support of this project and, frankly, of everything I do; I could not want for a more supportive community.

And to my dear friends, family, and adoring husband, Mark, who offered all sorts of gifts related to the needs of an editor on deadline, thank you—*thank you* for loving me that much.

# Editor's Introduction

I was in my forties and a returning college student when a professor asked why I was not writing about my ten years in the Marine Corps for her memoir class. Because I did not think anyone would care, I said. What she did not know is that for years, I had worked hard to repress most memories, and for good reason. I found it too painful to look back at what many would consider a failed military career, despite the ribbons and medals and writing awards I had accumulated in the 1980s.

But that evening after the night class, and while standing in the middle of a brightly lit parking lot, my professor issued what I took as an order. So I went to work, nervously, I might add. A week later I returned with a story about my first experience on a rifle range during which I had mostly hit everyone else's targets before finally learning to hit my own. However, the heart of the story, according to my professor and fellow students, was really about my struggle to balance a meaningful military career with marriage and motherhood. They urged me, *pushed* me, really, down the rabbit hole toward a deeper exploration of self and motive, which is exactly what I had been avoiding for years, yet exactly what I had to reveal, if I ever hoped my writing would connect with readers. In other words, what they truly wanted to read is what writer William Faulkner referred to as storytelling that reveals "the human heart in conflict with itself."

What I have learned in the years since is that everyone has a story. Everyone has a heart that at some point has wrestled with conflict. Everyone, if they live long enough, experiences loss and grief, possibly shame and humiliation, and hopefully love if they are fortunate and open enough to it. As the Hank Williams song goes, we'll "never get out of this world alive."

Maybe not, but we can certainly help one another along the way by sharing our personal survival stories. As memoirist Patricia Hampl states, "You give me your story, I get mine" (quoted in Robert L. Root's *The Nonfictionist's Guide on Reading and Writing Creative Nonfiction*). Maybe this explains why we are so drawn to true-life stories, or at least to the good parts where the human heart is in conflict with itself, for in doing so, writer and reader are making a most profoundly human connection with one another.

In your hands, unless you are reading this online, are thirty-two profoundly *true* stories that collectively represent an accurate portrayal of the American military story from World War II to Iraq and Afghanistan. I know of nothing else like this: thirty-two writers—veterans, military spouses, and now grown children of veterans—all sharing how their lives have been affected by military service.

I should warn you that this is not a warmongering, flag-waving, mission-accomplished collection. Nor is it a flag-burning protest collection; in fact, far from it. I received those types of submissions, sure, and I am grateful for the trust those writers placed within me for reading such intimate information, but in the end I selected stories that went *much* deeper on an emotional level. In other words, the events of some stories may be more shocking, but without the depth of emotional truth, they read as too hollow, too anecdotal.

Within this collection, however, I am sure you will gain a sense that every writer here is proud to have served our country, whether military service was rendered directly or indirectly. And every story here is *true*, as true as memory will allow. In "Memory and Imagination," also by Hampl, she writes, "The materials of memoir are humble, fugitive, a cottage knitting industry seeking narrative *truth* across the crevasse of time as autobiography folds itself into the vast, fluid story that is history" (from Robert Root and Michael Steinberg's *The Fourth Genre*; emphasis added).

Truth and history: you will find plenty of both in this collection. But you will also find a sense of yearning for a deeper truth, for a clearer understanding of that human heart in conflict with itself, for in the making, the stories in this collection unfolded, one by one, from tightfisted versions of themselves into no-holds-barred truth-bearing accounts of military life.

What I believe makes this collection unique are its truth-seeking searches that span generations of military service. As you will soon discover from a number of these stories, we are just beginning to understand and comprehend how children and grandchildren of veterans have been affected by military life—by military customs and traditions, the long absences, the tragic combat deaths, and a survivor's guilt. And sadly, because of a death rate of more than six hundred per day, we are losing stories from our World War II veterans—many of whom have yet to share their experiences.

One such cross-generational story in this collection comes from Leila Levinson in her essay "Prisoners of War." Levinson is the daughter of an Army doctor who served during World War II and helped to liberate one of the most horrific concentration camps. Follow Levinson's search for the truth as it takes her from research libraries into the living rooms of Holocaust and World War II survivors. What she discovers from their accounts helps her understand how her father's World War II war trauma drove her mother into madness—the sort of madness that led to institutionalizing in those days.

Christal Presley embarks on another cross-generational exploration—this time an actual thirty-day experiment in "The Thirty-Day Project," an excerpt from her book-length memoir with the same title, in an attempt to better understand her father's Vietnam War experiences that traumatized her childhood.

Other writers—Leah Hampton, Ronald Jackson, Beverly A. Jackson, Lorrie Lykins, Amber Jensen, and Carol Everett Adams—also examine the cross-generational impact of military service.

But there is also the depiction of the lighthearted side of life in the military. The silliness that sustains a combat unit and a ship of sailors too long at sea is depicted in such stories as Jeffery Hess's "Hulls in the Water" and Kim Wright's "How the Military Turned My Father a Genius."

So where to start? From page 1, right? Actually, there is no right or wrong way to read this collection. Start anywhere. Open somewhere in the middle and start with Brooke King's gripping portrayal of her Iraq experiences and struggles with post-traumatic stress disorder (PTSD) in "Breathe through Your Mouth," or at the beginning, with Matt Farwell's "Welcome to Afghanistan," and read chronologically, although the stories do not reflect a chronology of time. Rightly or wrongly, I have intermingled World War II experiences with those of the Cold War and Vietnam. You will find a Korea experience near stories depicting life during the Cold War and combat action in Iraq. And I have purposely intermingled the grittiest of true war stories with stories from loved ones—the dependents—back home. Rebecca McClanahan's story, "Dependent," is an excellent portrayal of life as a military dependent. In Lorrie Lykins's "Panel 30w, Row 15," she writes about innocence lost when her father, an Army officer and pilot, loses his best friend in Vietnam, and Lykins, just a child, realizes for the first time that her father, too, could be killed.

Pulitzer Prize–winning author Tracy Kidder provides us an unsettling glimpse into the world of a new second lieutenant during Vietnam in his story, "War Stories." Jon Kerstetter, in "Triage," reveals the controversial life-and-death decision-making process related to medical treatment on the battlefield in Iraq and beyond.

This collection also includes stories about Air Force pilots, those who crashed and died and those who survived; about Coast Guardsmen at sea; about sailors and Marines itching to put to use their training skills during the Cold War; and about Iraq and Afghanistan veterans—men and women—seeking help for post-traumatic stress disorder, being turned away or walking away from help, and learning to battle PTSD on their own. Military moms share their concerns about raising the next generation. In "Pictures Don't Lie," Cheryl Lapp struggles to hold it together emotionally during a lingerie photo shoot with a group of military wives, an event that was meant to be fun and to boost morale for their men in the desert, but was not so for Lapp.

What you will not find here, however, is a writer who offers up a whining apologia, for these are incredibly strong men and women who have weathered, in some cases, decades of trauma. So who are these contributors besides former veterans and military dependents? Several of them are college writing faculty and students in creative writing programs; some are writing-contest winners and published authors. A few here are even first-time writers, and they tell me that this writing experience helped to exorcise a few demons, to which I am enormously relieved.

No lie, I worried about some of my contributors, because, as Hampl also writes, "to write one's life is to live it twice." I know something firsthand about this. That story I wrote about the rifle range eventually morphed into a book-length memoir, *Eyes Right: Confession from a Woman Marine*, published by this very press in 2012, but the process of revisiting my past over and over again was nearly too painful.

So I was especially worried that I was triggering flashbacks by forcing my writers to go deeper in their work, toward that heart of the story—the one with the human heart in conflict with itself. We talked, we cried, and we e-mailed our way through draft after draft. At times I worried that I was pushing my writers to crawl back into holes too deep to crawl out of for the sake of meaningful storytelling.

In the end every writer persevered, and this collection of thirty-two unforgettable true stories is better for it.

Red, White, and True

# Welcome to Afghanistan

MATT FARWELL

It's three in the morning, and I am falling hard into a five-foot ditch. Like a cartoon character, legs splaying out in front of me, I land square on my back. The wind is knocked out of my chest. Luckily, the body armor and my helmet absorb most of the impact, and before the last profanity can even leave my mouth, the machine gunner walking fifteen meters next to me is there, pulling me up. Under the weight of sixty-five pounds of weapons, ammunition, body armor, and gear, I stumble to my feet and continue walking toward the mountain that we have to climb. We are looking for Taliban activity. It's not even light out yet, and I'm sweating my ass off, dirty and tired, hands and legs filled with tiny thorns. This day already sucks. Welcome to Afghanistan. As Drill Sergeant Berg would say, during rainy nights at Fort Benning, "Welcome to the motherfuckin' infantry."

Before I was climbing mountains in full battle rattle and falling in ditches, I shared a dive apartment with a capricious college roommate. Dwayne was touched, slightly. He liked to break plates and scream randomly at passersby from our second-story window. The apartment, in a rapidly gentrifying locale but still clinging to its shady, ghetto roots, was littered with the detritus of two overeducated children of privilege: books and papers stacked on every flat surface not already occupied with beer bottles, a sink overflowing with dishes, polo shirts and khakis strewn on the floor. Life was fun but filled with a certain amount of melancholy, the material maelstrom inside the apartment acting as a window into my conflicted brain. I'd never been particularly happy in college, and by the middle of my third year, things were beginning to reach a boiling point. The apartment and what went on there were just the physical manifestations of that slow boil.

My living conditions are a little different now. Instead of an apartment shared with just one whacked-out roommate, I now have nine crazy infantrymen all crammed into one room. It is thirty feet by fourteen, with dusty concrete floors and furniture roughly constructed out of unfinished plywood and two-by-fours. Spread about the room are the debris of nine men in constant flux and their cold-weather boots, dirty socks, a rolled-up carpet, half-drunk bottles of water, and partially eaten bags of beef jerky and ramen noodles on the shelves and scattered around the floors. Except for the four sets of body armor, helmets, and front-load equipment carriers containing 210 rounds of 5.56mm ball ammunition, Israeli tourniquets, canteens, and night-vision goggles hung neatly from each bunk, and the assortment of M4 carbines, squad automatic weapons, grenade launchers, and shotguns around each bed, it might look familiar to my friends in college who live in similar dumps.

"Dude," Clit says one night on guard duty, "I think I want to get a tattoo on my head when I go back to the States on leave . . . Think I'd get in trouble for that? I want, like, a big fucking dagger right on the top or maybe some bullet holes or maybe just cracks, you know, like my head is cracked."

Clit and I are sitting in the guard tower, staring emptily at the night below, panning the horizon for any movement. Clit speaks each sentence like it bears the utmost importance, but at least his sentences are always interesting.

"I always had a .38 and a TEK on me," he says. "The TEK fit perfectly under the seat. I wore gloves everywhere I went. We did a lot of illegal stuff. We used to go out on overpasses with bags of shit and piss and vinegar—like that's no joke, shit and piss and vinegar—and drop it on shit." He throws his cigarette butt over the sandbag barrier on the guard tower and stands up to stretch. He's one of the best guys in the platoon, a natural soldier and leader, smart and resourceful. He's got some great stories from before he joined the Army.

While I was growing up, my dad was in the Air Force, and when I lived in Turkey and Germany, practically all my friends were military brats. My brother served as a grunt in Ranger Battalion and the 25th Infantry Division before he became an Army helicopter pilot. As a kid, the thought of being in the Army had always been in the back of my mind. When it was time to start looking at colleges, I again thought about the military, applying for ROTC scholarships to cover the cost of Duke or Yale, and considered going to West Point. To figure out if I really wanted to become a cadet, I attended a weeklong recruiting session at the U.S. Military Academy; put the most delicate way possible, it sucked. The potential cadets seemed stiff, wooden, and out of touch. The actual cadets were either bitter because they were stuck at the academy on their summer break or too uptight to hang out with. The only one who seemed to have any sort of sense about him was a prior service infantryman who spoke with a thick West Virginia accent around the thick wad of Copenhagen that was perpetually shoved into his lower lip. Most of my days there were spent with a New Hampshire skater whose mom had tricked him into attending. He bugged the hell out of the straitlaced applicants and cadets by claiming to be a socialist or refusing to get out of bed in the morning because we were "An Army of one. A tired Army of one."

West Point was out.

Then I was rejected by my top two college choices. Not getting into Yale was crushing because my girlfriend at the time was a freshman there, and I had visions of happily ever after with an Ivy League degree. Not getting into Deep Springs, a bizarre all-male cattle ranch/college hidden in the middle of the California desert and populated by twenty brilliant misfits, was somewhat less of a disappointment, simply because it seemed so far out. So I went to UVA, or "The University," because it had accepted me into its honors program and I had in-state tuition. I decided on college because I was scared not to, because it seemed like the only thing for a smart kid graduating from an exclusive private boarding school to do. I really had no idea what I'd do once I got there.

Days here in Afghanistan, whatever they *are*, are not filled with the same sort of uncertainty that occupied my college era. Between the normal humdrum of trying to survive in the desert heat with the flies and bad food, there's the lingering knowledge that at any second, one of my sergeants could come into the room and tell us to get our gear the fuck on; we've got to go. Our best time is three minutes. We throw on our body armor—load-carrying vest and helmet—grab our weapons, and run out the door to our up-armored Humvees for response to whatever crisis might erupt.

· · ·

Eleven at night, UVA's Alderman Library stacks. I had twenty pages waiting to be filled with fleshed-out material from the couple of hundred note cards filled with citations, quotes, facts, and figures sitting next to the computer. The cards sat there mockingly, a cluster of white paper bones waiting to be animated into a body. An absurd amount of preparation had gone into that paper—hours and hours in the library, on the phone, cruising databases, on the phone with sources, chewing through dusty old archives. All that work, all that preparation, for nothing. Twenty blank pages, all waiting to be filled, all inconsequential pages. In the background, a pot of coffee was brewing. I'd just cracked a pack of cigarettes, and the facts were still there, waiting to be arranged. Yet I couldn't stop thinking: *Why even bother?* All this preparation for something that will be read halfheartedly by a TA and then thrown away. Another meaningless cluster of words carefully arranged and quickly forgotten. This paper seemed to represent nothing more than a microcosm of the whole college career—a bunch of seemingly pointless preparations from grade school on up for a piece of parchment that signifies nothing except that you can read, write, and show up to class on time. I was getting frustrated. More than a pot of coffee was brewing.

"Get your shit on and go to the trucks. Scouts got hit with an IED." The three guys from my platoon with whom I've been eating and I just look at each other for a second. Then we scramble, leaving behind our trays and running for the door. We run back to our barracks, half throw on our gear, and sprint to the truck while still buckling and fastening our straps.

"Radios on?" I ask, sliding into the back passenger seat, banging my M4 carbine and M203 grenade launcher against the seat's well.

"Yeah, they're good," says our driver, Bautista, as we pull out, while Burke is hopping into the turret behind the .50-caliber machine gun.

"How's the FBCB2? Is it showing the screen?" I look up toward the computer monitor next to our lieutenant's seat. The glowing screen flickers to life and shows our map location as we move.

"Yeah, it's coming on."

"Fuck, man."

"Yeah. Fuck."

. . .

The UVA scene was set. Seemed like every Tuesday night on top of the dilapidated frat house, James, Jon, me, and a case of Miller Lite. James and Jon were both products of an exclusive Manhattan Jesuit high school, overeducated and neurotic. They were half-discussing, half-debating Nietzsche and Heidegger like they did every time we got together. I sat outside the conversation, gulping at my beer, looking at the stars, contributing a comment here and there. I'd read those books, thought about them, written papers taking this position or that, but frankly, dead old German men ranting about the "thing unto itself" and the "Übermensch" wasn't interesting, not tangible at all.

As we got progressively drunker, the talk of Continental philosophy drifted a bit. Jon started playing his guitar; James began ranting about his father, his girlfriend—the normal bitching. Beer cans accumulated around our feet and were crushed. I was tired; I stumbled down the stairs and began the long walk back to my apartment.

"Who's going to get Rashid?" We pull up in front of the Tactical Operation Center, and Burke climbs out of the turret, jumping awkwardly off the hood while we are still moving and then stumbling toward our interpreter's room. Rashid, a twenty-three-year-old Afghani who picked up English while a refugee in Peshawar, comes running out toward our truck. We pass him his body armor and Soviet-made pistol and then wait to roll out of the gate. My hands are shaking slightly as I put on my gloves.

"Who's got batteries?" Burke asks. The sun will be going down in a couple of hours, and scouts are about that far from our location, so anything we do in the next twelve hours will have to be through the greenish glow of our night-vision goggles.

"I've got four," I tell him, "plus two in my camera if we're desperate."

Sara, the beautiful, smart, vivacious Cuban American senior I had a crush on for the better part of junior year, sat in her dorm room on the lawn designed by Thomas Jefferson. Half drunk, I slipped a note through her mail slot. It was a note a week in the making, revised over and over, a perfect profession of love and devotion. I received her reply two days later, two pages of beautiful red lettering. Each perfectly formed consonant and vowel was a knife to the heart; each overly precise sentence ripped chunks out of my ego. It was hard to look at the whole letter, so I read it in disjointed pieces, trying to amuse myself by putting the puzzle together. I already knew what it said in so many words.

I called James on his cell phone and told him, wirelessly tethering my burden to him.

"Fuckin' sucks, dude. She's a fuckin' bitch. Forget it. Me and Jon are smoking opium. Come over, it's pretty badass; feels like you're a couple of joints and a few Vicodin deep."

I hung up, drove back to my apartment, and demolished half a case of Heineken while watching overdue videos. My pillow was wet when I woke up.

Early December. I'd been cramming my brain for this exam—up all night, wired on Red Bull and nicotine, shoving public policy readings long neglected into my short-term memory. The exam was on the desk in front of me, a neatly typed-up sheet beside an open blue book. The first question was easy. But my mind was blank. I looked at the question, my mind still empty. I stared. For an hour I stared like that, while pens scratched on paper all around me. I got up, turned in the empty blue book, and walked straight to my dean's office.

"Sir, I fucked up my exam. I'm not sure I can do this anymore."

Within the day, the paperwork was filed, stamped, and put away. Officially, I'd withdrawn for the semester and taken a leave of absence from the university. The hardest part was telling my parents. I was now a college dropout.

"Dammit, I didn't grab any snivel gear." In my rush to get to the trucks, I hadn't grabbed any raincoats or fleece, nothing to keep me warm during the cold Afghani night. We sit up at the Tactical Operations Center awaiting permission from the battalion commander to enter the fray. We wait for ten minutes, which seems like an eternity, then twenty, and then an hour. We never actually get permission to go tonight, and when we return to our rooms, shedding our dusty gear, the adrenaline seeps from our bodies.

Still in Virginia, but no longer in school, I had taken a job at Lowe's, plotting my next move while hawking faucets and showerheads. Naturally, that got old fast, but I really wasn't planning on going back to college for a while. The Army had always held a certain romantic appeal, even if I had decided West Point wasn't for me. My job at Lowe's was going nowhere, college was boring, so shit . . . why not?

So one day after work, I walked into an Army recruiter's office and signed up for three years as an infantryman. The decision seemed logical—I'd get an adventure, get out of my head, and get away from, at least for a little while, my privileged white-boy roots for a life in which I was no more special than the next guy with an identical haircut and identical camouflage clothing.

I couldn't see anything else in the Army I wanted to do but pull a trigger, couldn't see myself repairing helicopters or decoding messages or anything like that. I just had the itch to carry everything on my back, strap a weapon to my front, and train to "close with and destroy the enemy."

Maybe that enemy was myself.

# 2

# Above and Beyond

LEAH HAMPTON

What did I know, what did I know
of love's austere and lonely offices?

—ROBERT HAYDEN

When I was a little girl, I used to have out-of-body experiences in military hospitals. Didn't matter where—base medical center, a VA, the gloomy purgatory of a pharmacy waiting room. In any frightening or ominous situation, the sensation that I was a swelling balloon would overwhelm me. During those interminable, agonizing hours of staring at broken people and waiting for my own or my father's meds, I would float up, out of my little body, above the uniforms and dependents below me. Rather than see what was happening around me, I stared intently at cracked ceiling tiles and glided through bleached hallways. My memories of these flights and floats remain clear and vivid thirty years on—unlike most of my childhood. I can tell you more about the tops of door frames and emergency sprinkler spigots than I can about my own family. Military children regularly divert their gazes. To understand—or survive—we have to look away.

I come from a family of lost men. I have great-grandfathers who joined in the Great War. My mother's father slogged through most of World War II as an adjutant while she and her siblings endured the incessant rationing and blitzing of London. My father went to Vietnam, among other places.

None of the men in my family died in a war. None of them were officers, few received medals, and only one great-uncle ever saw real combat. After they came home, my relatives disappeared. They weren't the only ones. Many veterans disappear into boring, middle-income jobs that never quite turn into careers. Some disappear into books or drop out of the system entirely, drifting, living on the streets, or going "off-grid" and starting organic farms. Others disappear into their garages, taking up hobbies and distractions that settle their minds, ordering the world through weekend carpentry or, in the case of an old friend's father, gingerbread houses. (All year, he makes scores and scores of gingerbread houses. It's the damnedest thing.) My dad liked cars, so he disappeared into an engine, barking orders at us when he was thirsty or needed a socket wrench.

My dad joined the Navy when he was sixteen with no high school diploma and no interest in sticking around dirt-poor Kentucky. When he was issued his uniform in boot camp, it was the first time in his life he'd ever owned two pairs of shoes. My father is a tall, broad man with a slightly red face, a face like his mother's that reveals Choctaw heritage in its jawline and stern, thin-lipped quietness. In the '60s when he was on leave in the Mediterranean, he would, on a lark and because he'd paid attention in geography class, convince people he was an Indian by reciting rivers with Native American names. Frenchmen thought he was speaking Cherokee. They bought him drinks.

My father also has the dazzling green, mischievous eyes of the Irish horse thieves who were his grandfathers. Mischief and rage, he got from them. I spent my childhood trying to avoid both.

The Navy put him on an aircraft carrier. My father claims that on his first day at sea, the first mate of the uss *Whatever* met him aboard a smaller craft that brought the new recruits in. They all gaped in backwoods awe at the size of the ship that would be their home. The first mate went down the line and asked if there was anyone who couldn't swim. My dad, who had never seen the ocean until a few days prior, stepped forward, thinking he'd be assigned a cleaning detail, something belowdecks. Fine with him. Two sailors promptly threw him overboard. Everyone on both ships watched and laughed from above while my father and a handful of other booters thrashed about, swallowing seawater, terrified and embarrassed, trying desperately to keep from sinking. Someone threw him a life preserver and called him a fucking pussy. A few weeks later he was in the Bay of Pigs. During that failed 1961 invasion of Cuba, CIA agents spooked around my father's ship and several attack carriers nearby. My father spent his seventeenth birthday on watch during the height of the invasion, waiting for the end of the world. That night on deck, he literally pissed himself with fear.

Later, the Navy taught him how to build airplanes.

Were it not for his headaches and his hatred of the cloying scent of jet fuel, I don't think there's a plane in the world my dad couldn't walk up to even today, take apart, and put back together. The Navy sent him and his remarkable mechanical mind all over the world, made him a good and proper Airedale. But first they sent him back to Cuba for the Soviet missile crisis in 1962. There are stories. I wouldn't blame him if he pissed himself again; I get scared just reading about those days.

Sometime after that, my dad got lucky and found himself on a cruiser in the Mediterranean. Nice weather, pretty French girls, decent work. And one particularly pretty English girl, whom he married as quickly as he could. He had a few good years, thanks to her. Unsure what to do next and more relaxed about the possibilities the military had to offer him, he reenlisted in the Air Force in 1968. The Air Force was classy. The recruiter, typical of those who finagled young men into the service in those days, promised to make him a radar man, promised him good pay, an easy ride far away from the horrors in the South China Sea. He signed up, and the Air Force immediately sent him to Phan Rang.

My father was not prepared for 1968 Vietnam. No one was, but an already nervous aircraft mechanic accustomed to the lights of Monaco was considerably less prepared than most for the height of that conflict. At Phan Rang, he was exposed to Agent Orange repeatedly and still receives special benefits because of it. Perhaps he had PTSD, too; his symptoms were textbook. But how could anyone tell? First, we would have to know what he saw and felt, which we don't. The term *post-traumatic stress disorder* wasn't even coined until the 1980s, and the volumes of literature on military PTSD deal almost exclusively with combat vets. Noncombat trauma has only just begun to be studied; it has taken the armed forces until the twenty-first century to acknowledge that assaults, accidents, and other atrocities can have the same, or worse, effects on its men and women as combat can. It's now called *post-deployment stress* or even *invisible wounds*. The definition of the invisible has been expanded to include rape, natural disaster, and injuries outside of a war zone, as well as the ancillary impacts on those who must live with the wounded.

But that's now. Back then (and still), no one was paying much attention unless you'd been out in the bush in Vietnam, patrolling the booby-trapped jungle. I know my father hated Southeast Asia and despised his government for going there. I know he got shot at on at least a few occasions. But that's all anyone knows. No one asked him. He was just a mechanic.

For the rest of his life, when his headaches were bad, my dad couldn't move or speak for hours on end. Most of the time all he had was Motrin—a Navy man's best friend, but little help when there's a spike behind your eyes. When angered my dad could put a fist through a wall and later deny he'd done it with wide-eyed innocence, even when confronted with the evidence.

Throughout my childhood he was jumpy, fearful of dark corners, planned persistently and obsessively for even the tiniest events in his life. Before she died, his mother, a jolly, wisecracking hillbilly from the Cumberland Gap, used to wonder aloud what the military had done to her sweet little boy to make him turn out that way.

Trying to separate the effects of Agent Orange, PTSD, or other standard unspeakables from the effects of *simply being in Vietnam* has always seemed pointless to me. Of course you would have night terrors. Of course you would lash out at people, even loved ones, for no reason. Of course you would get headaches and want to die. It doesn't matter what they sprayed you with or made you see, or didn't let you see, or gave or didn't give.

My dad was not a grunt or a GI. For at least part of his time at Phan Rang, my mother says, he was search and rescue. Once, only once, he described his duties to me. He would be choppered (by helicopter) in somewhere awful and ordered to fix a broken bird while other, stronger, men held the line and fired the rounds. If he couldn't fix that plane, nobody got to leave, including him. The helo was long gone, so whatever aircraft he was working on was his ride home. I don't know how many times he did that. Once seems enough to me, with or without napalm.

My mother, from the safety of a waiting-wives base in Kansas, wrote letters to her husband every day while he was in Vietnam. She did the same later when he was in Thailand or on TDY (temporary duty). *The children are fine; the weather is nice. Hurry home.* She didn't mean any of it. She was miserable for most of their marriage, always fearful of his return, uncertain of what would become of all of us. My mum would think of her father, who had lied about his age to join up against the Germans. He was too old, too poor, too short, but he went, and they won. She was so wistful about her country; I still don't understand why she married an American. "My father," she would remind us in lilting, tearful tones, "went to war in a busman's uniform." This was a point of pride for her—that her father, her country, had been so broke they didn't even have clothes to fight in. She wanted to worship her husband the way she worshipped her father, but what he was doing made no sense to her. Vietnam made no sense to anyone. From her vantage point, she saw men coming back limbless and angry, while her adopted country's government rattled on about domino effects and Watergates. And for what?

Soldiers glared at her, went crazy like in the movies, or folded up into themselves and shook violently. Her husband was no hero; he was just a mechanic. Time and the world seemed out of joint. She held my big brother and me close and debated leaving, going home to England, where at least, even if she was broke, there would be less anger and no cockroaches in the baby's crib.

My dad returned home in 1969. In California he couldn't wear his uniform off base for fear of being spat on and called a baby killer. He did remote tours in Thailand and Guam and came home for good in the mid-'70s. He felt ashamed of having been in Vietnam, but more than that, he felt anger toward everyone who hadn't been there. As if these things could ever be known, as if anyone who hadn't been there could understand. My father never, ever did drugs. He hated the stereotype of the strung-out vet, railed at the television during movies that showed soldiers sharing a little reefer to keep their spirits up. *I stayed away from that shit*, he'd say. *Nobody did that where I was. What. In. The. Hell. Actin' like it was some kinda goddamn party.* Then he'd tell us, me and my brother, that if he caught us toking reefer, he'd tear us a new one. I didn't smoke my first joint until I was twenty-five.

In 1976 we were sent to West Germany, and things were bearable for a while. My mum was back in Europe, where she belonged, and I went to a proper German kindergarten. My dad worked the flight line at Ramstein, readying jets for assorted duties, drowning out terrible memories of ships and jungles with the hum of propellers and the gleam of NATO fighters. To this day, I find the sound of air-raid sirens comforting; every day at noon, we'd hear the all clear, and I'd go take my nap.

But some things never settle. Occasional outbursts became regular and more terrible battles, until finally, after we returned to the States in the early '80s, it was impossible to get through a day without being berated, belittled, or beaten by my father. In Germany he would just yell or break one of our toys. Here, his headaches got worse, while his blood pressure skyrocketed. His knees were shot from years on a cramped ship and kneeling on unfriendly surfaces in stressful conditions. He suffered. One minute he would tell us we were worthless, and then he'd weep like a child. He retired a master sergeant at thirty-eight, and things got even worse. We'd move to a new town, near a base or a VA hospital, and he'd take a job and then quit over some imagined insult. Then we'd move and repeat the cycle again and again every year or so. It went on and on.

And so it did for everyone. What family stationed at Wurtsmith, or Scott, or Travis, or Seymour Johnson AFB didn't have times when they closed their doors to hide the shouting? For a time, we were at Marine Air Base Cherry Point, which made my father's angers seem like nothing. Marines. Marines do some crazy shit, especially if they've got invisible wounds. My mother didn't allow us out of the house that year.

The simplest answer, the go-to response, was detachment. This is not like denial; everyone knows bad things are happening, that their fathers and sons and wives are suffering and causing us to suffer in turn. We can all see it, but we just keep moving. Base to base, task to task. There is so much collective pain, but none of us is special. You just go to the PX and commissary. You just carry on. Because what else is there to do?

I figured all this out fairly early in life, which is probably why I started floating. That's what I used to call my out-of-body experiences. When things got bad, which was usually in hospitals, I would *float*. That feeling that I was a swelling balloon took over. My hands, my whole body, would puff up like a weird, weightless blister, and I panicked just enough to put myself into a trance. I left my earthly self, glided up to the ceiling away from the tension and the fear. I could see everything as I looked down, bloated and cocooned, bobbing along up above my corporeal six-year-old self. Everyone was always silent; no one noticed the bookish, bubble-curled tyke hovering above them.

I only vaguely remember the triggers for these trips, but it was invariably something a child shouldn't see. At an Army hospital one summer between third and fourth grades, I locked eyes with a man with no legs and one arm sitting in a wheelchair. He was alone, facing the faded green wall like a naughty schoolboy. He looked haggard and forlorn. He blinked at me meekly and turned away. The next thing I knew, I was leaving myself behind to drift out of there, coasting past light fixtures and fondling the high, soft pine boughs that hung over the sidewalk all the way home.

Once when I was very little, we were in the emergency room on base. I forget why; I think my brother had fallen on the playground. Suddenly, there were sirens and screams and a flurry of people in white coats. Words like *explosion* and *collision* hit me like a punch as bloodied, mangled men on stretchers began streaming in through the double doors. My mum put an arm around each of us and cooed nervously, "It's okay, it's just a drill. It's not real; they're just practicing." I believed her. I knew what drills were, and it was easier to disconnect and make everything real, but still less than real. Let's pretend. That may have been the first time I floated.

And so we went, on and on, until long after I'd grown up. My parents divorced. My big brother died in a car accident. Our family connection to each other strained and fell apart. My family had no hometown because we'd moved around so much all those years. None of us was anchored to anything. I settled in a place I'd never heard of and commandeered people I'd just met to be my new family. That felt safe. My father unwound and remade himself a bit. The last I heard, I think he was driving a truck in Texas. We don't speak anymore, so I wouldn't know.

*Aftermath* is a strange word. I've only just begun to calculate the effects of my father's experience in the Navy and Air Force. Before he joined up, my dad was a funny, lively man. I imagine he still can be sometimes, downright cool even. He's the kind of guy everybody, except me, wants to have a beer with. But every day, and for years after he came home, my dad sacrificed something. Some days it was a small comfort; other days it was a knee or an eardrum. Ultimately, it was his family. Despite counseling and medication and the best misguided efforts of the VA to support people like him, my father lost. This is incalculable: show your work.

Our armed forces have moved on now, on to other wars, other bases, and other forms of rehabilitation. We are all old enough and far enough removed from Vietnam to look back on it wisely. I need my country to do that, to be wise for its regular joes from now on. I've spent my life floating above my family's losses and pains because it was the only way to get through them. A little wisdom, a few of those coping-strategies workshops that are so popular now, could have helped bring me back down to earth, or helped my dad recognize what was happening to him. And for the record, my father's story isn't even one of the sad ones. My childhood memories are dotted with encounters of those limbless and angry men that so frightened my young mother and me. Their stories are much worse. We floated away from them, too.

When people say, "Never forget," I know what it means now. It's not only the grand campaigns and the bullets to the body. It's not just about Purple Hearts and white-gloved salutes. There are families and regular men and women, people like my dad, mechanics and cooks and nurses, who will be forever different, forever finely fractured in some indescribable, complex way, because of their time in the service doing menial tasks that kept the war machine running. They have no glory to remember, only workaday duty, which they performed willingly and complained about under their breath. So much was taken from them; so much was lost that they didn't even know they had to begin with.

What they could have been if we had only known or asked. If we hadn't all floated past them, pretending not to notice, trying to convince ourselves it was just another drill.

My father made it through his service with two bad knees, mild deafness, and no open wounds. He supported a beautiful wife and raised two intelligent children who feared and pitied him. He loved us and gave us everything he could, and he abused and humiliated us in the same ways he had been abused and humiliated.

Then one day we forgot about him. Each of us drifted up to the rafters, away from his nightmares and needs, and floated out of his life. He squared his shoulders and kept going, all by himself.

For that alone, they ought to give my dad a medal.

# 3

# Remembering Forgotten Fliers, Their Survivors

KATHLEEN M. RODGERS

My friend Petey white-knuckles the steering wheel when she's driving on base and a fighter plane screeches overhead, approaching the runway.

She still gets wiped out when she goes to a symphony concert or hears a trumpet solo.

It's been twelve years, or roughly four thousand days, since her beautiful, poetic music man/pilot died in a midair crash near a tomato farm in eastern New Mexico. The F-111 her husband was piloting was on a final approach when a civilian aircraft, flying in military airspace, collided with his jet. Roy and his navigator ejected, but the ejection capsule hit the earth like a two-ton brick. The altitude of the F-111 at time of impact was too low for the ejection capsule to function properly.

Roy Westerfield was taken too soon—when his song was just beginning. He was an exceptional pilot, husband, and father and a good friend of ours. Just the mention of his name and my husband, Tom, sighs with awe at how extremely talented and gifted Roy was. He was not your average jet jockey or musician. He was a masterpiece of a man. A walking, talking, flying composition in the making. He wrote arrangements on a baby grand piano in his home. If Roy had lived, his music would've winged its way into the professional world.

My last vivid memory of Roy was at the Cannon Air Force Base, New Mexico, chapel in October 1979. He played the "Lord's Prayer" on the trumpet at my wedding, and today I still get misty-eyed remembering the evening Roy conjured up a little taste of heaven out of the mouth of that horn. Shortly after the wedding, my husband and I moved to Arizona. Four months later, in a farmer's field only miles from the base chapel, the music died.

For those of us who knew Roy, a little bit of us went with him. My husband took the news like most fighter pilots do. He drank a beer for

Roy at the club at his new duty station and talked among fellow pilots about this latest "peacetime" crash. Then stoically, he stuffed the tragedy into one of those handy little storage bins in the mind and "pressed on." As all fighter pilots must do after a crash. It's called compartmentalizing, and they're all very good at it.

Six months later Tom would perform the same rituals again. Another friend, Sam Taylor, the son of one of the original Tuskegee Airmen, was killed just a few miles from where Roy had "bought the farm." Sam's F-111 just flew into the ground, as they say in the fighter business.

My husband, who'd wanted to fly airplanes since he was three years old, was "Captain Unemotional" during the day at work and at social gatherings where other pilots might be present. But sometimes in the evenings at home, when the flight suit had been unzipped and slung over the top of the bathroom door, Tom would let the walls to some of those little compartments come tumbling down. He used to sit in his recliner, sip a beer, and weep, silent streams running endlessly down his face, wetting the neckline of his T-shirt.

Then he would open up and mention all the names of all the men he'd known since pilot school . . . like John Sweeney, Lou Tallman, or Rick Cardinas, whose father flew the B-29 Superfortress that launched Chuck Yeager and the X-1 *Glamorous Glennis* into the history books and who found out only hours before he died that he was going to be a daddy.

There were others whom Tom never personally knew—the legends— like Colonel Tommy Thompson and A-10 Thunderbolt II demonstration pilot Sam Walker. I didn't understand it all back then. How a man like my husband could be one way in front of his fellow pilots—as if uncaring— and then so unabashedly emotional with me. That was years ago and I was young. Over time I've come to realize a couple of things about military pilots: that their lack of emotional demonstrations among each other is probably a defense mechanism and that, all too sadly, many of them die.

My first "reality check" took place three weeks after I was married. Tom and I were living in a little motel outside the gate of Davis-Monthan Air Force Base in Arizona. Tom was going through A-10 training, and I was nervous about him transitioning from the F-111 to the Air Force's newest single-seat attack plane.

One evening on the 6:00 o'clock news, as I sat waiting for Tom to come home from work, the television reporter announced that an A-10 from Davis-Monthan had crashed in the desert and the pilot had been killed. I thought it was Tom. I sat frozen for what seemed like hours, waiting, not knowing what to do. Then I heard Tom's car pull up outside the room, and I collapsed into him when he walked in the door. The pilot who died was Harry Whal. He sat next to Tom in academics.

There were so many pilots who died during the first year we were married. I look back now, wondering if Roy's haunting tune on the trumpet was a prelude of things to come in the fighter-pilot community. There would be more crashes. And someone else would play the trumpet. But it would be taps, and not Roy's sweet solos, that reddened our eyes.

After Harry Whal, Roy, and Sam were killed, I learned to live with fear. It kept me company during the day until Tom came home at night. Only then could I relax.

If I left the house during the day for a job or to run errands, I returned with a pit in my stomach. I remember turning the corner to head up the street, checking with caution that a blue staff car wasn't waiting for me in the driveway. Somehow, thankfully, I escaped that horrible nightmare that has become a reality for many women.

Like Jane Wallen. She learned in the wee hours of a spring morning in Alaska that her husband's A-10 was missing on a deployment exercise in Norway. My husband was one of the "death angels" waiting on her little front porch of the two-story eight-plex to deliver the news. A few days later the crash site was found, buried under an avalanche. How do you tell a young wife that her husband, the man she wanted to grow old with, was one second flying his airplane and the next second obliterated on a mountain halfway around the world?

Then there's Jeri. We sat in my kitchen one day, visiting. We have much in common. For instance, we were both raised in New Mexico and share a passion for our native state. We like many of the same things, and her daughter and my son are in the same class at school. The list could go on and on. We've both been in love with a fighter pilot and are former Air Force wives. But here the similarities stop. My husband recently retired and flies for a major airline. Hers is buried in the national cemetery in Santa Fe. Jeff "Burger" Watterberg made it home safely from the Persian Gulf War, only to die in a midair collision over Louisiana six months later.

Jeri and I talk about personal things: how tough it is now, being a single parent—on her own without the support of her best friend, lover, and father of her three children. So much of her life seems to have gone with Jeff. We talk hard, cold-reality stuff. What really happens after the accident and memorial services, once the tons of food, cards, calls, and people converging on your home have stopped?

How different things were handled in the movie *Top Gun*. After "Maverick's" backseater, Goose, is killed, the emotional emphasis rides on Maverick's character. Goose's widow and young son are soon forgotten in the glamorous flying scenes and love story. She's left standing . . . holding Goose's personal effects.

Hollywood didn't deal with the more realistic issues of an aircraft accident. It didn't show the wife and kid in a later scene, picking up the pieces of their lives and attempting to put the puzzle back together again. But it will never be the same—not with one of the pieces missing. What happened to Goose's wife? It still bugs me. Petey, Jane, Jeri, Betty Jane, and many others can tell us. They pick up where the Hollywood script left off.

Jeri can tell us about the aftermath of raising three children alone. Getting through the first Christmas without Jeff. Seeing glimpses of Jeff at every turn in the faces of his children. The Watterbergs had almost made it to their eighteenth wedding anniversary—Jeff, the president of his senior class, and Jeri, the former cheerleader whom Jeff lovingly referred to as his "burger queen."

Petey says she can get through Roy's birthday and their anniversary, but the day of the accident, February 6, is tough. She says it starts in January and builds. Petey has been remarried for years, but it doesn't take away the pain of loss. Her almost-grown sons are mirror images of Roy.

Betty Jane Thompson's grown son followed in his father's footsteps and became a fighter pilot. What went through her mind when her son flew F-16 Fighting Falcons in the Gulf War? And Jane, who is childless. All she has left of Carter are memories, even though the Norwegian government named the mountain Carter hit after him. It takes a special breed of lady to be married to a fighter pilot. Not all can handle it. Some leave the marriage, while others whimper and force their men to get out.

For the women who loved what their husbands did for a living and eventually lost them to that profession, they must be remembered. Never once did any of them whine or mentally bind their husbands' wings, for they had discovered that one little secret about most pilots: when they fly, they are happy. And every pilot's wife must learn to accept, at one time or another, that her husband just might not make it home for dinner. Ever.

Pilots and crew members who die in peacetime crashes are sadly the forgotten fliers, somehow less heroic because they didn't perish in combat. Make no mistake, these pilots and crew members died serving their country. We should all remember them. And the women and children they leave behind.

For every military jet that passes overhead, Petey is reminded that one day Roy took off and never made it back.

### Postscript
Petey remarried another fighter pilot, Lieutenant Colonel Matt Husson, and together they raised Roy and Petey's two sons. Writing under the name Maryellen Husson, Petey's poem "Taps," a tribute to her late husband, Roy, graces the opening pages of Kathleen Rodgers's novel *The Final Salute*. Petey died July 9, 2009, ten months after the publication of her poem in the novel.

# 4

# A Psychology of Rumor, a Psychology of War

CALEB S. CAGE

We fight wars because of rumors. A rumor of strength. A rumor of vulnerability. A rumor sent through diplomatic signals until it reaches someone who wishes to believe the rumor.

Rumors and war are inextricably linked. Spreading rumors is as much a part of human nature as is the strategic and tactical use of violence in warfare.

Robert Knapp published "A Psychology of Rumor" in 1944, a paper that studies rumors through the lens of World War II. His essay, a seminal work on the subject, defines *rumor* as "a proposition for belief of topical reference disseminated without official verification" and places rumor alongside myth, legend, and humor as another form of social communication. He writes that rumor is so powerful during wartime because it "thrives only during periods of social duress." The wartime necessity for secrecy together with enemy and friendly misinformation campaigns play upon that social duress to form the perfect landscape for rumor to flourish.

Knapp describes three major types of rumors from his experiences during World War II. There are "pipe dream" rumors that represent the popular "wishful thinking" of the public. There are "bogie" rumors that are, he writes, "derived from fears and anxieties." And finally, there are "wedge-driving" rumors, which are those intent on "dividing groups and destroying loyalties."

Pipe-dream and bogie rumors are opposites. The third kind, wedge-driving rumors, is what you might see in enemy propaganda.

Every day in Iraq we lived with these, the wedge-driving rumors, and with their intentions of dividing and destroying. They lived in our stories, in our thoughts, and in our everyday attempts to make some sense of our lives. Sometimes they comforted us, sometimes they tormented us, but however they made us feel, they were always working against us.

I had never heard of Knapp or his study on rumors when I was told I would be giving up my job as the company executive officer to take over a line platoon. Amazingly, I hadn't heard even a whisper about my job change before I received orders to helm a combat platoon, either. Leading a combat platoon was a dream job for me as a twenty-four-year-old lieutenant, and I became platoon leader for 1st Platoon, C Battery, of the 1st Battalion, 6th Field Artillery. What did I care, until later, that the rumor mill had failed me?

We'd only been in Baqubah, Iraq, along the eastern edge of the so-called Sunni Triangle, for about two months at that point. We were an artillery battalion out of Bamberg, Germany, and broken into something akin to a motorized rifle company. Our orders were to prepare Iraq for democracy by patrolling the streets, killing our enemies, and capturing the hearts of those we were there to protect. We called ourselves "the gods of Diyala," a reference to the province we were in and a less-than-subtle joke at the expense of our less-than-brilliant company commander, who insisted that, as Americans, we had the power of the Almighty in war-torn Iraq.

This was 2004. A year after the invasion, mere months into an insurgency we did not yet know much about, and years before the vaunted "surge" strategy that would, at least locally, tactically, and temporarily, win the day enough for the politicians to claim victory. Everything most of us knew about Iraq, about fighting with conventional forces against unconventional forces, and about so much else in our young lives was strictly academic—scenario training on infantry tactics, classroom training on Middle Eastern culture, and so on.

Before taking over 1st Platoon I often found myself sitting on a metal folding chair on the concrete floor in the company command post on our forward operations base, northeast of Baghdad. I'd listen to the radios, put together reports, and shoot the breeze with the soldier and sergeant who were assigned to work with me. The work was hardly glorious, but our position placed us in a key location to monitor information flow within the company.

The line platoons would come back through our area on the base before or after a mission and pass on the latest of whatever they had heard or seen in sector while on patrol. And the rumor flow didn't end there. Errant soldiers would pass through during downtime to use our Internet, letting us know what they learned through e-mail with their families and friends back home. Sequestered in our little square on the north end of the base, we received and shared with our fellow soldiers the scuttlebutt on the mood in the city, the mood in the battalion, and anything else that was going on. Later, when I traded my job as executive officer for platoon leader, I was able to come in from sector and pass along my own set of rumors to my replacement.

One constant rumor was whether our deployment would be extended. The standard deployment to Iraq for members of the U.S. Army was 12 months, but there was always a fear that what happened to our friends in the First Armored Division could happen to us: an additional 120 days fashioned onto the jagged end of a 365-day deployment.

There were never any facts that supported this particular rumor, but the possibility of an extension hung over our heads like a bad health diagnosis. Everyone had basically made peace with a 365-day mission. Minus a severe injury or worse, there was no way of really avoiding it. We had embraced the normal deployment calculus. In fact, you'd wake up 90 days in and realize you had completed a fourth of your tour almost without noticing. Then you would feel every minute of the next 180 days as if they were delivered through the rhythmic drips of water torture.

Eventually, you would spend the last quarter of the tour in an intense frenzy, trying to stay alive, trying to hand off the mission, trying to go home. It was a fact. Standard issue. We were fine with it, but an additional 120 days required an entirely different schema.

Rumors of an extension exaggerated our common fears of staying longer in Iraq, and perhaps dying. They played upon our helplessness, our inability to control the commanders and staffs at higher echelons, those who would make the ultimate decision. Rumors gave us a language to deal with an inconvenient possibility, and they allowed us to presuppose that we would all live through an entire 365-day deployment.

Our predecessors from the Fourth Infantry Division may have started the rumor of our extension—perhaps to mess with us, or maybe just to talk about fears they had nursed for the past year without having to admit to them. We certainly didn't want to discuss the possibility openly in front of soldiers who had just endured a year in combat. But the soldiers in the 4th ID, relieved and exhausted at the end of their 365 days in the desert, discussed it openly for us during the transition. They had nothing to lose.

We, on the other hand, still had plenty to lose. We needed to focus on learning the sector, which is a midsize city packed into a tiny collection of neighborhoods and villages along a bend of the Diyala River. We had to learn which neighborhoods were Sunni, which were Shia, and, more important, what on earth that information could mean to us during our patrols. We had to learn how to assess our threats and how to be friendly to a people we assumed were trying to kill us. We had to pull interminable guard shifts, drive in boring patrols, and escort important people and cargo around the city. We had to fight the strange and primitive virus of insurgency with modern tools and modern tactics, which meant that sometimes we had to stop and pick up pieces of people we loved and, at times, even pieces of insurgents.

Before we knew it we woke up one day and discovered a quarter of our time in country had passed. We knew the area better, and we knew the enemy better. Far more important was that by this time, we had grown to take comfort in knowing that even if we didn't know when the intense fighting was going to happen, we could control only so much. By this point a platoon sergeant or squad leader could lead a patrol or a raid or a sweep mission in their sleep. The soldiers learned that patrols, raid, or sweeps were unpredictable and that the best way to pass the time in between was to sleep. We had large, intense missions, and during firefights we came to expect and rely on the fact that our firepower, communications, and tactics were superior to the insurgents'.

But just as we were settling into a routine, the rumor of the 120-day extension started to seep into our psyche. It was about the uncomfortable uncertainty of combat, especially counterinsurgency combat, where even the knowns are unknown. It was about the desire to go home, the desire to be comfortable, the desire for predictability and for certainty. It drove some people crazy. One lieutenant, who was allowed to go home for his baby's birth early in the deployment, was staring down the possibility of not seeing his son until he was a year old. Others had more mundane reasons for fearing the extension—wanting to meet in person the girl they'd met online, wanting to see what their wives could possibly be spending their deployment money on, or just wanting to be out of the hot and violent country once and for all.

Many of the rumors were some sort of variation or corollary of the tour-extension rumor. One was the R&R (rest and relaxation) rumor. Every member of the battalion was authorized two weeks of leave at some point during the year, a chance to go home, to get out of the war zone, and to enjoy some time at peace. R&R was a much-desired pleasure for obvious reasons, but it also had disadvantages. Take R&R and you added the two weeks to your deployment. But for combat soldiers in Iraq, R&R was viewed as sort of a conjugal visit for a prisoner on death row.

That's why it was so devastating when word started circulating that Division was limiting the number of people who could go on R&R. They were doing this, the story went, by limiting the time frame available. This latter part added credibility to the rumor, because the faceless drones at Division were always disrupting our lives through slight policy changes or bureaucratic interpretations of regulations. The rumor stated that R&R would start in May and go through November, which made sense given that our 365 days spanned from February to February. The seven-month window in the middle of the deployment, the rumor went, would be increasingly limiting because only five or six people from a company could be gone at the same time and so only three R&R trips would be possible in a two-month period. Whether the policy change was ever discussed is unclear, but it is certain that everyone in our battalion, and likely throughout the theater, would be able to go home on his or her two weeks of leave during the deployment. After some bad press for making soldiers buy their own tickets home, the Army even started footing the bill.

Perhaps the worst rumor, though, was the one about us going home sooner rather than later. This one generated from word that the Third Infantry Division, which would be replacing us, was actually being spun up sooner than expected. This was a popular topic of discussion for my guys and me. It took us home. It allowed us to have some hope, to see that the light at the end of the tunnel was closer than it appeared. It was, of course, an absolute falsehood, a blatant rumor, created by us and for us.

Another rumor that correlated with the extension rumor came out of the bigger Army through friends and connections around the world.

Apparently, the anonymous "they" were telling the lieutenants at their officer basic courses, the rumor went, that the Army was planning to activate the Inactive Ready Reserve contract that every soldier had. Every soldier or officer, whether they had a two-, four-, or five-year active contract, actually had an eight-year total contract. The six, four, or three years beyond their active contract, called Inactive Ready Reserve time, was a time during which they could be recalled by the Army without any real recourse.

Of the many rumors this one was one of the most believable because we almost all knew someone who had been recalled. Everyone had heard of the star football player on the Army football team a few years ahead of us who had to leave a career in finance because he was recalled. Or the guy who had to leave grad school to fulfill the part of his contract no one really thought much about. For me, the idea that recalls had already started was an indication that another rumor was true: that the administration had not planned for the long war that the insurgents had in mind.

There was the rumor from day one in Iraq that the Army was going to close down the base that we had inherited and move to the brigade headquarters on the other side of Baqubah. We called this a quality-of-life rumor. FOB Gabe, the base where we lived, was awful. It was an old Iraqi Army brigade headquarters, complete with rusted-out vehicles, random strands of barbed wire, nonfunctioning toilets and showers, and barely livable buildings.

FOB Warhorse, on the other hand, sat in stark contrast with Gabe. Across town, FOB Warhorse, so we heard, had decent chow and plenty of women soldiers. Looking back, I think the rumor about the move to FOB Warhorse was just wishful thinking. Who hadn't dreamed of a more comfortable deployment there every time they had to deliver or retrieve something from Warhorse? For obvious reasons, this rumor refused to die.

Women were rarities on a forward operating base that housed a combat arms unit, and, accordingly, they were also the topic of many rumors. Nearly everyone on our operating base was male, but some members of our battalion were permanently stationed in the Baqubah "Green Zone" at the Civil Military Operations Center. They would run the same operations we did, and they had an additional security mission, but they also had a good chow hall, and they had local Iraqi women who came through their gates daily to clean the public areas used by the State Department and members of the Iraqi government. Before long rumors circulated that the Iraqi cleaning ladies were actually very inexpensive prostitutes. Although there was never even the slightest bit of evidence ever presented to support it, nothing closer than thirdhand accounts, this particular rumor grew and perfected over time.

I don't ever recall a time when we used rumors or tried to use rumors against the enemy. Of course, there were units in the area gathering intelligence through various sources. There were others using Information Operations and Psychological Operations tactics and techniques to "shape the information battlespace," as they said, but they were never quite rumors. There were fliers that attempted to sway public opinion through facts, such as fliers denouncing a local car-bomb attack as a vicious attack on the peaceful people of Baqubah by the more radical members of their communities. There were public service announcements on the joy of democracy. Maybe we were engaging in rumormongering to distort our enemy's image and the word just never trickled down to our level. Maybe we should have. The enemy was certainly using them effectively against us.

"If leaflets, newspapers, or radio broadcasts are likened to bullets," Knapp writes about rumor used as enemy propaganda, "then rumor must be likened to a torpedo; for, once launched, it travels of its own power." His description perfectly describes the sorts of information battles we faced as soldiers on the streets of Baqubah in 2004. The rumors were torpedoes, operating undetected and under the surface, moving of their own power, and destroying our abilities to have a meaningful and impactful conversation with anyone we met.

Many of the rumors that poisoned the minds of the local Iraqis against us were clearly the work of the insurgency. They spoke to the hearts and minds of their intended constituency, they confirmed their various biases, and they naturally fitted an enormous emotional need within the distressed community. They were the perfect tool for an insurgency.

They also perfectly mimicked the combat tactics of the insurgency. Rumors do their main damage by moving virally through whispers from person to person, quietly and far from public sight; like the message in a game of "telephone," they change shape and purpose with each telling; they use the perceived strengths of the American forces against them; and one of their key purposes is to undermine the legitimacy and power of their occupiers. Perhaps the biggest similarity between rumors and insurgencies, though, is the fact that, like an insurgency, rumors are nearly impossible to defeat through conventional means of communication.

The Iraqi civilians in Baqubah relied on their own rumors to deal with the environment we had visited upon them as well. In fact, rumors seemed to be an enormous part of the Iraqi survival plan—often by blaming their current crisis on the Jews, the Iranians, the Americans, or all three. We heard them constantly through our interpreters, through the Iraqi Army soldiers we worked with regularly, and through the conversations we had with the average Iraqi men on the streets whom we talked to during our patrols and hearts-and-minds efforts.

There was a thought that word traveled so fast because of an extraordinarily low literacy rate among Iraqi adults, a thought that turned out to be, at worst, a racially motivated myth and, at best, a rumor that made sense at the time. But whatever the literacy rates, rumors did, in fact, play an enormous part of the Iraqi psyche, just like they have and will continue to play in the future for any people trying to survive a war. They communicated regularly in the markets, schools, and other venues, passing information from person to person. They listened to their neighborhood mosques, as messages and sermons were passed either through their external loudspeakers or through the prayer meetings inside the mosques. And, of course, they read newspapers and watched satellite television channels that spoke to their collective and individual worldviews.

Most rumors that made it back to us were about the supposed sins of omission or commission committed by the Americans during the invasion or the early days preceding the insurgency and our time in Iraq. During our informal interviews on the streets with Iraqi men, we learned that Iraqis believed Americans turned the electricity off and on at random to maintain control of the people of Baqubah. We regularly heard through our interpreters that many of the locals believed that we could fix all of the security and quality-of-life issues but didn't, as part of the plan to gain domination of the Iraqi people.

One particularly damaging rumor was that the American forces that preceded us had left countless weapons—bombs, guns, and more—

unguarded in munitions depots following the invasion to ensure that we would have an insurgency to fight. That is, that we were there simply to fight and destroy the cities and infrastructure of Iraq and our warmongering couldn't believably do so unless we had an actual enemy.

These rumors drove a wedge between us and the locals. It is true that they could be interpreted as ways of making sense of the most powerful nation in the world being unable to restore order to the communities of Baqubah. But it is far more likely that we were hearing rumors planted into the Iraqi public by our enemies when we heard things like this, especially given that the aim of these rumors was to destroy any loyalties toward us that might have been felt by the locals.

Other rumors played perfectly off of anxieties of the people of Baqubah. These explained the American military prowess against a relentless but often incompetent enemy, sometimes taking them further still by invoking the American and Israeli alliance. After a particularly destructive firefight in the city, we would learn that some of the people from Baqubah were circulating ideas that the conventional soldiers in our unit were actually special-forces soldiers. Other times we would learn that there were more than five thousand of us on our base—a laughably high number about ten times higher than reality. Still other times we learned that we were actually a secret Israeli regiment.

The latter racism among the locals persisted in highly publicized rumors that wealthy Israelis were buying up all of the land in Iraq, were surreptitiously importing Israeli goods for sale in Iraq, and were causing most of all that was wrong or going wrong in their city at that time as well. Their nationalism and racial pride played into another set of rumors, too. On patrols after a firefight, I would ask anyone willing to discuss it if they knew who the insurgents were and if they were local. Faruk, my interpreter, would shrug and laugh when he translated their responses for me: all of the fighters that we faced in Iraq were actually soldiers from Iran, Syria, and anywhere else but Iraq. After one firefight later in the year, Faruk had the opportunity to talk to an insurgent who had been badly wounded while he was being treated. "He is not saying anything," Faruk said to me as he walked up, "but his accent is from Fallujah, not Iran."

There was no doubt that the Iraqis we worked with and talked to daily were surviving on rumors. They might have a whole month of

peaceful days, but they couldn't enjoy them because they had to antic-
ipate the next moment's chaos. Sometimes a rumor might spare them
from going to an area where there was a planned attack. Other times, a
rumor might console or comfort them by confirming their suspicions
or explaining their fears. The war was personal to them, as personal
as a secret whispered to them from a friend at a market or a mosque.

One real difference between Knapp's study and the reality of the wars in
Iraq is the way rumors impacted the American home front. He writes
that war "focuses and intensifies the emotional life of the public" and
that "rarely are the wishes, fears, suspicions, and hostilities of the public so homogenous in character" as they are during wartime. He shows
how this was true during World War II when he was writing and studying, but it would be hard to argue that the American mood was homogenous during the wars of the early twenty-first century. The American
people were not as engaged as the Iraqi people, not by any measure. The
information age took all of the fear and wonder out of it for most people, and for those few who had skin in the game, they could generally
talk to their loved ones daily or weekly. There were beliefs that seemed
akin to rumors—Iraq had weapons of mass destruction, George Bush
went to war for oil, and so on. The American people tended to believe
the things that confirmed their political biases, but they did not need
to create stories that explained their fears or gave them hope because
the wars during their time were so impersonal to them, so far away.

It was personal and present for us, though, and especially so during
the last quarter of the deployment. Just as we had calculated, we did
spend the final 120 days in an intense frenzy, trying to stay alive, trying to hand off the mission.

# 5

# Panel 30w, Row 15

LORRIE LYKINS

My father was assigned to the U.S. Armor School at Fort Knox, Kentucky, in 1968, where he taught battle tactics between his first and second tours in Vietnam. I was eight years old, and my brother was ten that year, which I would come to think of as the one in which everything changed.

As military brats my brother and I lived as we had the entirety of our short lives—within the cocoon that was the military post. We knew nothing but structure and routine and the comforting surety with which life unfolded each day. Years later, of course, we would understand that many of the things we accepted as ordinary were uncommon outside our cloistered world.

Every one of our friends had a dad, and everyone's dad wore a uniform to work, usually fatigues and combat boots. Most evenings after dinner our dad sat at the kitchen table dabbing a cotton rag at the mouth of a red, white, and blue–striped can of Brasso, methodically polishing his belt buckle. Then he brushed his boots, running the bristles back and forth in bursts of three: *snap-snap-snap . . . snap-snap-snap.* When he finished, everything was packed carefully into a wooden shoeshine box, round tins of leather polish, soft cloths made of discarded undershirts, the wooden-handled brushes. We knew better than to fool around with the shoe box.

Sometimes our dad went to work and we didn't see him for weeks or months at a time. But the routine didn't waver. Our mother, like the other mothers we knew, was firmly in charge. Our mom acted as den leader to my brother's Cub Scout pack that year, and she could build a fort in the living room with a gaggle of grammar school boys and then host an elegant cocktail party with no notice that evening. And she could pack a house for an overseas move in one weekend.

All the mothers were unflappable officers' wives who wore hats and gloves to church every Sunday and attended ladies' teas. There wasn't anything they couldn't handle. And any officer's kid who was out in the neighborhood acting foolishly could count on someone's mother dispensing with a scolding or even a swat to the ass. Didn't matter if she happened to be your mother or not. Certain things were expected of officers' brats. Misbehavior was not tolerated. We all reflected our dads. The line would be toed.

Like all of our friends, we moved at the end of nearly every school year and spent the summers exploring new neighborhoods. We reported for school in the fall with anticipation, hoping to be joyfully reunited with friends from previous posts. Sometimes there was the letdown of spotting the bully we dreaded when we lived in Fort Bragg, now terrorizing kids in the lunchroom at Fort Benning. No matter; our fathers were in the 82nd Airborne Division, and so we were part of a rowdy traveling tribe.

This is what I remember about 1968: columns of men jogging by our house in the mornings, the cadence of boots meeting pavement, their singsongs beating into my consciousness. I peddled my bike rhythmically, singing over and over, *"I wanna be a recon ranger; I wanna live a life of danger."* I heard those boots every night in my head, the tempo rocking me to sleep. I told my mother that I could hear soldiers marching in my ears at night, and she laughed, tucking me in tightly under my favorite bedspread that was embroidered with circus tents and trimmed with tiny white pom-poms.

I had a new best friend every year; that year it was Pam Fields, who lived a few houses away on the same side of the street. Pam's father taught at the Armor School with my dad. Major Fields had lost an eye in Korea, and he sometimes removed his prosthetic blue eyeball and casually placed it on a table, waiting for one of us to notice. Once he chased us around the front yard, holding the eyeball between his thumb and forefinger, his arm extended, gleefully shouting "I've got my eye on you!" as we shrieked and ran.

My family shared a common wall that separated the dining room areas of two homes with the Sesslers, who lived on the other side of our duplex. The sounds of the Sessler family's life blended with ours. The rhythms of conversation, forks against plates, and chairs sliding across linoleum merged and rebounded, creating intimate background noise one stops noticing after a while. The only exception to this was Sundays, when Colonel Sessler gleefully pounded on the dining room wall whenever his favorite football team scored against my mom's favorite team.

Some evenings my dad's friends—tall, muscular kinsmen with precisely chiseled crew cuts, Arrow shirts neatly tucked into Bermuda shorts—gathered in our carport to smoke cigars and shoot the breeze. My red Radio Flyer, packed with ice, served as a cooler, the necks of beer bottles bobbing and swaying in the sea of slush as evening wore into night. My brother and I went to sleep many nights to the music of the low rumble of their voices, punctuated by bursts of laughter, soothing and familiar.

Our dad occasionally brought home weather balloons and old parachutes that were no longer fit for their intended use and gave them to us to play with. We kept the parachutes—silky moss-colored confections—stuffed into an old wooden footlocker on the back patio, pulling them out after dinner to play a variety of roles in the make-believe we played with the other kids on our street. The parachutes became undulating tides of water or sinister mushroom clouds, tee-pees and fluttering sails of pirate ships, herds of wild horses and billowing sandstorms. If we had enough kids, we held the mellifluous fabric above our heads and ran, hoping to take flight, down the mossy hill that knelt protectively across our shared backyards. We formed a circle and pulled the edges taut and tried to toss one another around. On some evenings we flapped the parachute up and down frantically, certain that a breeze might be willing to be caught and lift us off the ground for just a second or two.

The things that mark the end of childhood don't seem so apparent to most kids while they're happening—sometimes from the safe ground of adulthood we can look back and pinpoint the event that signaled the emergence from the haze of not being aware of much beyond the daily details of our young lives. Usually, I think, it's a series of events—a confluence of elements that pull us out of childhood once and for all. It started for me that year in small ways, like threads of a seam coming loose. Those threads may weaken over time, the seam gradually opening, or something can catch and abruptly tear it wide. It was a combination of the two for me.

I became cognizant for the first time that summer of what despondency and powerlessness felt like. It came to me in the long, tantalizing evenings of the summer months, when the sun lingered in the doorway, looking back at the glorious day it had been, its fingers, long purple and peach streaks across the sky, wrapped around the doorjamb, hanging on, reluctant to go. I imagined I could hear the sun sigh as it relented and finally drifted over the threshold into twilight as my playmates twirled and collapsed on the cool grass, not noticing at all that the sun had left us. I usually missed sharing the appearance of twilight with the other kids because I had to heed my mother's call to go into the house and get ready for bed. Hearing the laughter of my friends still at play as I pulled on my pajamas was agony. I stood at my bedroom window and watched them chase lightning bugs, empty pickle and jelly jars poised for capture. They shrieked and laughed and ran themselves breathless without me, as if my absence didn't matter at all, and then I realized that it didn't. I looked forward to school starting again.

The elementary school we attended the year we lived in Fort Knox was close enough to our home that we walked to and from school each day. We walked quickly in the mornings, eager to get to school, where the playground featured stripped-down tanks and an old jeep we climbed into and pretended to drive. But our pace was deliberately slow on the way home. We dawdled, taking our time passing the brick row houses where the enlisted men and their families lived. Each day offered a glimpse into a world to which we were wholly unaccustomed.

Wonderfully foreign aromas drifted from the open windows—cigarette smoke and incense, spices, grease, and cooking meat. Wallops of raw, pounding music accompanied by crying babies, boisterous laughter, and rising and falling waves of conversation matched our steps. The buildings vibrated with life as we passed by staring, our mouths slack as if we were beholding a carnival midway for the first time. On good days a young woman with a frosty, white-lipsticked mouth and rollers in her hair the size of soup cans appeared in a window. She leaned on the sill, cigarette in hand, Nancy Sinatra singing about her boots being made for walking, a guitar whining like a running-down siren in the background.

This was our introduction to music outside the taste of our parents, who at the time were enamored of Gilbert and Sullivan operettas. They preferred the mincing melodies of the *Pirates of Penzance* and took great care with their 33-rpm records, gently easing the glossy black LPs onto the spindle of their Grundig stereo's humming turntable. They had purchased the blond maple console at the PX in Germany, and it was an elegant piece of furniture. Much too nice for the likes of Joe Cocker and David Bowie, whom we heard snatches of on our way home most days, along with the Who, Credence Clearwater Revival, the Beatles, the Rolling Stones, the Jackson Five, and Cream. This was dangerous alien music, and we loved it.

As we got closer to our home each afternoon, the row houses that hunkered on the edges of the sidewalk gave way to sober, trim lawns and the tidy one-story duplexes that housed officers and their families. This neighborhood was alive as well, but with different sounds, more reserved. Dogs barked and the sounds of hi-fis and television floated from each home we passed, but there was no element of danger. This was our first clear sense of a world outside our own, one that was alluring and exotic, yet still connected to our own, in which our play was interrupted each evening by the strains of taps. We stood silently, statues on the lawn, straddling bikes, or suspending jump ropes until the final notes drifted off. *All is well, safely rest, God is nigh.*

This changed one night that spring, when I awoke to the sound of the phone ringing, at first far way, then its volume increasing as if the phone had leaped from the kitchen wall and was marching down the main hallway, demanding to be answered. It rang and rang and rang, the shrill, jarring pitch of the rings reverberating through the house. Surely, the Sesslers next door were awakened, too. I heard my parents mumbling to one another, the sound of feet meeting the floor, their bedroom door opening, and then my father's slippers shuffling down the hall.

We had one phone in the house in those days, a plump black rectangle of a thing attached to the kitchen wall. My mother was adept at cooking while balancing its receiver on her shoulder, dialing numbers with the end of a pencil or a wooden spoon, the rotary face cycling round and round, clicking as she dialed.

The phone was suddenly silenced midjangle, and the only sound in the house was the humming drone of the rock tumbler in my brother's bedroom. Then from the kitchen I heard my father call my mother's name once, twice, then again, louder each time. The sound of the rock tumbler's gnashing monotone faded as I listened for my mother in the hallway. Silence seemed to hang in the air, and then I heard loud breaths, the kind of sound you make when the wind is knocked out of you. I had made this sound once when I'd fallen from a tree and lay rigid on the ground, gasping as I tried to inhale. Then came the muffled pitch of voices going up and down, sounds I recognized years later as abject anguish.

I slipped from my bed and tiptoed into the hallway that led to the kitchen. There were no lights on in the house, but I could make out my father, crouched on the black-and-white tiled floor in front of the sink, his arms spread wide, each hand gripping the counter. My mother stood over him, her arm cradling his head against her narrow hip, her gaze fixed on the telephone on the wall. I stood, frozen, staring at the scene for what seemed like a very long time. Neither of them saw me, and I turned and crept back to my room, holding my breath for fear of making a sound. I crawled into bed, pulling the covers tightly under my chin, willing myself back to sleep, knowing that something terrible was happening, knowing I wanted more than anything for whatever it was to stop, go away, leave us all alone, and knowing that it wasn't possible.

There are fragments of memory that remain, for whatever reasons, more fixed and enduring than others. The image of my parents in the kitchen in the middle of the night, seconds after learning that my father's dear friend John was dead, is one such inescapable and fixed memory for me. The way the moon shone through the kitchen window, backlighting my parents in a silvery tableau, remains the most vivid memory of my childhood. If I close my eyes today, more than four decades later, I see it in indelible detail—the quilted pattern of my mother's robe and the dark curls of her hair against her pale, slender neck. But as painful as it is to recall, I cherish this image of my mother and father in that moment. They weren't my parents; they were two dazed young people, grief-stricken and clinging to one another in the way I imagine two people who knew the same fate could befall them would. The idea that a mortar shell could destroy their world and everyone in it, that phones could ring in other homes in the middle of the night, bringing the most terrible news imaginable, was not an idea at all. It was real and it had happened to someone they loved, and they were in that moment destroyed.

On March 2, 1969, an enemy mortar shell hit the 191st Assault Helicopter Company's operations center in Kien Hoa Province, Vietnam, killing six men, including the company commander. The commander was my father's close friend. John was thirty-two years old—the same age as my father. John's wife, Linda, was my mother's dear friend. The oldest of their three children, Joanie, had been my playmate. John died that spring day with five young men who were under his command, all of them in their twenties: Dennis, from Monroe, Georgia; Carl, of Sanford, North Carolina; Rob, from Fresno, California; George, from Urbana, Illinois; and Ken, from LaCrosse, Wisconsin. The men were buried together in a bunker that took a direct mortar hit. For a short time, the men were listed as missing in action, until the bunker in which they were entombed was excavated and their bodies recovered.

I learned these details through my own research, because my parents preferred not to discuss it. This was following a business trip to Washington DC thirty-two years later (nearly to the day). A visit to the Vietnam Veterans Memorial wasn't on the agenda, but a walk following dinner had wound me up there, searching for John's name with a reluctant young colleague in tow. Andrew, my company's most junior employee, confessed he knew little about the conflict even though he had taken plenty of history courses in college, and, hearing this, I insisted he accompany me as I checked the directory. We located Panel 30w, Row 15, and I stood gazing up at the name of my father's friend. Two women nearby held a piece of paper against the wall, one rhythmically passing a stick of chalk back and forth across a name. Others milled silently or spoke to one another in low tones. It was nearly dusk.

My colleague was clearly distracted by a gathering of a small group of Vietnamese people a few yards away from where we stood. They, too, had come to find a name. They sat in a circle, looking up at the wall, chanting in a low, hypnotic murmur. The smell of incense and the sound of a gong drifted over to us. Andrew edged closer to the group, watching, and when one of the members broke away, I watched him approach Andrew. The older Vietnamese man spoke softly and gestured to the wall, guiding Andrew by the elbow to get a closer look. Andrew nodded, raptly attentive. When he rejoined me he said that the group had come to honor an American serviceman who had helped some of their family members during the war. We stood wordlessly, looking at the wall for a long time, and then walked its length, stepping carefully around offerings and mementos that had been left there: a pair of tattered combat boots; faded photos; letters; dog tags; flowers; a black plastic government-issue ballpoint pen clipped to a red, white, and blue–bordered airmail envelope; a Purple Heart ribbon.

We made our way along the edge of the reflecting pool and then sat at the top of the steps leading to the Lincoln Memorial. As the moon rose over the water, I tried to explain Vietnam to Andrew, who grew agitated as I spoke. He hung his head and said he didn't remember learning about it in school and wished he'd made a point of educating himself about it sooner. He said he felt ashamed and was overwhelmed by the specter of the wall and the number of names set into it and all the lost lives each of those names represented—not only the men and women who had died, but their mothers and fathers, sisters and brothers, cousins, grandparents, sweethearts, friends. For each life lost countless others were forever altered in one fashion or another, and the scope was unfathomable. Andrew mused about how different the world might be had so many young people from one generation not been lost. He asked me about the name on the wall I had come to see. I told him about the terrible night in 1969 when we learned about John. Andrew asked if I remembered him. I told him I didn't remember John, only the effect his death had had on my parents.

When I returned from the business trip, I asked my parents to tell me more about John and what had happened to him. They seemed surprised by the clarity of my memories of the spring of 1969 and equally reluctant to revisit it, except to say that John and Linda had been like family to them. They said that the loss was as painful—and in some ways more so—all these years later, because his absence from the lives of everyone who had loved him seemed more poignant with each year that passed, each milestone marked. The randomness, senselessness, and abject unfairness, the magnitude of it all, haunted my dad, especially. He told me once that he believed he hadn't been worthy of coming home. Better men, much more deserving men he had known, had not made it home, he said, and he couldn't understand why he had been spared. Nothing he could ever accomplish in life could reconcile this in his mind.

My parents met John and Linda in 1960 in Ulm, West Germany, where both men had been stationed. They lived in the same building, and the two couples became fast friends. They discovered that they had all been born and raised in Ohio and quickly bonded over their common roots and, in the case of John and my father, ethnic background. The two sometimes exchanged phrases in a hybrid of Slovak, the language spoken by the elder members of both their extended families. Both couples were newlyweds and away from home for the first time, and so they formed a family of sorts with a few other young couples who grew to depend on one another for everything. They shared holidays and birthday celebrations and the births of one another's children. My dad thought of John as his brother, and they remained close after returning to the United States.

The year before John died, my parents took my brother and me to spend Easter with John and Linda and their three kids in Fort Rucker, Alabama. Photographs snapped that day are of their daughter, Joanie, and I standing side by side in our new dresses, beaming as we clutch our Easter baskets. Our mothers wear wide-brimmed hats and smile, squinting in the sunlight. On Sunday morning we ran around the yard searching for eggs, and then John and Linda and their kids attended mass at the Catholic church, while we attended services at the area Episcopal church. We regrouped afterward for Easter dinner.

My parents drove from Fort Knox to Dayton, Ohio, for John's funeral, leaving us at home. My brother and I were sent to stay several blocks away with my father's colleagues, my brother with a family that had two sons, and I with Major Halstead and his wife, Gabby. Their daughter, Debbie, had been our babysitter and had recently gotten married. I slept in her old room, which was daintily decorated in yellow, still a little girl's room with frilly curtains and matching daffodil bedspread, but it seemed sad and vacant. Gabby had had Debbie's wedding bouquet preserved, a process that involved dipping it in wax, and it sat in a vase on the French provincial dresser, the mummified flowers inert, their colors muted.

Gabby was a petite German woman with dark hair she wore in an elaborately upswept beehive. Her dense accent required that I pay acute attention when she spoke to me. Much of the time I was unsure of what she was saying, so I nodded a lot and remained quiet, preferring Debbie's room, where I spread my Little Kiddle dolls around my bed, picking each one up and holding the doll's hair to my nose, inhaling deeply the smell of home. The Halsteads had a towering black standard poodle that had apricot-hued rings around its eyes, giving it the effect of wearing a mask. It was a gentle dog, but it stalked me, tracking my every movement, lingering in the doorway of Debbie's room and eyeing me so intensely that I felt that I was never alone. When it was bedtime I lay awake, thinking about my playmate Joanie, thinking about my own dad, thinking about death, wondering if my dad would die too. These thoughts terrified me. I wanted my parents to come home. I wanted to sleep in my own bed. I didn't want to think about death and what it meant, but the thoughts persisted, sometimes pulling me back to wakefulness after I drifted off to sleep.

At the funeral Linda wondered aloud if John was, in fact, dead and asked my father to check the body in the casket to be sure. He was overwhelmed at the prospect of asking the funeral director to unseal the coffin and remove the Plexiglas cover that had been fitted over John's body—a standard procedure carried out by the Army's morticians in preparing bodies to be shipped back to the States from Southeast Asia. He left the room, but he couldn't go through with it. He waited a few minutes before he returned and reassured Linda, even though he hadn't asked to examine the body. He berated himself afterward for not doing what Linda had asked, even though he was convinced it wouldn't have been right to disturb John's remains.

When they returned from the funeral, my parents collected my brother and me and took us home. Life went back to our normal routine. But for me everything was different. I wanted to warn my friends that their dads might not come home from work. The evening news with Walter Cronkite got my attention for the first time. Now I knew why my parents watched every night after dinner. I realized what the nightly KIA and MIA reports meant, that these were more phone calls and more dads who would never come home. More kids who wouldn't see their fathers ever, ever, ever again. The fabric had been torn wide open. I was afraid of a lot of things now, and the world had become a very scary place.

We moved to Florida at the end of the school year that summer, and my father left for his second tour in Vietnam. This time I understood why there was a terrible crying scene at the airport with extended family members gathered around in a tight, mournful huddle, my grandmother weeping until she hyperventilated. I watched my parents embrace and heard him say quietly into my mother's ear as he held her, "I don't want to go." Then he pulled away and strode across the tarmac, his flight bag in hand. I was sure he was not coming back, just like Joanie's dad. Not ever.

I had insomnia. I was terrified to go to sleep, afraid I wouldn't wake up in the morning, afraid I would die, afraid my dad would die, afraid the phone would ring. This new knowledge and understanding of the end of existence was terrifying to me. When my mother came into my room one night and sat on my bed, I told her I felt cheated. I wished I hadn't known about John's death; I wanted life to go back to how it was before I learned what death is. My new bedroom was unfamiliar, and I was often disoriented when I awoke, uncertain of where I was. I was a third grader in the grip of an existential crisis. Life had changed forever.

And living in the civilian world was bewildering and difficult. I felt exposed and alien for the first time in my life. I instinctively knew not to mention to the older kids in our neighborhood who wore tie-dyed T-shirts emblazoned with peace signs that our dad was in Vietnam. But word got around, and when a girl sidled up to my brother in the school lunchroom and hissed, "My mom says your dad kills babies," we knew we were in for it. And we were. We never told our mom about those things or how tough that school year really was for us, and I was sure to tell anyone who asked that my dad was a plumber and that he was away on long business trips a lot. But most everyone knew the truth, and it made life at school hell for us.

Our mother coped by sitting at the dining room table every afternoon without fail, writing long, newsy letters to Dad in her elegant, looping longhand. She stored his letters to her in a hatbox on the top shelf of her closet. After dinner each evening we gathered around the television, watching the news, hoping to catch a glimpse of him in the jittery film footage of the war zone a world away. It was the longest year of my life.

My dad returned from his second tour in Vietnam in the summer of 1970, and we moved to Fort Leavenworth, Kansas. It was a relief to be back in the refuge of a military post and among people who understood us. No one asked awkward questions, and there was no need to be anyone other than who we were.

Linda visited us that fall, leaving her children in the care of their grandparents in Ohio. She and my mother spent a lot of time talking quietly, just the two of them. Sometimes they went into my parents' room and closed the door to talk. When I came home from school, I could hear the sound of hushed murmuring and weeping interwoven with laughter. Once, I overheard Linda telling my mother that someone at church had asked her why she hadn't removed her wedding ring yet. "I just can't," she said. My brother and I crept around the house, careful not to disturb them.

Linda went to work as a teacher, raised her three children alone, and never remarried. She was a single mother in an era in which it was uncommon to be one and later became a source of comfort to other military widows as a leader in the Gold Star Wives organization. She gave an interview to her local newspaper decades after John's death and spoke about the final days they spent together in Hawaii, where he was on leave, the December before he was killed. "There was this feeling between us that this could be the last time."

It's self-indulgent to suppose that I have any right to ruminate about the death of someone else's father, especially in the context of how it affected my life. If anything, I should be writing about gratitude and the good fortune my family had that my dad made it home. My family was reunited. After a year in Kansas we returned to Florida, where my dad was stationed at MacDill Air Force Base at what was then called the U.S. Readiness Command Center, later U.S. Central Command. My brother and I joined a competitive swim team, made new friends, and began to put down roots for the first time. When our father was stationed in Germany two years later, our parents decided he should go alone so that my brother and I could stay in the civilian world and go to the same junior high and senior high schools. At long last we had a home and a mostly normal life.

But every Christmas my thoughts were drawn to Ohio and the family John left behind when a card arrived in Linda's sweeping handwriting that closely resembled that of my mother. I was eager to look at the photos of the children Linda enclosed each year, anxious to see if Joanie still wore her brown hair short and if the boys had freckles. And I thought of them every March, which I had come to associate with the ringing of a phone in the middle of the night—a sound I dread to this day—and witnessing what was surely the most terrible moment my parents had shared so far in their marriage.

Mostly now, I think of the granite wall to the east that rises from the earth, a great dark wave bearing a generation, a sea of names. I think of the lives unlived, of the pilgrimages that have been made to the wall, those yet to come, the stories behind each one, and the infinite ripples that flow from those. I think of how we are all inescapably tied to that wall, each of us connected to the loss, memory, and regret it represents, the depth of which no words exist to adequately describe.

# 6

# Past Perfect Tense

KEVIN C. JONES

I go to the bar. Buy a beer. Buy two. I forget that I'm still holding a half-full bottle from a few minutes ago that I haven't finished. Confused, I put it down on the counter and pay for the new ones, dollar bills tucked in the cheap leather folds behind my green military ID card. Geneva Convention Category I. If captured by a foreign army, I can be made to do most anything they ask, a description not wholly unlike my current status as a lance corporal in the U.S. Marine Corps. I open both bottles, drink one as fast as I can, chase it with the other. I'm still thirsty. I don't know if it's the cigarettes I've been chain-smoking or the acid I dropped a couple of hours ago. Can anyone in the bar tell that I'm tripping? *Am I tripping?* The room seems to bend. Walls move closer to me at concave angles. Gel filters cover all the lights, making everything blue. I'm in the Wave, a bar in Waikiki. It's supposed to look like everyone's underwater, dancing on the bottom of the sea. It makes me feel like I can't breathe, so I suppose it's working. There's a girl across the room who shouldn't be here. She should be in California, like I should, not in Hawaii, both of us strange fish pulled up from faraway shores. Blonde hair, shaved on the sides, black skintight pants, long-sleeved scoop-neck shirt, flats. She looks like an albino Audrey Hepburn, notices me noticing her, floats over. In my drug-addled brain, the crowd parts, and suddenly she is standing before me, smiling. Whispering in my ear.

This isn't now. This is more than twenty years ago. This is happening to someone who used to be me. Who I used to be. Who I still am, somewhere, in the unchanging, past perfect tense of memory. Like an infant's cognitive abilities, the past exists in colors and shapes. Motional residue. Impressions, not actuality. In the future imperfect tense things fall apart. Jobs, marriages, friendships, family relationships. Good people die and bad people live.

In the future I wonder how I got here.

In the past I feel the girl's breath against my skin and miss what she's said.

"What?"

She moves her mouth even closer. "What's your name?" she says. When I write a story about this in twenty years, I will characterize her voice as "rich, melodious," but the truth is I won't remember what her voice sounded like at all.

I write the story in graduate school, in a place where everyone else seems to be crafting tales about small southern towns, and homecomings, and coming to grips with their past and who they are now. In a place where I am the only Californian for the entire first year of school, I write about none of these things and all of them, just like everyone else. We are all trying to write about what we know when what we're really doing is digging deeper and deeper into ourselves to explain what we barely understand. What I barely understand. So I make the girl into a character. Give her a melodious voice.

One of the things I learn at my southern graduate school, and later from living in the South, is that the truth does not always make a good story.

"Jones," I almost say to the girl, because I am a Marine and, therefore, do not have a first name, but I catch myself. "Kevin," I say, and the name feels strange in my mouth. I've been in the Corps for more than a year and in that time have gone to a war and back without ever saying my name. It feels like it belongs to someone else. Somewhere else. Not to here, and the military, and camouflage, and guns, and boredom, and tediousness, and anger. Not to then.

She smiles at me, and I notice the tribal tattoo etched into the right side of her head where the hair has been shaved down to stubble. It looks like a spiky black comma arching over her ear. I ask her the dumbest tattoo question of all, the question I will get in the future, which is to say now, in the present, when people see my fully sleeved left arm:

"Did it hurt?"

All tattoos hurt. The outline alone for my sleeve took twelve hours and left my arm looking like a toddler attacked me with a ballpoint pen until I went back for my next session. My sleeve is colored from the outside in: first the outline, then the black work, then the initial color, then more color, then detailed shading, on and on, for months. Sometimes it takes years. The future of my tattoo is yet to be determined. The afternoon I spent getting my elbow shaded in was to be one of the most painful physical experiences of my life. But it is my pain. My choice. Part of a continuing effort, decades after the girl and the bar and the acid, to carve myself out of the rest of the world's marble.

"The guy pinned my head to the table, held me down, and said, 'Bitch, your ass is mine, now.' Then he went to work." She tilts her head slightly, like a dog looking at a particularly interesting object. "Felt like a jackhammer all the way through to the other side."

I try to follow what she's saying, but it's hard to sit still and I wonder if she can tell that I'm high. I'm three hours into my trip, and though she doesn't look like the type of girl who would be put off by a little dope, you never know.

Buying the dope wasn't easy. I went through a friend of a friend who knew someone in the motor pool who'd scored some acid when he was on leave back home in Long Beach. In the short story I wrote for graduate school, most of the details are true, but I changed the acronyms because back then, right now, in the bar, there is no NCIS. In the past tense the Navy has the Naval Investigative Service, or NIS, but I change it in the future because people have heard of the television show so I don't have to interrupt the narrative to explain what I wrote.

Graduate school teaches that, too. Not to interrupt narrative momentum, like explaining things, or making your reader do math, or joining the Marine Corps when you're an unemployed twenty-year-old community college dropout with shit else to do. One year and one war later, I can think of plenty of shit to do that doesn't involve humping a ruck twenty-five miles down the road at two thirty on a Friday morning. Or cleaning rifles for twelve hours. Or being under the complete control of a psychotic redneck platoon sergeant who can't form complete sentences.

In real life, buying the drugs was much more dramatic than in my story, because actually committing an act is an order of magnitude more terrifying than writing about it. To be honest, I wasn't the one who bought anything. The guy's friend did and then gave me some, but that's too difficult to explain in a short story, and not nearly as interesting, so the truth gets changed again. In the past perfect tense events spool out in sequence, naturally, like a film you've seen before, because, of course, you have.

I ran KT, this giant hill in the middle of the base, all the time on Kaneohe Bay. First, I hated it. Later, as an NCO (noncommissioned officer), I got good at it and used it as an equalizer against larger, stronger Marines who got out of breath running up a ladderwell. I could see everything from the top of that hill. Beaches on the other side of the officers' golf course. The flight line. Coconut Island, home of the University of Hawaii's Marine mammal program. Most of it I wasn't allowed to go on or near. Like many things, they were beautiful and out of reach.

I didn't think about the war as much as the character in my story did, but I've thought about the Marine Corps every day since I got out. The Marine Corps, as much as I hated it, has become perfect in my past. While everything in the future is imperfect, changing, unreliable, the Marine Corps has remained the same. I did not understand this then. I appreciate it now.

Like the short story, I took acid in an effort to deprogram myself. I was becoming more and more acculturated to the Corps, and it frightened me. Young and foolish, I thought that I was missing out on the greater world of civilian life. In actuality, my friends were doing the same stupid things while working the same interchangeably shitty jobs. I was stationed in Hawaii. Even then, even now, in the bar, I know how lucky I am to have drawn Hawaii from the permanent-duty-station deck of cards. I have friends who were sent to Yuma, Arizona; Twentynine Palms, California; Camp Lejeune, North Carolina.

Iraq.

Afghanistan.

Friends who killed people in combat, something I never had to do.

In the bar the girl knows I'm high. She tells me. She takes me by the hand out onto the sidewalk on Kalakaua Avenue, past the 7-11 and the people waiting in line to get in the club. She takes me down to Lewers Street, and we stand on the corner, watching Marines try to pick up on tourist chicks going into Moose McGillycuddy's. In my short story the girl asks me if I've ever read poetry and explains that every word is a paragraph, every syllable a sentence. Only she didn't say that to me. Someone else will, in the future imperfect. She's now part of my perfect past as well, existing entirely in a single freezing January in Charlotte, our affections bursting like overripe fruit in the hothouse environment of an MFA program. Like all writers, I am a thief, and I stole her words for my story long after our imagined future no longer existed.

I never had sex with the girl from the bar. Of course, I did in my story. The recovery of the war vet through the transcendental experience of congress with someone who may or may not be real. I left the woman in the story deliberately ambiguous. Was she real? Something supernatural? Unknowable?

I tell the girl I need to get back to base. I never say "home." She takes me to her car, a black MG convertible, and drives me back over the Pali Highway to Kaneohe. When we get to the front gate, I almost panic. She doesn't have the proper documentation to get on base, and I'm still loaded. Fortunately, I don't get into any trouble with the MPs. The guard at the gate remembers me from Marine Combat Training back at Camp Pendleton, before Desert Storm. He waves me through. That's it. Easy-peasy. She parks in the battalion parking lot. We walk up the back ladderwell to the second deck and down to my room at the end of a long, linoleum-covered hallway. I put on Nirvana's "Smells Like Teen Spirit," but at a low level. I'm not trying to be romantic. It's 0400 and I don't want a bunch of hung-over Marines barreling down the hall looking for a fight, not to mention the amount of trouble I can get into if the duty NCO comes along.

We lay on the bed together, the drugs slowly leaching out of my system as the sun rises over the Pacific and through my window. She has been telling me something that I wish I could remember, but it's gone, forever maintaining its perfection. The last bit of the evening remains like a silent movie on damaged film. Just flashes. White-blonde hair. The tribal tattoo. Her deeply tanned skin, bare feet on my lap as she lay with her head on the opposite side of the bed from me. The incongruity of an attractive woman against the olive-drab wool of my blanket, the industrial furnishings of the room, the faint smell of pine oil and weapons lubricant existing at the molecular level of everything Marine Corps.

I am still there, in the past, lying with that girl on my bed, walking her down the hallway, down the back stairs, across the grass to the battalion parking lot. Putting her into her car, closing the door. No kiss. No phone number. Watching as she drives away.

In the future it is January in Charlotte, and snowing, and I am leaving a small house in North Davidson for the last time. It is not the past perfect yet, but will be, then it is, then it fades.

In the future imperfect I teach college. Work with veterans of new wars. Help them write about what they know, who they are. I search for words. Sometimes I have them; sometimes I don't.

7

## Tom

ALAN JONES

Some of the best things happen purely by chance.

We were flying back from gunnery training in Tripoli, spring of 1956. That spring was part of a serene interval, three years after the Korean truce was signed and before the Suez war and the Hungarian revolt in the fall of '56.

Usually, we flew in flights of four, and the whole squadron flew back together at five-minute intervals. This time Tom and I had finished qualifying and were ordered to return to Etain, our base east of Verdun, as a flight of two. Tom was from the yellow-tail squadron, I from the blue, but we had flown together a few times and had a couple of drinks together.

We checked out of Wheelus, the big military air base east of Tripoli, around 0900, with a flight plan to Pisa, where we always refueled. As usual we listed our alternate as Rome Ciampino, even though military jets weren't allowed to land there. The Italians feared the jet noise and vibration would damage the ancient buildings. In those days the airlines were still flying DC-6s, Constellations, and some strange Air France birds, all propeller driven. The flight-plan alternate was a formality in most cases, and there was no other jet-friendly airport along the west coast of Italy.

Taking off in formation, the lead at 98 percent power so the wing could keep up, we cleaned up gear and flaps and climbed out toward Italy. We switched to our side channel to talk and were just about abeam of Malta when Tom called in his easy Texas drawl, "This airplane is sort of a dog. I'm having to roll in a lot of left trim to keep it level." I double-clicked in response, and we flew on in silence, admiring the view, until we were over Sicily.

Flying over the Med was usually very peaceful, sailing along over flat blue water with land always in sight. There were the speck of Malta

0

and the humped mountains of Sicily, and then the stretched-out coast of Italy angled off to the right. But this time was different.

"Two, this thing is getting worse," Tom said. "And I'm starting to burn internal fuel." That made the problem pretty clear. One of his two-hundred-gallon drop tanks wasn't feeding, which meant we couldn't reach Pisa and he would have to do something about the tanks. We switched to Channel 3, and Tom radioed Ciampino. "Rome control, this is Air Force 592 en route to Pisa. I am short of fuel and request permission to divert to Ciampino, estimated arrival in thirty-five minutes."

Rome asked for details and cleared traffic for an emergency landing.

"Where are you gonna drop the tanks?" I asked.

"We'll see," he said. "I may try to land without dropping."

That didn't sound good to me. Two hundred gallons of JP-4 was about fifteen hundred extra pounds hanging on his right wing, and it didn't do much for his flight performance, let alone landing.

We sailed along in silence again, homing on the Ciampino low-frequency range until the Italian coast swam under us. In those days we had Omni stations around the States, but in Europe we used the old low-frequency radio beacons: a whole system of instrument approach and letdown procedures was based on it. On this particular day it didn't matter because we were CAVU (ceiling and visibility unlimited), but following the beam meant you didn't have to navigate. You only had to take up your heading and sit back. Things could go wrong and sometimes did, but that's another story.

Ciampino had cleared out traffic, and we made a fighter approach—at twelve hundred feet, pitch out at the end of the runway and pop the speed brakes, lose speed on downwind and lower landing gear and flaps at 185 knots, and start descending as you begin the final 180 turn and over the fence at 140 knots.

Tom's plane was eating fuel at a pretty good rate, so we didn't waste time. I entered the pattern with him until he made his 180 onto downwind with the heavy wing on the outside of the turn, and then I climbed out to sea, watching him land. He carried some extra speed over the fence and eased onto the runway before it could stall and drop the heavy wing. It was a neat bit of flying.

"Ciampino tower, this is Air Force 2," I called. "I'll be burning off fuel for about fifteen minutes. The emergency aircraft has landed."

The tower was good with that, and with speed brakes out I burned holes in the air off the coastline, which I had pretty much to myself. A lovely spring day with no clouds in sight, no boats, no airliners. A few dinky islands with three thousand years of history.

After about ten minutes, the tower got nervous and called for my status, so I headed in and made a routine landing. We were the only jets in sight. Could have been the only ones in Italy.

Tom was waiting at operations in the terminal, chatting up the airport personnel, whose English was no better than our Italian. The Italians secured the aircraft, and we spent about an hour contacting Etain, which promised to send a T-33 down for us, with repairs to follow. They needed to load a maintenance crew and equipment and find a cargo plane to get them to Ciampino. Etain said it would take a couple of days.

We pulled our B-4 bags out of the ammo bays—the only storage space in the 86—and walked out front to get a taxi. No one had credit cards in those days, although there was American Express, so we always carried some cash. This was an era when we got eight dollars per diem while traveling and turned a profit on it. The hotel in Marseilles, where we would overnight on the way to Tripoli, cost around a thousand francs—three dollars at the official rate of 350 to 1, although if you took greenbacks into the economy, you could usually get 400 or 450. Same with the lira, which was something like 1,500 to a dollar.

At any rate, we taxied into town and, taking the driver's advice, found a room in a rather impressive hotel. We stashed our bags, washed up, changed from flight suits to civvies, and went downstairs for dinner and a drink at a sidewalk café under the arcade that runs around the piazza. In the center of the roundabout was a huge fountain, very baroque and bigger than any I'd ever seen, very Italian. Many years later I figured out we were staying on the Piazza della Repubblica. I don't know if the hotel is still there, but it was definitely very swanky then. (It may be the Exedra today, going for about three hundred a night.)

Tom and I got moderately buzzed on beer and wine, took a ramble around the area, and turned in early.

The next day we pumped the hotel clerk for ideas and then hired a taxi for the day to show us all the sights he could manage. He was very good. We saw the Appian Way, the Colosseum, the Forum, Gina Lollobrigida's house, the Pantheon, the catacombs. You name it, we saw it. Even the marble typewriter, the monument to Vittorio Emmanuel II, first king of reunited Italy.

The driver dropped us off at St. Peter's in the early afternoon. As it happened, Pius XII was holding a public audience, so we wandered in. The basilica was jammed. A men's chorus of fifty or sixty sang something ecclesiastical, and—remember, we didn't speak any Italian, let alone Latin—the audience went on for quite a while. We were impressed by the grandeur of the place, but more interesting was the sound of English being spoken behind us in the crowd by girls with American accents.

Tom never missed an opportunity like that. Before we left St. Peter's, we had arranged to meet two of the girls that evening for dinner. I can't say the Vatican is a good pickup joint, but Tom was good at improvisation. The young women—there were four or five—were schoolteachers on the grand tour, and they were probably ready to speak English with some countrymen.

The details are hazy, all these years later, but it did not turn out to be a carnal evening. It was memorable, though. We went to dinner and then hired a horse-drawn carriage for a moonlight tour of ancient Rome and of the same sights we'd seen in daylight. The ruins by night were even more spectacular. After two or three hours behind the horse, we jumped in a cab and went to an open-air nightclub somewhere on the outskirts. A floor show was going on, with a magician, a girl singer, and the like. We didn't understand a word, but the magician was cool. Tom and I each had a beer; the girls had Cokes. I still have the tab somewhere, and we were astonished at the amount. The beers were about two dollars a piece, and the Cokes three dollars, upwards of fifteen thousand lire. This in an economy where the hotel room was only five or six bucks.

The teachers' tour moved on the next day, but we still had a day or two left in Rome. We did more desultory touring and walking about and found a lively nightspot in the heart of Rome that evening. Tom struck up with an Italian girl and disappeared about nine o'clock. I drank an hour or so more and went back to the hotel.

I didn't hear Tom come in, but he was full of it the next morning. After an elaborate evening, he said, drinking and the usual foreplay, he ended up in the girl's apartment. After a satisfactory round of sex, he got ready to head back to the hotel when the girl suggested he pay her a few thousand lire.

"I was shocked," Tom said with a straight face. "I told her, 'But I thought you liked me. I didn't know that you were . . . ,'" and in the end he escaped without paying, except for dinner and wine, of course. Tom could do that. He would talk about the Texas girls he knew in high school and after and some coming-of-age stories. His teen sex life was a lot better than mine, or at least his stories were.

Tom was very much a Texan, but he wasn't one of those ten-gallon phonies. For a Texan he was understated, with a dry sense of humor and an *aw shucks* manner he could don effortlessly. With women it didn't hurt that he was tall, reasonably good-looking—at least the Air Force nurses back at Etain said so—and a happy sort of guy. He was also a good pilot, better than average in our wing, though perhaps not on a par with the few who had combat experience.

The rest of our stay, a day or two more in Rome, was relatively routine. Not boring. A twenty-five-year-old American should never be bored in Rome. We had some good meals, explored the city on foot, and checked in daily with Etain.

Eventually, Etain sent a pilot and a t-33, and we met him at Ciampino in midmorning. With the T-bird leading, we made a formation takeoff, which is pretty interesting with mismatched airplanes. I had to throttle back to stay with the T, but with a long runway and cool morning air, we made it off without incident and flew back to the base. I don't know when the 561st got Tom's f-86 back or who went down to get it. Tom and I had bragging rights all year as the only pilots in the wing who were tourists in Rome.

I saw Tom only a few more times after that. We all had temporary duty on other bases, and we stood one-hour alert together back in Germany. He wasn't one of us who hung out at the O club bar or the craps table in the back, although he would take a drink from time to time.

As fighter-bomber pilots, we flew ground support for Army maneuvers over near the Iron Curtain, making low-altitude runs against a simulated enemy, directed by a forward air controller. It was exhilarating work, but it was close to the ground. The Army colonels knew nothing about air-to-ground work, but they loved a low-level air show, and we gave it to them.

A few months after our Rome adventure, Tom drove his airplane into the ground on a routine training mission. It's always a "routine training mission" until somebody gets killed. One of the 561st pilots told me later that Tom just got too low and pancaked it on a mock strafing run. No reason, except bad judgment and bad luck. The same old story.

It could have been me, and then Tom would be writing the story.

# 8

# Middle Passage, Morning Watch

ANNE VISSER NEY

It's not the towering sail,
but the unseen wind that moves the ship.

—SAILOR'S ADAGE

I

Day breaks holy on the morning watch. Night recedes as twilight emerges beyond the ocean's rim. The false horizon disappears, and before dawn the quartermaster fixes the ship's position using a timepiece and sextant. In those precious minutes of nautical twilight, the star's reflection in the sextant mirror is aligned with the sharpening edge of the sea. The precise time is marked at the moment the angle between star, ship, and horizon is properly sighted.

The fix is reduced and plotted on the navigational chart. Sunrise is observed and recorded in the ship's log. The new day is gauged by wind direction and effect on the skin of the water, by cloud type, the sky's appearance, and the barometer's change.

These were my duties during my first permanent Coast Guard assignment as quartermaster of the watch. I loved each task, but I shot stars in reverent witness to light and motion, sensing the enormous responsibility of wayfinding across the sea.

On watch then I often thought about where the ship would carry me and what lay between where I was and the beckoning borders that lay ahead. Now, after a thirty-one-year service career, I wonder at the tenacity I had to answer those questions. If I had known then the full journey, would I have had the courage to sail on?

II

Stowaway stories are as old as Jonah. Individuals slip onto a ship for illegal passage for many reasons—to escape God, poverty, or the law; to seek family, fame, or adventure. But after the September 11 attacks, these and other conventional narratives appeared to ignore obvious possibilities concerning the nation's border security. After 9/11 the U.S. Coast Guard and its DHS (Department of Homeland Security) partners immediately focused on securing maritime ports of entry into the country; stowaways were but one aspect of border control.

Ten years ago, in 2003, one hundred million metric tons of goods landed in U.S. ports every day, much of it in sealed, fully packed intermodal containers that shuttled across the globe with use and reuse. It is impossible to search each "box" landed without halting the global economy. DHS officials wondered: could a bomb be in a container? Maybe.

Merchant ships flagged in dozens of countries were often registered to shell corporations that obscured true vessel ownership within a tangle of legal and financial instruments. Did Bin Laden control freighters? Nobody knew.

Foreign mariner documents often served as de facto passports, although many were issued to seamen without a background check. The problem of absconders—registered crewmen who abandon ship and disappear into port cities—was as old as that of stowaways. Might any of these travelers manipulate document loopholes as part of a terrorist plot? The possibilities were obvious and frightened the country as it reeled from the terrorist attacks.

Fact-backed conventional wisdom said that maritime travelers sometimes accompany illicit cargo hidden on a vessel: narcotics, for example. Until America was launched into the Global War on Terror, officials had not seriously considered that mariners or stowaways might accompany arms, biological weapons, or radioactive material destined for dirty bombs—all of which could be hidden in the millions of containers moving from the ports by rail or truck toward every city in the country.

The 9/11 Commission (the National Commission on Terrorist Attacks upon the United States) did not release its report until August 2004. Yet it was clear that government agencies had failed to share information that might have helped to uncover Bin Laden's plot. Not needing the official report to remedy this failure, the Coast Guard began to establish interagency support teams to bolster security in and around the nation's largest ports. These teams included DHS partners: Customs and Border Protection (CBP), Immigration and Customs Enforcement (ICE), and Border Patrol; Department of Justice agencies including the Federal Bureau of Investigation and Alcohol, Tobacco, and Firearms; and deputized state and local law enforcement officers. These teams allowed information to flow between investigators and intelligence officers scrutinizing similar problems from different viewpoints and enhanced communications between agency leaders responsible for the enforcement of overlapping statutes.

America's porous borders are a mixed blessing. Our generally robust economy, melting-pot culture, and intellectual strength relate directly to open trade policies and a willingness to allow people and ideas to flow. Yet anyone involved in counterterrorism work is keenly aware of the darker possibilities of unlimited movement across borders.

Each agency had its own version of this problem of enforcing laws that continue to reflect the nation's competing priorities of freedom and security. CBP must deny and allow entry of goods and people. ICE must investigate smuggling, including of humans, but also determine whether illegal migrants have a valid basis for being issued a visa. The Coast Guard senior officer in a given port, titled the captain of the port, including my CO (commanding officer) at the time, must ensure that commerce flows smoothly through secure, safely operated port terminals and hazardous material facilities.

This is the milieu I stepped into in October 2002. Exactly twenty-three years after I became a Coast Guardsman, when borders of citizenship and personhood seemed without limit, I reported to the interagency port security team at Charleston, South Carolina. There, every day, I had to reconsider the physical meaning of border. As I did so, I began for the first time to fathom the deeper meanings of separation and connection that define our lives in so many ways.

It was the night I attended my first stowaway interview that I came face-to-face with my old questions and discovered new ones stirring inside. As the interview proceeded, I began to glimpse the depth to which we are shaped both by the promise of our horizons and by the waters flowing under the bridge as we navigate between our origins and endings.

III

When I graduated from high school I was already desperate to escape my small Ohio town: cornfields and dairy farms. I rated colleges by their distance from home. Once there I ditched studying for extracurricular activities. By 1979 I stopped even pretending to care about academics.

One bright morning that April, I lay on a seawall along a causeway somewhere in the Florida Keys, soaking up sun in my turquoise bikini. I tipped onto my elbows, squinting across the blue-green Florida Strait so I could study a man-of-war's translucent balloon. It drifted with the wind, trailing its stinging purple tentacles closer. The sea breeze skimmed my belly.

Traffic whooshed along the coast road that connects Maine to the southernmost point in the continental United States. There, in Key West, A1A terminates at the famous red and yellow marker with its sign that points ninety miles to Cuba. Trucks trundled along A1A, once in a while honking approval. New crops of college kids on spring break roared past, whooping greetings. *My* break had ended weeks earlier. My roommates, long gone, were finishing the semester back in Ohio, while I lazed in the sun, dreaming about my future.

I pulled on my older brother's white Navy shirt that I used as a beach cover-up. When I appropriated it on my way south, Tim tossed in advice for free. "Whatever you decide, don't join the Navy."

"How about the Coast Guard?" I teased.

He shrugged indifference and then added, "Make sure they guarantee you an 'A' school after boot camp."

"You mean a school?"

"No, *an* 'A' school. It's your job training. Like, I was an operations specialist, so I had to go to OS 'A' school."

The conversation rolled around in my head as I explored the Keys. After a month or so, when the sun perfectly set, I climbed back in my car and headed home and called a Coast Guard recruiter.

I see now that nothing prevented me from pursuing my adventures: driving south, flirting with men-of-war, looking across the ocean toward countries that seemed so close yet lay completely beyond my experience or understanding. Dream chasing is in many ways a uniquely American privilege. My ideas of border and boundary were identical: nonexistent or, at the very least, infinitely accessible.

By 2003 and the night of the stowaway's interview, I was painfully aware that I had done nothing prior to 1979 but grow into these freedoms. They were simply an accident of my birth.

## IV

The four-hundred-foot cargo ship moored as my DHS team waited along the seawall. A CBP inspector would interview the stowaway; ICE agents might arrest, detain, or place him into custody; other assignments were based on the participating officer's unique jurisdictions and authorities. I would gather information on the vessel and the foreign ports where it had called, sifting for recommendations that could tighten port and therefore the nation's security.

After the gangway was in place, we climbed aboard and reassembled around the stowaway, who sat cross-legged on the steel deck, waiting. His gaze flickered up our legs, across our eyes, and out onto the terminal, where glaring halogen and sodium lights must have silhouetted our uniforms and haloed our ball caps. I glanced around. Yellow gear—forklifts—buzzed around the dock, in and out of the shadows between canyons formed by stacks of containers marked MSC, COSCO, or APL (Mediterranean Shipping Company, Chinese Overseas Shipping Company, Asian Pacific Line). Huge cranes rumbled and beeped as cargo was lifted from the ship's forward holds to the pier. Longshoreman hustled around us intently as they worked the offload.

I studied the stowaway. A thin wool blanket hung around his shoulders even though sweat soaked my T-shirt and heavy uniform in the July night. His torn T had once been white. He wore pink shower shoes. He smelled unwashed.

The inspector began his interview, already stymied because the stowaway had no documents. "Where do you come from?"

"Rwanda," the stowaway answered in a lilt that suggested fluency in another language. He folded his hands and fixed his gaze on them. "I walked across Africa." Ah-free-cah. He parted his hands as if to show the distance he had come measured between calloused palms. To me, his voice resonated a continent of misted forests and lakes a thousand meters deep. "It took me five years."

He said he was born in Kigali, Rwanda's capital. I guessed him to be thirtysomething. His mother was Ugandan, his father Hutu. She went missing during the genocide; he was dead. "Did he die in the genocide?" the inspector asked. The stowaway looked away dully, almost sullenly, as he answered. "*Non.* Just died."

When there was nothing left for him there, he walked away from Rwanda. He slept where he could: in abandoned cars or on the ground. He crossed through the Congo. The police arrested him in Angola and then forced him to fight alongside rebels for three years. He fled to Gabon when he escaped. From there he slipped across the border to Angola, where he scraped together a living as a longshoreman and eventually embarked the ship that brought him to the United States.

I mentally assembled Africa based on my fifth grade classroom's roll-down world map, color-coded by a nation's official language: pink (French), yellow (English), mint green (German), and powder blue (Dutch). Rwanda was green. The former German colony lies two thousand kilometers east of Africa's Atlantic coastal nations of Angola, Gabon, and Equatorial Guinea. A thirty-eight-hundred-mile spur of the Kinshasa Highway connects Kigali to Libreville, Gabon. Luanda, Angola, where he hired on as a longshoreman, lies just north of Libreville.

As he spoke I recalled my own passage from home.

v

The recruiter was eager to sign me up when I walked into his office in the summer of 1979. The Vietnam draft ended in 1973, drying up the Coast Guard's applicant pool. In 1975, when the Coast Guard gender integrated, new possibilities opened for women, and for recruiters who had been left scrambling to fill enlistment quotas. Remembering my brother's advice, I refused to join without a guaranteed "A" school. When I convinced the recruiter he would not sign me up otherwise, he handed me a *Ratings Description Brochure* and told me to pick a school.

I skimmed the entries for a job that would take me to sea. "Quartermaster," I announced, pointing to the page that showed the QM insignia—a ship's wheel—and described his duties: navigation, Morse code and flag-hoist signaling, weather, logs, and shiphandling. "That'll get me on a boat, right?"

"Cutter," he said. "Coast Guard ships are called cutters." He hesitated and then shook his head slowly and suggested I think about yeoman or storekeeper: an office job. There were only a dozen or so female quartermasters, four gender-integrated cutters, and mixed-crew ratios of 10 women to 150 men. Billeting was tricky. For me to land a sea assignment, the cutter would have to have a female berth available at the same time one of the three junior quartermasters rotated ashore.

"But it's possible," I said. Either my determination or his looming quota sped my request along. I signed the contract when my guaranteed orders were approved on the crisp blue morning of October 21, 1979. I raised my right hand and swore the oath familiar to all military personnel, to "support and defend the Constitution of the United States against all enemies, foreign and domestic . . ." The recruiter clapped my shoulder, shook my hand, and handed me orders and a plane ticket.

At the airport my stepdad, a World War II combat pilot, hugged me proudly. My baby sister, faced with the prospect of being the last, lone sibling at home, wept fat teenage tears. My mother kissed her oldest daughter and sniffled into a tissue. Soon, my plane taxied and rose away from northeastern Ohio's orderly farms. Two hours later the jet circled into Philadelphia. The Atlantic Ocean stretched beyond my window like a blue scrim of infinite possibility.

Long after dark 170 other kids and I boarded the Greyhound Special to Cape May. The bus rolled southeast onto the turnpike, past fewer and smaller towns and over more and larger inlets, each waterway alive with the lights of buoys and boats. I trembled as we approached New Jersey's southern peninsula and the air grew pungent with salt, diesel fuel, and the smell of low tide.

I wondered was it like for the stowaway when he began to sense the ocean beyond Africa's hills and savannas. Was he excited? Or did he cry, finally realizing he had reached this milestone without his missing mother, dead father, and family? Did he leave home to run away from boundaries or toward new borders? And which was true of my own journey?

## VI

The inspector asked the stowaway why he left Africa. He shrugged as if to say, who knows why we do what we do? The inspector pressed. Had the police wanted him? The stowaway squared his shoulders beneath his blanket and raggedy shirt; he pulled his chin in and frowned. He was never in trouble. He thought often about leaving to find a better life. He began to study the chalkboard posts announcing vessel arrivals and departures. One day he left.

It was my turn to ask questions. He had chosen a ship of American registry either by chance or by design. Why this ship? I asked.

He waved a hand along the deck rail behind him. "It has low sides." His amusement convicted the ignorance that must have shown on my face. "The last day before this ship left, I swam to it. I chose it because I could climb up the side." He lifted his arms to show how he had used drainpipes and scuppers for handholds. He looked directly into my eyes while he spoke, as though we were old comrades reminiscing about a shared experience. I held his gaze longer than required and then glanced toward the ship's outboard side. My arms ached as he described his clandestine boarding.

"Then, I hid."

I still wonder if he crept on deck late at night to see the ocean's dark blanket of stars. Did his heart sink as the Southern Cross dropped low in the sky, a visible reminder that his home was now just a memory? Did his heart quicken as the Northern Hemisphere's brighter constellations rose higher each night?

I wanted to ask him foolish things. I wanted to know if he recognized Orion.

## VII

The winter constellations rose higher every morning during my eight weeks of boot camp. My company commander, a chief petty officer (quartermaster), marched his eighty-two recruits to breakfast every morning for our first two weeks of training. The autumn stars glittered over the peninsula's chilly air as we waited at attention for our turn in the galley. One morning the chief ordered his fledglings to locate Orion.

This constellation is notable for its clarity and the large number of fifty-eight selected navigational stars in its vicinity. Betelgeuse glitters strangely red, and new ship's lookouts often report it as a UFO or flare. Blue-white Rigel sits on Orion's left knee. The Hunter's Belt and the constellation Aries scribe the celestial equator, a useful, if imaginary, navigational construct. Aldebaran in Taurus, the Pleiades' Seven Sisters, Capella in Auriga, Castor and Pollux in Gemini; finally, opposite the belt from Aries, Sirius, the Dog Star, shines brighter than any other star visible from Earth.

Only the sun and moon, four planets (Venus, Mars, Jupiter, and Saturn), and the selected stars are used to fix a ship's position by sextant. Discerning them is crucial to wayfinding at sea. Oddly, in practice the navigator must know the ship's general whereabouts in order to plot the exact latitude and longitude calculated from the sight; in other words, a precise location can only be fixed when the approximate position is already known.

I knew nothing of these tools and concepts the day I joined the Coast Guard. In my ignorance the stars were beautiful. But they told me nothing and implied no way ahead.

Could I have pursued my vague dreams of exotic places and new experiences alone? What if nobody had shown me those stars or helped me to approximate my position so I could determine my place in the world?

### VIII

The stowaway pointed to the bridge, six decks up. "After five days I knocked on the windows. I was thirsty." He said he had been treated very well by the crew.

As the interview wound down, I went inside the ship to find the master—the vessel's captain—chugging pink bug juice in the air-conditioned, brightly lit galley. Merchant marine masters are under tremendous pressure to stay on schedule. Docking fees run to thousands of dollars an hour; time lost is money lost. Stresses mount enormously when things fall behind, particularly when resolving a delay is beyond a master's control: Weather, port holds, offload crane breakdown. Or stowaways.

"Asshole," the captain said after he offered me an icy bottle of water and a chair. He assured me that his crew was hypervigilant about security, locking every door, window, and hold 24-7. The house—the ship's central tower where berthing, galley, offices, and the navigational bridge are located—was always locked, even in U.S. ports. "That's why he had to bang on the windows when he got hungry. Scared the living shit out of the watch," he added.

"He said he was thirsty," I said.

"Yeah, whatever. He's lucky we're Americans. I know guys would've tossed him over right then and there." He turned away to discuss offload operations with the third mate before continuing. "I hate stowaways. We tried to get rid of him at every port between Lagos [Nigeria] and here, but he doesn't have papers, so nobody would take him." Off-watch crewmen came and went, quaffing cold drinks and devouring cake. Red gingham tablecloths with matching curtains lent the mess deck the air of a cheerful midwestern diner.

I said, "He's a man without a country. I can't take him off or order him to stay on board. It's up to ICE. But I guess you know that."

"Just get him the hell off my boat. We're due in Houston in two days." He drained his drink bottle. I wished him good luck with Customs and let myself out of the house.

I passed the stowaway as I headed toward the gangway. He was ensconced in his assigned quarters: a small unventilated compartment meant for mooring-line storage. Its open door faced the harbor. A stiff breeze had sprung up, coming off the North Atlantic and past the Sullivan's Island Lighthouse marking the coast.

He had no papers, no ID card, no vaccination record, no passport, not a thing to prove where he came from or who he was or why he was here. He had his story, the shirt on his back, a borrowed blanket, and a pair of plastic shower shoes that barely cushioned the soles of his feet.

The merchant ship he had climbed aboard had since called in a half-dozen African, Mediterranean, and European ports. At each stop the master had tried to put the stowaway ashore. But no sovereign nation would admit a man without proof of existence or country. Neither would any nation readmit a citizen lacking proof of citizenship. That night he sat in limbo at the ship's next-to-last stop before it began a new round-robin voyage across the Atlantic.

After the DHS debrief, I drove through the port gate and onto the Cooper River Bridge's twinkling spans. If he had known what to look for, the stowaway might have seen my car passing over the river that the ship had navigated to reach the port.

What would happen to him? Did he feel the same frustration as I did when borders lay just beyond my grasp? Did his dreams shimmer also for him like bright rainbows whose ends impossibly vanish the closer they are approached?

# IX

My career started out with flying colors. I graduated from basic training with a four-time honor company. Our seventy men and twelve women together had earned nineteen out of twenty possible teamwork ribbons. Along the way I was awarded expert marksmanship medals for the M16 rifle and .45 pistol. Thrilled with my new life, I barely paid attention to world events that would irrevocably shift and blur America's borders in the coming years.

In November 1979, while I learned to shoot a weapon, Islamist revolutionaries stormed the U.S. Embassy in Iran, taking fifty-two Americans hostage and ushering in a new age of international engagement. Now, I do not even remember how I learned what had happened in Tehran. At the time I certainly did not understand the geopolitical concept of borders or sovereignty any more than I grasped the conflicts that the gender-integrated Coast Guard had stirred up within its recently males-only ranks.

Ten days after boot camp graduation I flew to Orlando for signalman and quartermaster "A" school: twelve weeks of U.S. Navy–sponsored training. The five male Coast Guard students and I, the only woman in our thirty-man class, easily took top rankings. When the time came, I requested assignment to one of the four cutters that had been opened to women.

Two weeks before my class graduated, the Coast Guard chief in charge summoned me to his office. I reported as ordered and stood at attention in front of him with my eyes "in the boat," staring straight ahead at the wintry Florida sun streaming through the blinds over his head. Had my orders arrived?

Soldiers and sailors have amazing peripheral vision while at attention. The chief balanced on his chair's back legs with his feet on the government-gray desk. He laced his fingers behind his head. I saw the soles of his black patent-leather shoes. Finally, he said, "Visser, you are not going to make it. Not as a quartermaster. Not as a sailor. Not in the Coast Guard."

I was chagrined: orders to sea these comments were not. "Do you hear me, Visser?" The chair's front legs slammed to the floor as the chief dropped his feet from the desk.

"Yes, Chief," I said. I did what I hoped was a sharp about-face and marched back down the hall as my newfound poise melted into a slow burn. What did he see or know that I did not? Could he be right?

### X

The morning after the stowaway interview, I briefed the captain of the port before sending paperwork up the chain of command. The man remained on the vessel, which had sailed before dawn en route to Houston. Unwilling to hold the ship and unable to investigate the man's claims of Rwandan citizenship in just a few hours, ICE had referred the case to their Houston office.

"What will happen to him?" my CO said, although neither of us could know.

"I don't know, sir. It's Houston's call now."

"But what can they do in Houston that they couldn't do here?" he said.

I said I didn't know, mumbling about the ship's schedule and the man's situation due to his lack of papers. I rubbed sleep from my eyes, hoping to erase the previous night's dream.

It hovered around me like a fog. In it the stowaway and I were far out to sea on the ship of ghosts that can never go home, *The Flying Dutchman*. Seamen believe anyone glimpsing this mythical ship portends doom. My uneasiness hung on all day.

### XI

In the end my "A" school chief was wrong about my future. From 1979 until my retirement in 2010, along with many Coast Guardsmen of the same era, I challenged, broke, and renegotiated dozens of gender barriers women encountered as they grew up in the once all-male service.

I received orders to sea from A school. On Good Friday 1980, I reported to the 378-foot high-endurance cutter (WHEC) *Mellon* homeported in Honolulu, Hawaii. I qualified as an underway quartermaster of the watch within two weeks of my arrival. In subsequent years I reached many female nearly firsts—boarding officer certification (1982) and recruit company commander (1985). By the late 1980s I graduated into Coast Guard history as their first female chief quartermaster (1988) and first female chief warrant officer (boatswain specialty, 1990).

I discovered along the way that setting precedent is usually difficult and sometimes impossible, and it nearly always leaves scars. Borders cannot always be crossed or barriers broken at a given time and place. In 1992, when my son was eighteen months old and my job required frequent travel at odd hours throughout the Caribbean, my only option was to request release from active duty into the selected reserve, a choice I gladly made. (In 1993 this policy was changed; now, all Coast Guardsmen are offered care-for-newborn sabbatical—a two-year unpaid leave followed by guaranteed reinstatement at the last rank held.)

The day of the September 11 attacks, my reserve (and active duty) background included seaport security, counterterrorism, interagency and international government coordination, maritime law enforcement, and "boots-on-the-ground" (field) intelligence to support the Coast Guard's busy southeastern U.S. missions to interdict narcotics and illegal migrants at sea. For twenty-three years borders had defined my Coast Guard service.

I stood my last watch at sea in July 2002 as a deck officer aboard *Mellon*'s aging sister ship, *Dallas*. From there I returned to active duty, charged with helping to redefine the concepts and enforcement of borders in the nation's fourth-largest container port at Charleston. There, I grappled again with the same questions I had posed of my own life decades earlier. Where are we going? What challenges lie between our past and our future? With what tenacity will we pursue our dreams of freedom and choice?

## XII

I never saw the stowaway again. I remember how he smiled at me, the smallish blonde tucked between the team's burly men. The woman who failed to grasp the value of a ship with sides that, in spite of difficulties, a man might climb. I never learned his fate. He arrived illegally to the United States, and, once ICE determined his nationality, he was likely deported back to Africa. The odds of being granted a visa were not in his favor.

During the interview the inspector inquired if the stowaway had received help—a question meant to flush out unsavory associations or the name of a coyote, a middleman who moves illegal migrants across borders. The stowaway seemed surprised by the question. Again, our eyes met. The ship and port lights reflected from his face.

"No accomplices? No help?" the inspector repeated.

"No," he said. He gazed again toward the city. He squatted, perched on his heels as though suspended between the dark Atlantic, across which he had come, and the port's golden lights. "There was nobody."

His answer haunts me still. Not because he was alone. I believe that a dreamer's determination rises to meet the challenges presented by the dream. Nor do I regret not having done more for him. I gave him what was mine to give: eye contact as one traveler to another and a good-natured nod to my ignorance about the possibilities inherent in the American ship's construction. I gave witness to his story even as I struggled with the questions that it raised. Acknowledgment of the other is a small but significant kindness.

What haunts me is the possibility that his future may be as bleak as his past apparently had been. Who would show him the proper stars and teach him the basics of a few simple tools that might enable him to find his way?

I don't know the answers. Maybe there are none. But I do remember those first morning watches I ever stood. How clear everything seemed as I looked through the sextant toward the sharpening horizon, in the half light between night and the sunrise that would usher in a new day and all that it would bring.

# 9

# The Thirty-Day Project

CHRISTAL PRESLEY

"Dad says he'll do it," my mother tells me.

My hand is suddenly sweaty as I press the phone against my ear. Two days earlier I'd called my mother to ask if she would relay a request to my father. I'd decided that would be the best way to gauge his reaction without actually having to deal with him directly. I wanted to know if he would be okay with my calling him every day for thirty days to ask him about his experiences during the Vietnam War for a writing project.

I had been writing for years to work through some emotional issues, leaving out anything related to my father or to Vietnam. Those subjects were too painful, and I was too afraid of what would happen if I opened that Pandora's box.

But as much as I wrote—about my botched marriage, the emotional turmoil I felt, and my failed quest to find contentment—I remained stuck. Blocked in both my writing and my life.

Then one day a guest speaker at a writing workshop posed a question that hit me right between the eyes: "What if you wrote about the thing you fear the most?" He said that he'd been trying to find happiness for years, but nothing had made him happy until he started to explore and work through his fears. Although he would never have expected it starting out, doing that was the way he'd finally become happy.

Frightening as it was, the idea also intrigued me. Could the key to finding happiness really be so simple? Nothing else I'd done had made me feel fulfilled, and I was tired of being miserable. I was willing to try just about anything.

I knew exactly what I feared the most: my father and the war he had brought home with him from Vietnam. For so long I'd tried to repress memories of the tall wooden gun cabinet in the bedroom, my father leaning inside to get the gun with which he threatened to blow his brains out a thousand times. I'd tried to erase images of the little girl who hid in her closet, reading books and writing stories by the light of a flashlight. These were the last things I wanted to write about. I'd spent the past thirteen years of my life trying to put Vietnam behind me, and I'd gotten pretty good at pretending to be happy. But on some level, I must also have known that I wouldn't ever be truly happy until I'd addressed all the unspoken questions and issues with my father that I'd been trying so hard to ignore. Until then I'd be stuck not only in my writing but in my life.

When I asked my mother to ask him, I thought I was finally strong enough to go through with it and hear whatever he had to say. But when he agreed, I realized that my initial bravado had been resting precariously on my deep-down certainty that my father would never say yes. He wasn't *supposed* to say yes. Although I hadn't consciously been aware of it when I made the call to my mother, I must have subconsciously believed that when he refused, I'd be able to tell myself I'd tried and go right on being angry with him as I had for as long as I could remember.

But he'd said yes. Now what?

Too late to back out now. I'd just have to figure it out along the way.

The following morning I decided to go back into therapy for the first time in two years, just for a month, in case I needed some extra support to get me through the next thirty days. I thought I'd been doing well. But what if the plan I'd come up with to move me forward actually wound up setting me back? I didn't want that to happen. I needed to stay strong.

The therapist I found, Dr. Louise James, was older than I expected, old enough to be my mother. As she read through the lengthy questionnaire I'd just completed, I sat across from her, silently counting the framed photographs adorning the walls and the potted plans scattered about the office.

I've always hated the first day with a new therapist, and there have been many. By the time I went to see Dr. James, I was highly skilled at sizing them up. I could tell right away if someone would be able to help me. Or if it was someone whom I *wanted* to help me. I liked Dr. James. Her voice was kind, and she didn't try to impress me with her qualifications.

As ridiculous as it now sounds even to me, I remember clearly the first thing I said when I walked in the door of her tidy, homey office: "I've had more therapists than I can remember. I'm not here to begin therapy again. I only need you for thirty days because I'm doing this project with my dad. Once a week for thirty days—that's all I need." That's how I thought of it—as a project. Like a school assignment I'd complete, hand in, and then file away and be done with.

She must have been doubtful (and who could blame her), because the first thing she said was, "I will only be here until February. After that, I'm retiring. You might want to go with someone else. Someone who will be here longer."

I kept assuring her that wouldn't be a problem. It was only November. My thirty-day plan meant I'd be out of there before Christmas. Finally, she just shrugged.

"So you say your father has post-traumatic stress disorder and there were times when you were growing up that you didn't speak to each other for days, even weeks, on end?" she asked. "But he and your mother are still together, and you lived with them until you were eighteen, correct?"

Her questions stung. I knew that my relationship with my father was broken, but hearing those words spoken aloud somehow made it seem that much worse. I nodded.

She wasn't the only therapist to ask about my father. They all had. But I had never been willing to talk about what really happened back then until now.

"And now you're going to talk to him every day for the next month to try to get to know him?"

I took a deep breath. "Yes."

"When was he diagnosed with PTSD?" she said.

I shrugged my shoulders. "I was in elementary school," I muttered, staring down at my lap. Just thinking about that time in my life made me nervous. "He's had symptoms since I was five, maybe longer."

"And you say you, too, have been diagnosed with PTSD. When did you start having symptoms?"

"I don't remember, around that same time maybe."

I always knew there was something wrong with me, but it wasn't until I went to a therapist when I was in college that anyone had put a name to my problems. Although there's no official illness known as intergenerational PTSD, it is well known and acknowledged that the children of veterans with PTSD may develop symptoms of their own that are related to dealing with their parent's symptoms, and this is sometimes called secondary traumatization.

"What are your parents' names?" Dr. James asked.

I looked down. "Delmer and Judy Presley," I said tentatively, not quite sure why she needed to know this.

"Okay," she said. "If we're going to do this together, I want you to start a journal. Write down all the things you feel angry about. What your conversations bring up for you. What you remember, and how it felt for you as a child. Do you feel angry right now?"

Did I feel angry that minute? I didn't know. I thought I was past that. Did I *sound* angry?

I handed her my co-pay and closed the door behind me. My mind was already churning. I'd agreed to keep the journal, but where would I start? It had been twenty-six years since I first realized something about my family was horribly, terribly wrong. Twenty-six years that I'd been hiding from my father.

I was barely out of the building when I was surprised by the words that suddenly flashed through my mind: *Dear world*, I would write. *You missed it. I was dying back then, I couldn't tell you, and you goddamn missed it . . .*

### Day One

I force myself to make the first call.

"You're still doing the project with me, aren't you?" I ask when my father picks up the phone. I bite my lip. Knowing how difficult this is going to be suddenly feels overwhelming. Would we be able to handle whatever came up? What if I failed? Where would we be then? I almost cry when I hear his voice, but I don't. "It'll just be some questions, Dad," I say, trying to keep my voice light but hearing it tremble in spite of myself.

"Questions about what?" he wants to know. He sounds suspicious.

What's that about? Mom said she'd explained it all to him. We'd do this thirty-day project together, and I'd write down our conversations as we went. I'd always used my writing as a way to process my feelings, and maybe I'd be able to turn our conversations into a book. She said she'd told him that, too.

I hold my breath. "Questions about the war. About *Vietnam*."

That unspeakable word is a cancer in my throat when I say it. It's the word my mother and I only whispered, if we ever dared to speak it at all.

"I don't want to talk about the war," he says. "I don't know anything about a war."

I feel as if I've just been slapped in the face.

Even though I had initially hoped, and assumed, that he'd refuse to talk to me, when he said yes, I got my hopes up. Now they are dashed again, and I am flooded with memories of all the sudden, unexplained mood swings he'd had when I was growing up and of how frightening they were to me.

All I can do is hang up the phone.

### Journal

*I remember the first time I was afraid of my father.*

*I was five, home from kindergarten and tucked away in my house made of sofa cushions, watching "Tom & Jerry" reruns. I was eating crackers, dipping them in potted meat, blowing away the crumbs when they fell onto my lap.*

*We lived in a trailer, in a trailer park called New Garden Estates, in Honaker, Virginia. I had a ten-gallon aquarium with a black pop-eyed goldfish. I had an orange and white cat named Tiger that I pushed around in a wagon. I had two dogs, Smokey and Rusty. My favorite drink was the lemon-lime slush from IGA. My mother had just quilted me a "My Little Pony" bedspread and purple curtains to match.*

*Since I clearly remember the day I first became afraid, I know that my dad and my life had once been different, and my mother has the pictures to prove there was some normalcy even after everything changed. But I can't remember much about those times.*

*"Your father used to hold you," she says, as she points to the pictures of my father and me that she has arranged in a scrapbook. She looks happy when she says it. She really remembers us that way.*

*It must help to have something to hold onto like that.*

*On that day when I was five, my father came home from work, his eyes wild and his face unshaven. He was a welder who worked on mining equipment and came home with his clothes black and thick with grit. His habit was to put down his lunch box, take off his work boots, and strip down to his underclothes as soon as he came in the door. My mom* would come in to greet him, put his dirty clothes in a plastic bag, pick up his empty lunch box, and take them into the kitchen. On this day, however, as he collapsed into the rocking chair in the corner and struggled to untie his boots, his hands trembled and his breathing was labored.

"Daddy?" I whispered. He did not respond, didn't even acknowledge I was there. Something was wrong. This was not my father. Everything about this man seemed unfamiliar to me, from his countenance to his actions. It was as if some supernatural force had invaded my father's body and made him act strange.

My mom came in as usual and helped him back to the kitchen. I hid behind the sofa, knees pressed into the shag carpet, and held my breath as I tried to hear their frantic whispers. At some point, when no one was looking, I escaped to my bedroom and hid in the closet. I did not come out for dinner. I remember clutching a little plastic toy called a Glow Worm that my father had bought me for my birthday that year and peering through the slats of my closet door. The black pop-eyed goldfish gulped for air at the top of its tank.

Back then I had not yet heard of Vietnam, did not yet realize that a war in which I'd never fought would shape the course of my life.

This was the moment it all came undone, and after which it would never go back to normal.

"You are smiling in all the pictures," my mother says, every time I see her. "Look how happy you were."

I don't remember being the girl in those happy photographs, but she's right. It's me looking out from all those pictures, and I am smiling. I'm smiling in every single picture my mother put in the scrapbook.

"This is your childhood," she says proudly, pointing to a picture of me when I turned twelve, sitting behind a birthday cake with a horse drawn in icing on the top. She made that cake herself, and gave made me a whole cup of icing, and let me eat it with my fingers because she knew I didn't like the cake part. That's one thing I do remember.

"Look at this one," my mother says. I am nine, trying to bounce a basketball on the grass behind our trailer. There's an azalea with pink flowers to my left, a freshly tilled garden to my right. A little bird feeder is attached to the pole on our clothesline. "You used to run through that garden barefooted," she says. "You'd eat Fruity Pebbles while you ran. Do you remember that?"

I nod. This is one of the few good things about my childhood that my brain has not erased.

"The mind is a mysterious thing," one of my first therapists said. "When we block out the trauma, sometimes we block out the good memories too."

Sometimes, however, it feels as if I kept the trauma and blocked out most of the good things. I am still not convinced my mind works like everyone else's, but if there's one thing I do know, it's that my mother has always loved me. She loved me so much that she erased the devastating effects of the war as best she could and cleaned it all up so I wouldn't be so afraid. But it didn't work. You can't pretend something isn't happening at the same time you're having to deal with it on a daily basis. And not talking about it actually makes it seem worse instead of better. When I look at those pictures, all I see is the unspoken war and nothing else.

I was a seriously disturbed child, but no one saw it, and if they did, no one mentioned it.

In elementary school I changed my classmates' answers on tests so they would not receive one hundreds, stole a beach picture from my neighbors, cut their heads off and replaced them with those of my own family, and then took the picture to school.

"We went to the beach this weekend," I told everyone, including my teachers, while flashing the picture in their faces. "Just my mother, my father, and me."

Their eyes grew large as they stared blankly at the clumsily doctored picture, cocking their heads to the side in confusion. They nodded and then looked away as fast as they could.

I faked sick whenever I could, often holding the thermometer next to the heater to raise its temperature. I ate poison ivy and stapled my hand to see what would happen.

I felt invisible, as if I were a part of the world but not of it.

I developed a facial tic, my eyebrows dancing oddly up my forehead whenever I spoke.

I did not enjoy the company of others. I preferred to be alone. Put me in a room with people at close quarters, and before long I'd be dying to get out of there.

I liked hiding in my bedroom closet, away from everyone and everything. I'd turn off all the lights so I could read by flashlight.

*I had friends, but they did not know me. I didn't want them to.*

*Leave me alone, and I would be just fine.*

*Everyone else was unpredictable; you could not trust anyone but yourself.*

When I was seven, my father tried to teach me to play the guitar. I remember sitting on his lap, our arms intertwined, as he pressed my fingers against the strings. I had never realized his hands were so calloused. It was the first time I recall his touching me in a loving way, even though I'm sure there must have been many others before then.

"This is C," he said. "Remember C."

"C," I repeated, although I knew I'd never remember anything except the roughness of his hands.

"Someday, you'll be able to tell people you took guitar lessons from the best in the world," he said. I nodded.

"Ralph Stanley asked me to play with him once," my father said. "Turned him down."

I could feel his breath against my neck.

"Know why I turned him down?" my father prodded.

Dr. Ralph Stanley lived—and still lives—not far from Honaker, deep in the Clinch Mountains of Appalachia. Way back before Stanley wrote his haunting melodies for the movie "O Brother, Where Art Thou" my father was a die-hard fan. Years ago he had sent Stanley some tapes of him playing the guitar, and Stanley was so impressed that he called my father and insisted he come to his house and play with him.

But a blizzard arrived the night my father was supposed to go, and he never rescheduled.

I had heard this story many times, but it never got old. It was easy to pretend I didn't know what was coming next.

"Why didn't you play with Ralph Stanley, Dad?"

We both sank deeper into the chair.

"Because I am the best in the world, and the best in the world doesn't play with just anyone."

"This is D," he continued, pressing my fingers against the thick wires and holding them there.

"Could have made it in Nashville," he muttered under his breath, more to himself than to me. "Could have been famous."

*My fingers stung when I pulled them away. They had dents in the tips the exact width of the guitar strings. No one had said that learning the guitar was going to hurt.*

*My father paled, his face gray, as he examined the rawness of my fingers. He turned them over and over in his hands. With a look that was part frown and part fear, he pushed me softly from his lap. I slid to the floor in a heap. I was sure I had done something wrong, even though, looking back, it's much more likely that he was afraid he had hurt me.*

*He never gave me another guitar lesson after that, no matter how much I begged.*

### Day Two

I'm afraid to make the call to my father tonight. Afraid of what he'll say—or what he won't. I sit there with the phone in my hand, dreading the emotions that will come either way.

It's why I've stayed away so long, why I go home only once a year. This year I am going at Christmas. I am always careful to keep my visits brief, never more than two or three days. Pop in. Pop out. Fulfill my duty for the year. Leave before I lose my mind.

I don't like who I am when I'm there. I become jumpy. Irritable. Guilty. I keep remembering the glassy-eyed deer heads that used to be on the living room wall of the trailer my parents no longer live in. Those dead deer eyes witnessed everything, but, like my mother, my father, and me, they did not speak about any of it.

"Please come home," my mother cries and begs over and over. "I miss you. I love you."

And still, I don't go.

"Look how happy you were in the pictures," she persists on my rare visits home, trying to convince me. "You are smiling in every one, such a pretty little girl."

I'm thirty years old, and no matter how much I prepare and swear to myself that this visit will be different, year after year, it is always the same. As soon as I pass Abingdon, at the first glimpse of the mountains, I start to feel Vietnam all around me. For me the word *Vietnam* has never signified a country or even a foreign war. To me it has always been synonymous with my father and the undeclared war that raged within our home. The jaggedness of those mountains always triggers memories of that secret war that threatens to destroy the bulwark of the life I have carefully constructed for myself. It's as if I've foolishly lifted my head above the rim of my carefully dug foxhole and given the enemy a clear shot.

When I imagine walking through my parents' door, the images in my mind are always the same—I see my father curled in a fetal position on the sofa, his back toward me. I try to ward off the darkness of these memories by reminding myself I don't live here anymore—I've moved out of the war zone.

At this point in the journey back home, I try to imagine I'm inside a bubble made of thick, impenetrable glass. I take deep breaths, count to ten, work hard to keep my muscles relaxed.

"You should come home more often," my slews of aunts, uncles, and cousins say, in the brief moments of each year's visit when they see me. "Such a city girl you have become. You stay gone so long. Don't be such a stranger, you hear."

I look them all dead in the eyes, put on a smile, and then breathe a sigh of relief as I walk out the door.

I wonder what it would feel like if they really knew me. If they had asked back then.

If I'd told them the truth.

If I'd felt safe enough to tell.

I snap out of it and force myself to dial my parents' number, hoping no one picks up. Truth to tell, I really don't expect anyone to answer because I'm calling on a Wednesday evening when I know they go to church. We always went to church three times a week—Sunday morning, Sunday evening, and Wednesday evening.

"Hello?" my father says on the third ring.

I close my eyes.

"Hi, Dad," I say with trepidation. "I called to talk, but something came up just as I dialed your number. I'll call back tomorrow."

I hang up before he can respond.

I don't know if I can do this. I've already wasted two days and we've exchanged no more than a few words. I'm still angry from the first conversation, and if he's not going to talk about the war, I really don't know what we have to talk about. But if I don't talk to him, how can I ever put the past to rest? Suddenly, it seems like a no-win situation I've gotten myself into.

### Journal

*I was six when my father went to the* VA *hospital for the first time because he was so emotionally disturbed and his hands shook so badly that he knew he shouldn't go on working and that he needed to qualify for disability insurance. That's when he was finally diagnosed with* PTSD, *but it would take six years before he was approved for full disability. Meanwhile, he just kept on working.*

*As a young child, "post-traumatic stress disorder" was just a bunch of words. All I knew was that it had something to do with my dad's brain and he seemed to be going crazy. And I knew it was bad because my mom told me that if anyone found out how sick he was, they'd come and take him away forever, and they'd take me away too, and she couldn't live like that. If he had to be that sick, I wanted him to have something everybody could understand. So I picked brain cancer.*

*When I was six, I envisioned a map of the human brain like I had seen on television.*

*"Here is a normal brain," a doctor in a white lab coat would say solemnly. He would use a pointer to show his audience the parts of the brain displayed on a screen. Each one would light up in a different color as he talked about it.*

*"Now, here is your father's brain," the same doctor would say, shaking his head as my father's brain appeared on the screen. This one didn't look like the other brain. The doctor could not point out the individual parts. Everything was a jumble of mush and sharp wires all clumped together.*

*"Nothing we can do about this one," he'd say, and move on to the next. Did my brain look like everyone else's, I wondered, or was I a freak too? I was not normal. That was for sure. When I went to school on a Monday and the teacher asked, "How was your weekend?" I couldn't fathom answering that question honestly, the way the other kids did. I felt as if the world I inhabited was different from the one in which everyone else lived.*

*When my father shut himself in his room for weeks on end, or took his gun and went to the river, I made plans to tell everyone at school that he'd died of brain cancer and talk up all the gruesome details. He'd been fishing, I planned to tell them. His brain hadn't been right for a while. Suddenly, it gave out. Just like that. Like when your heart stops beating. His brain stopped working, and he fell right in the water. They found his waterlogged body with his head all bloody washed a mile downstream. He'd hit his head on some rocks. That's why there was so much blood.*

*Everyone at school would feel sorry for me if I had a father who died of brain cancer.*

*My father threatened to kill himself so many times, and the events surrounding each episode were so similar, that it was hard to separate them in my mind. He would already be depressed. Then something would happen—maybe he'd hear a loud booming noise or he'd get a bill he couldn't pay. Maybe the lawn mower would break or the car would get a flat tire. Things that would simply annoy or mildly upset anyone else would be enough to throw him over the edge.*

*Then, keys jingling in hand, he'd march through the hall toward the bedroom, unlock the gun cabinet, and grab his rifle. He kept it cleaned and loaded, so it was always ready. A man on a mission, his rifle cradled against his chest like an infant and his pupils so dilated you could hardly see the whites of his eyes, he would march back through the house and out the door, but not before uttering a single sentence: "I'm going to the river to kill myself."*

*We used to try to stop him, but there was no use. I cried and wailed, but to no avail. For a while, my mother even threatened to kill herself if he so much as left our property with that gun. But he knew she'd never do it. She wanted to get to heaven, and according to her beliefs there was no quicker way to hell than to commit suicide.*

*So in the end we just had to let him go. Naturally, we were nervous wrecks the entire time he was gone, always imagining the worst. We ate junk food to comfort ourselves and slept huddled together tightly in my bed. We didn't talk about what was happening or how we felt. Instead, we made small talk about my fish, my dogs, or the Bible to fill in all the spaces between the things we did not mention.*

*And somehow, several hours later, my father always came back.*

*I never really knew why he came back, and I've never asked him. I'd like to believe it was for my basketball and softball games, to strum his guitar on the back porch. I'd like to believe he came back to anchor the roof on our trailer so it wouldn't blow away, to till the ground so my mother could plant flowers, so she could have a garden every year. At the time, however, I actually thought he came back just to torture us some more.*

### Day Three

The next day I can't work up the courage to dial my parents' number at all. When I finally do call on Friday, I think my father will be at home, but he isn't. I have forgotten that he and my mother were going to see a play about the Carter family called *Keep on the Sunny Side* at a local theater. It's become a tradition for my parents to go to a play there at about this time every year, which reminds me that he has improved. He's getting better. Isn't he?

I'm disappointed he isn't available, yet also relieved.

I don't leave a message. I will see him in person tomorrow. We're meeting at a gas station just outside Knoxville, Tennessee, which is more or less halfway between my home in Atlanta and theirs. I'll meet them there and bring my mother back to my place for Thanksgiving. We'd arranged all this a few weeks earlier because, as much as I wanted to see her for the holiday, I was anxious about returning to Virginia.

We're meeting at a gas station, a spot we'd chosen because it wouldn't be too noisy or too crowded and it could be reached without my father having to drive on a major highway. Noise, crowds, highways—any of these things could have triggered an episode of PTSD. My mom isn't really comfortable going too far from home either, but she's willing to take the chance and suffer the discomfort in order to spend time with me.

I don't know whether seeing him in person will be easier or harder than trying to talk on the phone. Either it will be a good way to break the ice and plunge in, or it will torpedo the project before it's really begun. With my father I never know what to expect. Just about anything could set him off.

### Journal

*I remember one day when I was eight, sitting at the kitchen table with my father on a Saturday morning after my mother had left to work the drive-through at the bank, which was then open a half day on Saturday. He seemed distant and preoccupied, using his fork to push his food into a large pile in the middle of his plate as I sat opposite him in total silence.*

Then, somehow, I knocked over a glass of water. I tried my best to catch the glass before it hit the floor and shattered, but it was too late. The noise sent my father into a fury, his eyes wild, bulging, and unblinking.

"I'll clean it up," I said, my voice trembling. "I'm sorry. God, I'm so sorry."

An apology wasn't good enough. He had already been triggered. There was no going back.

He came after me without warning, without saying a single word. I ran around the table, turned over a chair in front of him to buy time, ducked to my room, and locked the door.

"You open this door!" he yelled at last, beating at it with thunderous fists. "You open this door or I'll bust it down!"

I pressed my body against my dresser so hard I saw stars, but I managed to push it in front of the door. Then I threw open my closet door, curled up in the far corner, heart pounding from exertion and terror as I watched through the slats and tried to catch my breath.

His knuckles cracked against the wood. He was going to kill me, and my mother wasn't there to help. I put my hands over my ears and prayed. I had never felt God in my life, but I prayed because it was the only thing I knew to do. I pressed my hands tighter over my ears, shut my eyes, and hoped that dying wouldn't hurt too much. I began picturing myself standing in front of Jesus, himself. He would make the judgment call, put me on the right or on the left, get out his checklist of all the things I had done wrong, and size me up.

Please forgive me for my sins. Forgive me for my sins, I prayed over and over in my head. I hoped my prayers would be answered at the exact moment before I died. That way, there would be no time for further bad thoughts to enter my mind. If I had a bad thought after I'd asked for forgiveness, I'd go straight to hell, meet the devil with his pitchfork, be doomed to beg for water forever.

Still, I was willing to take my chances. Even hell would be better than this.

But neither the devil nor Jesus showed up in my bedroom that day. I must have blacked out or fallen asleep, because the next thing I knew, I was on my bed with my mother beside me, holding me in her arms. Had she come home from work and found me in the closet? I didn't think about it then, but she must have been able to open the door even with the dresser pushed in front of it. Which means that my father could have got into the room if he'd really wanted to, or tried. Her voice trembled as she read verses from her Bible aloud, put her hand on my head, and prayed. We lay that way until I stopped shaking.

"Don't leave me," I cried. "Promise that you won't leave me." I held onto her for dear life.

"It's Vietnam," she whispered. "Vietnam." Her face was pale. "Your father loves you. You have to know that."

"Can't we go away from here?" I whispered. I always had a bag packed and stowed in the back of my closet—just in case. I needed to be ready.

She held me closer but didn't answer my question.

"Don't ever tell anyone about this," she whispered through her tears. "Your father is a good person. This isn't his fault."

"I think we need help," I whimpered. "I don't want to live like this."

She pressed her Bible tight against her chest and closed her eyes. "We have to pray harder," she said. "If we pray to Jesus and follow his word, he'll make everything okay." Pray harder. That was her answer for everything.

I didn't say a word. I just curled up like a baby and turned my back against her.

# 10

# The Lack of Weight

GERARDO MENA

So here I am, six years after the last day of my life. I guess I should be more specific. Six days after the last day of my previous life. The life I was proud of, where what I did mattered. The one where I had brothers willing to sacrifice themselves to protect me, and I for them. But that life is over, and now I write. I write about war. Our war. I write poems and essays about our experiences in combat, the deaths of friends, begrudgingly waxing poetic about the true meaning of bravery. I have won contests and awards for the experiences I have written about, but it always leaves me feeling empty, leaves me with an insatiable void impossible to fill. I couldn't even place or describe this feeling until recently, until I realized that what was weighing on my disposition wasn't a weight at all, but a lack of it. A lack of pride. A lack of patriotism in anything I currently do.

For the first six years of my adult life I lived with the elite Reconnaissance Marines as a special amphibious reconnaissance corpsman under a full combat load in spec ops: thick plates of body armor, a rifle with a full magazine, an overstuffed med bag, and an excruciatingly heavy rucksack. And the more miserable the mission, the happier I was. I had a sense of duty back then. An appreciation of hardship because the suck always made the reward so much sweeter. But after I watched and held several of my friends as they died in combat, suddenly the proverbial grass seemed so much greener, and I bought into the notion that I could accomplish much more for our fallen, and for the special-operations community as a whole, if I was a civilian, passing on our wild and amazing stories through literature.

I believed this lie right up until last year when a close friend and mentor, one who should've been invincible, was shot through his scapula in Afghanistan. And I know I should've been ecstatic that he lived, but I couldn't shake this feeling of guilt that I wasn't there to patch him up. I wasn't there to laugh and tease him for being weaker than a tiny bullet. I wasn't there to tell him to get up, return fire, and stop whining because we still had "man shit" to do.

No, instead I was at home in Missouri, sitting in a college creative writing class and talking about my flowery feelings while listening to a bunch of eighteen-year-olds write poems about how much they hate their parents, hate the government, and, of course, how nobody understands them.

Most days it takes everything I have not to vomit when I hear them open their mouths or grab them by their shoulders and shake them hard enough to make them rattle to keep them from drowning in their own bullshit. How honorable of me.

Then I thought hard about what I was doing and what I was really accomplishing as a civilian. I thought about the old platoon and wondered what they were doing now. Were they kicking down the front door to a bomb maker's house? Were they partying like rock stars in Thailand, again?

I thought back to those days filled with fun and danger, and I longed to lace up my worn combat boots. I longed to see if my fingers still remembered the motions to buttoning up an old pair of cammies. I longed to heave a heavy rucksack and med bag on my back and teeter under the weight until I caught my balance. I longed to muss my four-year-old son's curly brown hair, kiss my wife passionately on the mouth, and walk out the door and into the night to hunt terrorists.

But that dream is done. It died when Kevin Dempsey, Jonathan Simpson, Kyle Powell, Jose Galvan, Nathan Krisoff, Gary Johnston, Dustin Lee, Luke Milam, Michael Ferschke, and David Day were killed in action. It died because they had no one to tell their stories.

It died because it was a greater sacrifice for me to bury my rifle than to keep pulling the trigger. Needs of the platoon over needs of self. Never above you. Never below you. Always beside you. Semper Fidelis.

# 11

## War Happens

LINDA ADAMS

I recently ran into a man who was struggling to understand why soldiers enlisted in the Army. To him, it looked like signing on the dotted line was an expectation of death. This was offensive, but I set aside my anger and explained that no one who enlists seriously comprehends that. They're all thinking of their own personal reasons. Some want to travel overseas.

For me it was a job. In early 1989 I was twenty-four, and jobs in Los Angeles were hard to find. It may have been a sign of the fall of the Berlin Wall that November and its subsequent damage to the Los Angeles defense industry. But Army enlistment guaranteed a paycheck. I mean, what kid pays attention to news of overseas deployments?

So when Saddam Hussein invades Kuwait on August 2, 1990, the idea that I might actually be going to war crashes into me. Fear becomes a gray taste that I wake up to every day.

*War.*

A scary thought, and it's being helped along by the media. Everywhere we look in 1990 the news is waving a flashing sign about Iraq's chemical weapons and how they are going to gas the troops. *USA Today* publishes a haunting op-ed picture showing a soldier with a skull.

I am a soldier. To sell newspapers the media are already predicting I am going to die.

My truck company deploys at the end of October 1990 to Saudi Arabia as part of Desert Shield. I'm a private first class, which is a worker bee in the company. We have about a hundred men and eight women. Most of the women are lower enlisted and younger than I.

In the last few weeks before our deployment, everything goes completely mad. We're going. We're not going. We're going. We pack our two duffel bags and stack them in the company's basement. Then the packing list changes, and we have to unpack and repack the bags. It's not like packing a suitcase. Everything assigned to that specific duffel bag *has* to be in it. But it's a tight fit. Packing a duffel bag is a combination of precision, art, and disaster. One wrong move and that bottle of shampoo spews floral notes all over your combat boots.

Just as we think we've finished, my squad leader announces, "Dump 'em. Some joker in first platoon forgot a pair of socks. We have to inspect everyone again."

As if to emphasize his point, an alarm clock in one of the duffel bags goes off, declaring it's time to wake up from this nightmare.

I think our squad leaders and platoon sergeants are trying to keep us busy, but instead it advertises how frightened they are.

Then, as we pack all the supplies onto the trucks that will be shipped by boat, things settle into the eye of the hurricane, into an impossible calm. We *know* now that we're going. But there's an odd sort of comfort in knowing that. Reality is marching into war and taking us with it.

We board a civilian 747 jumbo jet to Saudi Arabia. So many soldiers are deploying that the military is relying on commercial airlines to get everyone to the war zone. I've never seen a jumbo jet before. It has four engines hanging on the wings, so enormous that I wonder how they can stay attached. The wind whips around me, carrying the roaring whine of the engines mixed with jet exhaust.

The flight attendants greet us, but their smiles are plastic and their perfume isn't strong enough to hide the thickness of the tension in the air. They see our rifles, and all they think is hijacking. It doesn't matter that our rifles aren't loaded.

"Please place your guns in the overhead compartments," the attendants tell us. Weapons of war as carry-on luggage.

Once the rifles are out of sight, the flight attendants visibly relax. They proudly display a poster they all signed for us. It almost makes up for their fear of us.

Almost.

But it's on this trip, I think, that the river of war begins carrying us downstream, wearing us down. The long trip over is quiet. Gone are the men boasting about how they are going to kill the enemy.

It's like no one wants to speak because that would reinforce the reality of what is happening.

We land at an airport in Saudi Arabia in the dark. Outside, I am sweating and it's ten at night. The air has a vaguely foul odor, like rotting garbage.

Our transportation is late, but we don't even know where we're going or what's going to happen next. No one tells us anything. While we wait my squad shares a bottle of ice cold water. It's the best thing I've tasted, and too soon it's gone.

At last the buses come, and we collapse on board. Not only does every muscle ache, but the ache has gotten into my bones. We finally stop at a truckport and wearily unload our bags. I feel like a zombie, well past exhaustion.

We look for familiar faces. Mine is my best friend, Rebecca (not her real name). We're the only two women in my platoon and both privates. She's thirty-two. She throws her duffel bags to the asphalt, sprawls across them, and is out.

I'm not so lucky. I lie on the hard ground, too tired to sleep and too tired not to. Rebecca's snoring curls around me, jabbing at me as the greasy odor of engine oil from the asphalt pokes at me from underneath.

All I can do is think, and it's the last thing I want to do.

The first thirty days are relatively easy. We lie to ourselves, pretending war is just like training in the field back home. We'll be going home soon, we tell ourselves. In the first thirty days, it's easy to believe the lie.

We're living in tents in Dhahran, on the shore of the Persian Gulf, the first of eight locations for my unit. The Gulf is blue, sparkling, and pretty. One of my sergeants talks about fishing. Anything to make the world look ordinary.

Thanksgiving comes. President Bush (the first one) visits us, and we get a big Thanksgiving meal of everything traditional. Turkey, stuffing, mashed potatoes, cranberry sauce. The mess tent is filled with smells of home and holidays. I think about potluck Thanksgiving dinners outside in Southern California, ten thousand miles away.

But this is the best meal I've had in a month, and we all stuff ourselves because we know, somehow, it's the last good food we will see for a long time. So when I come across the MARS candy bars scattered on the center table, I fill up my pockets.

But Thanksgiving also has the finality of making us realize that we're here for a while. Of course, we don't know that right away. The realization is creeping up on us, one by one. The threat of war is there, however: a constant presence.

"Burn your envelopes," my squad leader says one day. "If the enemy gets your home address, your parents might get a call from them saying you're AWOL."

And we're ordered to watch for any vehicles following us because the enemy might be trying to get information on our troop numbers and what kinds of equipment we have. Even a truck backfire causes us to hunt for a sniper, and a rumor goes down the truck lines about a soldier who found a bullet lodged in his helmet. Paranoia has settled in.

The first to fracture is Rebecca. She has a boyfriend in our unit, one of the sergeants. He's told her he's not marrying her, but Rebecca has convinced herself she can change his mind.

"I don't feel complete without a man in my life," she says. She reads romance novels and sighs dreamily over "happily ever after." She loves her boyfriend. Isn't that enough?

Before the war she could live in the fantasy, but it's hard to have a fantasy when you're a target for death. Rebecca tries. She binds her cracking relationship with anything she can find to keep the fantasy alive. But all they do is fight when they're together, yet they can't not be together. So Rebecca brings me along to lunch because when I am with them, they don't fight.

I eat, but my food is tasteless because I'm too conscious of interrupting their conversation. They include me, but there's an awkwardness as if they're trying to figure out what to do with me there. They want normal—a normal without fighting—and they want me to facilitate that new normal. But all I can think about is the enemy out there, somewhere, and what's going to happen next to all of us.

No one seems to notice but me that Rebecca is slowly coming apart. She smokes more and more, as if each draw on the cigarette fills a crack inside of her. And now she never leaves the tent without two packs of cigarettes stuck in her uniform shirt pockets. Her hands shake when she fumbles with the buttons to get at the cigarettes. Her uniform reeks of an omnipresent brown-smoke stench.

And then one day, she finally takes her anger out on me. She blames me for something she did. We're working in twelve-hour shifts, pumping fuel for trucks hauling artillery, and she was due to relieve me at dinnertime. Lately, she's been arriving later and later, and eventually I struggle just to make it to the mess hall before it closes. I don't understand at first, what's going on with her, and then suddenly I do: she's lingering over dinner with her boyfriend.

Her selfishness angers me. Forget friendship—we're living under the threat of war and have to rely on each other. Yet Rebecca's fantasy romance needs have consumed her. My gut tells me that if I talk to her, she'll react like a cornered animal. Asking her to relieve me on time threatens her romantic life and fantasy.

So I mention the dilemma to the sergeant in charge of fuel point. He's older than the other sergeants and is also a veteran of the Vietnam War. He takes Rebecca aside privately and quietly, and then afterward she blows back at me.

"You should have come to me!" she screams. "He yelled at me and royally chewed my ass out!"

Even the sergeant in charge is surprised at her reaction. "Rebecca, c'mon, you know I didn't raise my voice."

I get a heat blast again a few days later when my squad leader tells me to take garbage out to the trash dump. It's a ten-minute trip. When I return Rebecca launches another diatribe full of fury.

"I had to fuel up a convoy while you were taking out the trash. You're just lazy!"

I say nothing, but my temples are pounding with fury. A trip to the latrine would have taken just as long. Would she have chastised me for needing to pee?

Things with Rebecca are never the same after that.

It's Christmas, a lonely, empty time for soldiers. Even lonelier for me. Since I arrived I've received only bills in the mail. It's very hard for a soldier because we don't have much contact with the outside world, and the mail takes two months. I have no idea during this time frame that my father is unemployed because of the defense-industry collapse and that money is running out for my family because of my mother's cancer treatments. The world is happening around me, and I'm in this bubble in the desert and can't see beyond it.

The mail clerk notices my lack of personal mail and sends *any female soldier* packages my way. I get an orange towel in one package. The color is like a lifeline. I try to soak up its brightness. It's the first color besides green and brown that I've seen in a long time.

Our latest move puts us in Thumamah, seventy miles from the border of Kuwait. We build guard posts out of sandbags and dig foxholes. The 82nd Airborne drops in at our mess hall as they're preparing for the coming deadline. The Marines steal one of our latrines.

January 16, 1991: Desert Storm starts at 0300, while we're all asleep. A day later we're awakened by the screams of SCUD missile alarms. We dive face first into protective masks and then into foxholes under the cover of darkness. The mask closes me off from the world, and all I can smell is the rubber. I listen to the sound of my breathing and wonder what is happening.

But nothing more happens, and it's the worst thing because we don't know what's going on, and we have no control over it, either.

The sorties are the first barrage of battle. They zoom over us, headed into Kuwait, but never come back our way. One day when a crane drops a forty-foot cargo container, the boom sends us scurrying for cover.

Later, I hear on the radio that a woman soldier is captured. She is lower enlisted, as I am. Could this happen to me?

On February 24—now it seems a lot shorter than thirty-eight days—the ground war begins. We stare out where we know the war is and listen to the artillery barrage. We're two hours away, and the booms still thunder nonstop for two days.

Then silence.

But before the silence, at the base, no one is getting along anymore. In basic training, we were taught to trust our sergeants and chain of command, and this was pounded into our heads over and over. But the war hammers at us mercilessly, and it's like we all realize at once we can't trust anyone—maybe not even ourselves.

I'd like to say the rift with Rebecca was triggered by a specific incident, but it's more like a gradual seismic shift.

By now the relationship between Rebecca and her boyfriend is dead, even if it hasn't quite stopped kicking its feet. Like the seismic shifts everyone else is suffering, the war, or threat of war, shreds their relationship into pieces. Even the boyfriend is snappish, enough that the privates on the walls hear things like: *What's wrong with him? I asked him a question, and he nearly bit my head off.* And, *I heard first sergeant is keeping an eye on him.*

Rebecca is even worse, because her happily-ever-after fantasy is dead. Loss or fear or whatever it is seems to push Rebecca into rage, and she's unleashing that rage on everyone, including me.

"You don't understand!" she screams at me when I offer to help.

The other soldiers tell me to fix her. But what am I supposed to do?

The war for us ends March 3, 1991. We hear about it on the radio, and the news seems too good to be true.

A few days later we stop at a phone on a street in Thumamah. When I call home my father's first words are, "You didn't get the Red Cross message?" No, I didn't get the Red Cross message about how my mother is dying.

I hate that I break down and start crying when I tell my squad leader. He talks to the first sergeant to see if they can locate the Red Cross message. We've moved so many times that no one knows where we are.

Soon, however, I am on my way home. The Army wants me to go to my duty station first and then fly home, which is on the same coast and costs thirty dollars less. I end up paying for the trip and barely get home in time to say good-bye to my mother. Shortly after the funeral service, I have to return to my duty station.

Rebecca is there, too. The relationship with the boyfriend is finally over, and they have to work at saying hi to each other. She still jokes and tries to have fun, but it's different. It's as if the war ate away the best parts of her.

She has concluded that since she can't have her boyfriend, she might as well take the next available man. No one likes the man she picks, though she will marry him and divorce him a week later.

Finally, she decides she just wants out of the Army, so she intentionally fails the physical training test three times. The Army kicks her out, and it's the last time I see her.

She's not the same anymore.

Then again, no one is.

It's been more than twenty years since I was in Desert Storm. Sometimes things catch me, and I get a queasy feeling about what might have happened had some things been different.

In 2001 a terrorist sends anthrax through the mail, and I think about what would have happened if a terrorist had done that during Desert Storm. With all the mail coming in, anthrax would have contaminated everything long before anyone caught it.

In 2003 Jessica Lynch is captured after her convoy gets lost in the desert and drives smack into danger. I will watch *Saving Jessica Lynch*, the bad movie made about her experience, and will nearly have a meltdown. Because the same thing could have happened to us.

But the one thing that always comes back, that stays stuck in my head, is a conversation I had with another soldier back in the States after the war.

The soldier looks at Rebecca and then at me. Then he blurts out, "You grew up . . . She grew down."

War. It's such a terrible thing to happen to a person.

# 12

# The Wing Shed

BEVERLY A. JACKSON

*Saint-Vougay, Brittany, France, 2008*

The day before yesterday I was standing over my father's grave in the Brittany American Cemetery in the village of Saint James. His remains had been moved there, after the war. But today I am 240 kilometers west, in another French village, to visit the locale where he fell when the Nazis shot down his airplane.

I was only four years old at the time of his death in 1942. My mother soon married another military man, who didn't like reminders that his wife had once belonged to someone else, so any discussion was verboten. I knew my father had been a tail gunner in a downed B-17, but mostly he remained a mystery to me, a hollow in my solar plexus that I spent a lifetime filling with "what ifs."

I never knew where he was buried. A writer friend of mine, Vanessa Gebbie, whose father survived the war and served in the Royal Air Force (RAF), swapped war stories with me. When she realized how disconnected I felt, she took it upon herself to unearth my father's whereabouts with a simple Internet search, doing what I never dreamed possible. I had no idea all this internment information was available. Once I found out where he had lain all these years, I began immediately making plans for a pilgrimage to visit him. I cashed in a chunk of the small inheritance my mother left me, caring not that it was my retirement fund, and booked the flights. Single-minded, excited, perhaps a little crazed, I researched and networked with all kinds of people who could help me once I arrived in France.

One clue linked to another. One contact linked to the next.

On the Internet I found history I'd never known. When the United States joined the war against the Nazis, the first American strategic bombing command was based with the RAF in England, near Ixworth in Suffolk. That is where my father was assigned duty.

Each revelation led me to another, like following bread crumbs. Not only were burial records available, but so were personal accounts by pilots, even the original *Day Raid Reports* of men returning from bombing sorties. I identified my father's unit, the 97th Group, and narrowed the search to the exact day.

There it was, the report for October 21, 1942, stating that at 10:30 a.m. ninety planes from four different groups took off to bomb the submarine pens in Lorient, France. Seventy-five bombers returned because of bad weather, mechanical failure, or enemy action. Fifteen B-17s, all from the 97th, my dad's group, got across the Channel. They also hit bad weather, but twelve of them managed to reach Lorient and unloaded thirty one-ton bombs over and near the target of submarines.

But three of the fifteen planes were reported lost. The surviving crews reported that about thirty-six Focke Wulfe 190 Luftwaffe fighters struck down those last three planes.

The *Big Bitch*, my father's plane, was the last airship in the formation and totally unprotected from a rear attack. A B-17 loaded with bombs was an elephant in the sky, easy prey for the Luftwaffe. It wasn't until 1944 that the United States developed the Mustang fighter with enough fuel to fly deep into Germany and defend the bombers. The RAF had Spitfire squadrons that helped out, but not on this day.

My father's tail gunner's compartment at the rear of the plane was the tightest, next to the ball turret. The tail gunner sat on a modified bicycle-type seat in a kneeling position for the majority of the mission. The tail was drafty, and the gunner had to constantly battle frostbite.

I imagined the view from the tail gunner's window—storm clouds, enemy craft, bullets hailing on the glass. A horror, yet no help to fight them off.

The Luftwaffe made their first hit on the *Big Bitch* at about the fifteen-thousand-foot mark. After three attacks a fire broke out in the bomb bay and flight deck, one engine blew out, and its controls were shot away. With the radio out there was no communication between positions, but the copilot and navigator seemed to have the fire under control. Because they were flying level, they thought they might make it to the Channel, if not to England, on the engines for flight controls.

On another website I discovered there were three RAF Spitfire squadrons that were supposed to defend the rear of the 97th's formation. But in the stormy weather they reported they couldn't see any aircraft—bombers or enemy fighters—and thought all planes had abandoned the mission.

The RAF could have changed the history of my life if they had been able to fight that day.

These are the stories that I never heard, growing up, if my mother even knew them. I couldn't wait to get to France.

The staff member of the cemetery, an American named Alan and a docent of sorts, told me that all of the American dead, sailors and soldiers buried all over Brittany, were transferred to Saint James after the war. Acres of lush, green hillsides are dotted with white marble crosses, row upon row, manicured and tended, not unlike Arlington's acres of headstones. It flattened my heart to see that vista of white markers. Alan picked up a protocol bucket of sand gathered from Omaha Beach and led me through the maze of paths to find my dad. I had brought a bouquet, but someone had already put little American flags and fresh flowers on his grave. Alan said it was a welcoming gesture done by a member of Brest 44, a national French society dedicated to keeping alive the memories of World War II liberators. As the gray sand was rubbed into the three-line engraving on the cross marker, the lettering became legible. "Now you can see it's your father," Alan said gently.

Andrew L. Jackson
Sgt. 341 Bomb Sq 97th Bomb Gp (H)
October 21, 1942

Then he left me to be alone. Taps chimed from the chapel bells and floated on the morning air over acres of graves. Sun in a cloudless sky threw shadows behind every cross, cloning them skinny and flat across the lawns.

Everything clean and serene, I stood at my father's grave and waited. I stood there, fearful of an emotional avalanche. But nothing came. There was no one there for me to talk to. I stood among the dead, as if on an empty stage. After the many battles of a terrible war, there were only silent tombs, not only in this cemetery but so many others gravesites in France—Normandy, Ardennes, and Chapelle.

My father's bones were interred beneath my feet, but his spirit was not there.

I drove my little rented Fiat to the last place on my itinerary: Saint-Vougay, a village three hours west of Saint James, where in 1942 the Nazis had originally buried my dad in a churchyard. I had coordinated this visit in advance with the Amicale, a group of Saint-Vougay farmers who had formed their own local memorial society, similar to the national Brest 44, since World War II had bestowed a historical trophy—a crashed airplane—on them.

I got lost twice in the pouring rain, but I finally made my way to a farm where a reception had been set up in a barn, and a few dozen villagers waited for my arrival, almost an hour late. Iffig Palud, the president of the Amicale, and his wife, Martine, were my hosts. Mayor Madame Marie-Claire Henaff welcomed me as if I were visiting royalty: champagne, my own translator, a visit to the shrine to lay flowers and flags, and later, in the passenger seat of an authentic World War II jeep, driven to a spectacular banquet. The ride, courtesy of Brest 44, was with young Frenchmen dressed in American GI uniforms who beeped the horn all the way to the restaurant where I was toasted and presented gifts, including a 1942 *Life* magazine with photos of my father and his crew. The next morning two more Amicale members took me sightseeing.

The churchyard where the Germans buried their enemies was ancient and charming, with roses growing on walls around the graves. My French friends showed me the section the Nazis had used for Canadian and American war dead. Those barrows were long empty, remains moved to Saint James, and to my disappointment my father's spirit wasn't present there, either.

Today the Amicale is excited about our final sojourn. We have parked the cars off an isolated farm road, to visit the Wing Shed. It is an old-fashioned lean-to, long abandoned, really just two walls on some poles stuck in the soil. Its weathered walls are pale-gray metal, constructed from their prize, the wing of the *Big Bitch*. After decades of hard winters, the metal structure cants perilously, sinking in tall weeds. A somber little group of nine, we congregate on a muddy cow path alongside an irrigation ditch.

Huddled under umbrellas in the spring rain of Brittany, we have to cross an irrigation ravine to get to the shed, which, after sixty-five years, is bonded to its surroundings. Grass sprouts from the crevasses of its seams. Under this flat gray sky, I feel like a melancholy child in my old body—a woman close to seventy. A father could not recognize his child in this gauzy light. Drizzle greens the checkered farmlands all the way down to the sea. Tongues of smoke waft above the distant chimneys of squat stone houses. Brittany is gripping in its stark beauty, but this is not a place where I would choose to die.

Our Amicale host, Hervé Simon, owns this farm and addresses us in French. I can understand every third or fourth word and am grateful that Iffig, their president who speaks fluent English, translates for me.

"Hervé is telling you the farm has been empty since his father, Jean-Yves, died," Iffig says. "It's now for sale, but as you can see, it needs a lot of work." Iffig gestures to a small yellow farmhouse and rickety barn sitting just beyond the shed. "We plan to escape this rain and share a bottle of wine indoors afterwards."

"The English Channel is there?" I ask, pointing north, thinking of the bombers that crossed the Channel and France on every mission to Germany.

Iffig nods and gazes out over the vista of farmlands. Under the umbrella his face is shaded, his eyes pensive behind rimless glasses. "Hervé's father worked this land all his life. Farming is much easier today. Life was hard during the war," he says, "and the Germans were despised. When they blew up your father's airplane, farmers ran into their fields to try to save victims and to hide anything that might aid the Nazis, like maps or weapons. It was said that a machine gun was thrown into a brook near my home, but it was never found. The farmers needed any materials they could salvage, for almost any supplies were scarce. Mothers made shirts and clothes, even wedding gowns, out of parachute material."

I remember my mother complaining about war shortages. No gasoline, no nylon stockings. But she hadn't lived in an occupied country. She hadn't even loved my father, I think, surprising myself with a newly birthed paternal love of my own.

Iffig continues, "Jean-Yves took his horse and cart into another farmer's field, searching for what he saw drop. The wing of the aircraft landed about two kilometers from where the body of the B-17 crashed." He stops to point to the distant left of us. All I see is a stretch of gentle farmland.

"Jean-Yves knew he had to rush," Iffig explains, "for soon the soldiers would arrive, looking for survivors and to collect the spoils. Metal was a treasure during the war, so he was making a dangerous risk. He got the wing tipped onto his cart and tied, then dragged it back to his farm to hide it in his barn under hay and manure. It stayed there until the Nazi occupation was over. Fortunately, the Germans never searched Simon's farm because it was so far from where the, uh, what do you call the body?"

"Fuselage?" I offer.

"Ha, it's the same in French, fuselage! Anyway the wing fell far away from the main crash. Farms closer to the main wreckage were searched and searched again for airmen in hiding."

The Amicale members chat among themselves, their umbrellas bobbing as they shift in the rain. All kindness, all in attendance for my benefit.

I say to Iffig, "I read that the plane tried to turn back to England, but it made a violent jolt and headed straight down after some kind of explosion."

"Possibly the bombs loosened and tore a hole," Iffig says. "There are still witnesses alive who were children standing at the window of the schoolroom here in Saint-Vougay when that plane burst into flames and fell from the sky."

"Did you yourself see it?" I envision the silver ship spiraling downward, explosive flames igniting the heavy cloud cover. I wonder where the tail landed. I am hungry for details.

Iffig laughs. "No, I was not here in 1942. You think I'm so old, eh?" His eyes twinkle. Indeed, he has to be twenty or thirty years younger than I am. My father had just turned thirty before he died. I'm embarrassed by my eagerness and illogical question.

The citizens of the tiny village of Saint-Vougay formed their Amicale to build a granite memorial to the crew of the *Big Bitch*. For decades it has been their personal symbol of liberation from the Nazis, and they welcome all interested visitors with grateful enthusiasm to share it. But as an immediate relative of one of the crew, I get the full treatment. They act as if I'm family, as if they want to fill my loss with their love. I learn such societies thrive all over France, honoring American, Canadian, and British dead warriors.

"If it was not for these heroes," Iffig says, "we would be speaking German today."

Firsthand accounts from those old-timers, who as children looked out the window of the one-room school, say that when the plane exploded in the air, only two parachutes dropped from the sky. Pieces of airplane and bodies fell, widely scattered over nearby farm fields. But precisely who and where are lost to history.

The pilot and the navigator, in parachutes, were the only two of a ten-man crew to get out alive. The pilot, John Bennett, managed to escape for a week, fleeing on his knees with two broken ankles, passing out from pain, hiding in bushes, starving, until he was finally discovered by a startled farm woman. She helped him inside her barn and fed him, but called the French police since she was alone and frightened. The police collected Bennett and turned him over to the Nazis that same day.

The other survivor, the navigator, wounded and unconscious, was captured immediately and taken to surgery in a German infirmary. Both men were ultimately sent to Stalag Luft III POW camp (subject of the film *The Great Escape*) for the duration of the war. They both returned home in 1945, lived into their eighties, able to relate all they knew. The other eight crew members died that October day.

Tired of waiting for the rain to let up, I break from the group and scramble down the ravine. The mud fills my shoes and soils the hem of my jeans. The rain seems like a torrent now that I'm no longer under Iffig's umbrella.

"Be careful," Iffig cries out. "Wait, I'll come with you." I turn and see Hervé and Jean-Claude follow Iffig, large men wading comically across the ditch, umbrellas tilting on their up-stretched arms, with Jean-Paul sloshing right behind. These members of the Amicale are visibly pleased to have me see their treasure. Muddy and soaked, the rain runs down our faces, and we break into laughter at the sight of each other.

The metallic shed is dull and marred by decades of Brittany storms. It is pierced with holes of various sizes, corroded at their edges, some smooth, others ragged and rough edged. It would be hard to count the number of bullet holes that pepper the wing. I tentatively touch them, some so large I can put three fingers through the holes. The metal feels hot to my touch or icy cold. I can't tell. The thought of being airborne, high off the earth in the crosshairs of thirty-six Nazi fighter planes, is hard to hold. The movie versions bear little resemblance to the emotional reality of seeing these raw wounds in metal. The noise, the smoke, the courage and fear are all bitter tastes in the back of my throat.

Iffig sends me to the end of the shed where the metal shows a faint outline of one of the points of the large American star that once emblazoned the wing. At first it is hard to see on the stained and streaked surface, but looking closer, the shape, a triangle, one arm of a large star in a slightly lighter color, becomes apparent, like an abstract ghost of itself—a weathered memory of the other ghosts who died here. It is like seeing the American flag or hearing the national anthem in this faraway, alien land where the man I never really knew was lost to me forever. I am glad for the rain. Iffig circles my shoulders with his arm and says, "Let's have that cup of wine."

The Simon farmhouse is tiny, a series of dollhouse rooms crowded with mildewed overstuffed furniture. Our Wing Shed group mills in the old-fashioned kitchen, sipping wine, eating Brittany shortbread from decorator tins. The Amicale members whisper among themselves and file in and out of a back room. Iffig engages me in light conversation, his eyes darting back and forth, and I'm aware of secrecy and excitement.

Finally, a package appears in front of me, wrapped in brown paper, tied with packing string. It is flat, oblong, and heavy. Glasses raise in a toast. Faces beam around me as I untie the string to reveal a hunk of battered gray metal, corrugated on one side and smooth on the other. Handwritten in French with black marker is a brief history of the crash of the *Big Bitch* with my father, Andrew Lexington Jackson, named in particular. And beneath these words are the autographs of the members of the Amicale. It is a piece of the actual Wing Shed that has been cut away for me to take with me. For me to keep.

My thoughts tumble. I am a skeptic, not one to quickly trust. I am a loose fish who no longer has expectations of people or of life. I am the daughter of a dead American hero. And without a doubt, in that uncanny mystery of a force beyond reason, I know that my father, Lex Jackson, or whatever part of him left on this earth, still alive, sits right here in my hands.

# 13

# Triage

JON KERSTETTER

October 2003, Baghdad, Iraq. Major General Jon Gallinetti, U.S. Marine Corps, chief of staff of CJTF7, the operational command unit of coalition forces in Iraq, accompanied me on late-night clinical rounds in the U.S. Army combat surgical hospital that occupied a captured Iraqi medical facility. We visited soldiers who had been injured in multiple IED attacks throughout Baghdad just hours earlier. I made this mental note: *Soldier died tonight. IED explosion. Held him. Prayed. Told his commander to stay focused.*

In the hospital, the numbers of wounded who survived the attacks created a backlog of patients who required immediate surgery. Surgeons, nurses, medics, and hospital staff moved from patient to patient at an exhausting pace. When one surgery was finished, another began immediately. Several operating rooms were used simultaneously. Medical techs shuttled post-op patients from surgery to the second-floor intensive care unit where the numbers of beds quickly became inadequate. Nurses adjusted their care plans to accommodate the rapid influx. A few less critical patient beds lined the halls just outside the ICU.

The general wanted to visit the hospital to encourage the patients and the medical staff. We made a one-mile trip to the hospital compound, late at night, unannounced, with none of the fanfare that usually accompanies a visit by a general officer in the military. After visiting the patients in the ICU, we walked down the hallway to the triage room.

One patient occupied the triage room: a young soldier, private first class. He had a ballistic head injury. His elbows flexed tightly in spastic tension, drawing his forearms to his chest; his hands made stone-like fists, and his fingers coiled together as if grabbing an imaginary rope attached to his sternum. His breathing was slow and sporadic. He had no oxygen mask. An intravenous line fed a slow drip of saline and painkiller. He was what is known in military medicine as *expectant*.

Some of his fellow soldiers gathered at the foot of his bed. A few of them had been injured in the same attack and had already been treated and bandaged in the emergency room. These fellow soldiers stood watch over the expectant patient. The general and I stood watch over them. One soldier had a white fractal of body salt edging the collar of his uniform. One wept. One prayed. Another quietly said "Jesus" over and over and kept shaking his head from side to side. And another had no expression at all: he simply stared a blank stare into the empty space above the expectant patient's head. A young sergeant, hands shaking, stammered as he tried to explain what had happened. The captain in charge of the expectant soldier's unit told the general and me that this was their first soldier to be killed—then he corrected himself and said this was the first soldier in their unit to be assigned to triage. He told us that the soldier was a good soldier. The general nodded, and the room fell suddenly quiet.

The general lay his hand on the expectant soldier's leg—the leg whose strength I imagined was drifting like a shape-shifting cloud moving against a dark umber sky, strength retreating into a time before it carried a soldier. And I watched the drifting of a man back into the womb of his mother, toward a time when a leg was not a leg, a body not a body, toward a time when a soldier was only the laughing between two young lovers—a man and a woman who could never imagine that a leg-body-man-soldier would one day lie expectant and that that soldier would be their son.

As I watched the soldiers at the foot of the bed, I noted their sanded faces, their trembling mouths, their hollow-stare eyes. I watched them watch the shallow breathing and the intermittent spasm of seizured limbs and the pale-gray color of expectant skin. I took clinical notes in my mind. I noted the soldiers—noted the patient. I noted all the things that needed to be noted: the size of the triage room, the frame of the bed, the tiles of the ceiling, and the dullness of the overhead light. I noted the taut draw of the white linen sheets and the shiny polished metal of the hospital fixtures. A single ceiling fan rotated slowly. The walls were off-white. There were no windows. The floor was spotless, the smell antiseptic. A drab-green wool Army blanket covered each bed. Three beds lay empty. I noted the absence of noise and chaos, the absence of nurses rushing to prepare surgical instruments, and the absence of teams of doctors urgently exploring wounds and calling out orders. There was an absence of the hurried sounds and the hustle of soldiers in the combat emergency room one floor down. Nobody yelled, "Medic!" or "Doc!" Nobody called for the chaplain. Medics did not cut off clothing or gather dressings. Ambulances and medevac helicopters did not arrive with bleeding soldiers.

The *Merriam-Webster Online Dictionary* defines *triage* as "the sorting of and allocation of treatment to patients and especially battle and disaster victims according to a system of priorities designed to maximize the number of survivors." All dictionary definitions refer to the origin of the word *triage* as deriving from the French verb *trier*, to sort. The essence of the meaning is in the sorting. In the context of battle a soldier placed in a triage room as *expectant* has been literally sorted from a group of other injured soldiers whose probability of survival was deduced by a sort of battlefield calculus implemented by a medical officer or a triage officer. The sorting occurs rather quickly—usually with minimal, if any, deliberation.

A military physician trains for triage situations. I trained to make combat medical decisions based on the developing battlefield situation and limited medical resources. I read about triage. I role-played it in combat exercises. When I first learned about the role of triage in combat, I reasoned: *Of course, triage is necessary. It's part of war. You do it as part of the job of a medical officer.*

More than twenty years ago, when I was a newly minted captain, I attended the two-week Combat Casualty Care Course at Camp Bullis, Texas. The course was designed to teach medical officers combat trauma care and field triage techniques. The capstone exercise included a half-day mass-casualty scenario, complete with percussion grenades, smoke bombs, and simulated enemy forces closing on the casualty collection point. The objective was to give medical officers a realistic setting in which to perform triage decisions and to initiate medevac protocols, according to standard operating procedures. About twenty moulaged patients mimicked battlefield casualties, ranging from the minimally injured to those requiring immediate surgery. Each medical officer in training was given five minutes to perform the triage exercise and to prepare an appropriate medevac request. Providing treatment was not an option; the exercise focused exclusively on making triage decisions.

All the participants could have easily completed the role-play within the time limit. Nothing, of course, is that straightforward in Army training. There is always some built-in element of surprise to test how well trainees cope with chaos. In this case the element of the "unexpected" was a simulated psychiatric patient who was brandishing an M16 rifle and holding a medic hostage while threatening to commit suicide. To maintain the element of surprise, the doctors who had finished their turn were whisked out the back of the triage tent, not to be seen again until the after-action review some hours later.

My turn. I entered the tent at the shove of my evaluator. The mock "psych" patient was screaming and threatening to kill a nearby medic. Other medics were pleading with the disturbed patient to lay down his weapon and let the wounded get on a helicopter. I was to take charge and get control. I did. I approached the screaming patient with quick confident steps. I got about halfway through the triage tent when he pointed his rifle directly at the hostage and yelled, "One more step and the medic is dead!" I backed off slowly, turned sideways, and quietly pulled my pistol. In an abrupt and instantaneous movement, I reeled around and shot the psych patient with my blank ammunition. "Bang— you're dead!" I yelled. A nearby evaluator took his weapon and made him play dead. One out-of-control psycho eliminated. I finished the triage exercise within the five-minute time limit. My evaluator laughed. "Damn," he said.

I felt great. I had control.

In the after-action review I was asked about my decision to shoot. "Time," I answered. "I only had five minutes, so I maximized my effectiveness by eliminating a threat. It's combat," I argued.

One fellow doc asked if I would really shoot a patient in combat. A debate ensued as to the ethics of my decision. Nobody else had shot the psych case. Nobody else finished the exercise in the allotted time. Some trainees had considered shooting the crazed soldier but failed to act. Some managed to talk the psych patient into giving up his weapon. Those physicians had taken nearly fifteen minutes to complete the exercise— minutes during which some of the simulated patients died a simulated death. In the end it was decided that my decision to shoot, while potentially serving a greater need, may have been a bit aggressive, but that it was in fact *my* decision, and my decision met the needs of the mission. All ethical considerations aside, I felt that I understood the necessity and the theory of triage. I understood it as part of my job.

Military triage classifications are based on NATO guidelines and are published on numerous websites and in Department of Defense publications. The triage categories in the third edition of *Emergency War Surgery*, the Department of Defense bible of military medicine, are listed as follows:

Immediate: This group includes those soldiers requiring lifesaving surgery. The surgical procedures in this category should not be time consuming and should concern only those patients with high chances of survival.

Delayed: This group includes those wounded who are badly in need of time-consuming surgery but whose general condition permits delay in surgical treatment without unduly endangering life. Sustaining treatment will be required.

Minimal: These casualties have relatively minor injuries . . . and can effectively care for themselves or can be helped by nonmedical personnel.

Expectant: Casualties in this category have wounds that are so extensive that even if they were the sole casualty and had the benefit of optimal medical resource application, their survival would be unlikely. The expectant casualty should not be abandoned, but should be separated from the view of other casualties. Using a minimal but competent staff, provide comfort measures for these casualties.

The text of *Emergency War Surgery* further notes, "The decision to withhold care from a wounded soldier, who in another less overwhelming situation might be salvaged, is difficult for any surgeon or medic. Decisions of this nature are infrequent, even in mass casualty situations. Nonetheless, this is the essence of military triage." Triage requires assigning patients to those various categories based upon a rather quick and semiobjective assessment of a patient's injuries. If the triage officer calculates that a patient falls into the *expectant* category, treatment is withheld in order to allow medical teams to more efficiently concentrate on those soldiers with potentially survivable injuries. Preserving the fighting force is the central tenet of the process.

I have read and reread the official triage definition. I suppose I might have used it in a classroom of medics that I instructed. I am intimately familiar with the words that describe each category and with the professional commentary about the mechanics and ethics of sorting injured patients, yet I repeatedly come back to those words that try to clarify exactly what might be involved in the process of triage. I find the words weak and innocuous. They undercut the gravity and scope of a real-time triage experience. Here's the rub: the official commentary about the decision process focuses on the essence of triage as being the *difficulty* of making that decision. The difficulty is a given, but I think there is more. I think the essence of military triage is the *necessity* of making the decision when the combat situation demands it. It is the necessity of triage that requires medical staff to assign expectant soldiers to their death in order to provide an accommodation to a calculated greater good—a cause measured by the number of combat survivors. It is an accommodation that has not changed since the trench warfare of World War I.

Modern military medicine provides battlefield casualties with more sophisticated treatment and much faster aeromedical evacuation than in prior wars, but the process of triage remains essentially raw and unrefined as a standard combat operating procedure. Combat physicians encounter an overwhelming number or complexity of casualties. They make a rapid medical assessment, render a decision based on incomplete information, assign a triage category, and move to the next patient. Done. If they are particularly adept, they can triage several critical patients simultaneously.

Saving lives is the end point of all triage. Let one life go, save three others, or five, or maybe ten. The ratios don't matter; the benefits do. And a benefit in war always comes at a cost. On the surface, of course, the ultimate cost of a triage decision is a soldier's life. One decision, one life; perhaps one decision, several lives. But there are other costs not so easily calculated, like the emotional cost to survivors or the psychological cost to soldiers who make triage decisions. Textbook definitions are silent on how military physicians prepare for, or react to, the demands of making a triage decision. No chapter in a military textbook instructs combat physicians in the multidimensional complexity of decision making that serves to deny life-saving interventions for soldiers. There are chapters on why triage decisions must be made and chapters on how to apply established medical criteria in making those decisions. But what to do next, after the triage decision has been made—not covered. And that vacuum of knowledge leads to a feeling of exposure and vulnerability, both of which cannot be tolerated in war.

The act of triage is subsumed under the assigned duties of medics and physicians. I am not suggesting that the process fall to someone else or that the criteria used to make triage decisions should be discarded for a different process. I know of no other way of quickly sorting and categorizing patients when the critical nature of combat demands that it be done. I am, however, declaring that the practice of triage obligates doctors and medics, whose principal duty is the saving of lives, to perform tasks that share in the brutality and the ugliness of war—tasks that are tantamount to pulling a trigger on fellow soldiers.

In the final analysis the decision to withhold medical care is not a decision that can be practiced, and rehearsed, and fully prepared for outside of the realm of combat. How could that ever be accomplished with any modicum of reality? Could a medical officer simply say, as I did in training, "Bang, you're dead" or "Put the black tag on this one," and, with that, feel the same gut-ripping tension that combat evokes? No, the reality of triage tends to hit more like the force of a bomb blast. In an instant fragments of stone and metal explode through the air with such velocity that when they hit a human target, even if the target is not killed, it is stunned and bleeding and breathless. It is that environment in which a military doctor or medic makes a live-fire triage decision and then must stand against the ballistic force of its consequences.

Somewhere in the process of making notes about the expectant patient, I paused and moved toward the middle of the bed. I put my hand on the patient's leg, just as the general had done. I laid it there, let it linger. From where I stood I stared directly into the expectant soldier's face. I watched his agonal breathing, a long sighed breath followed by an absence of movement, and that followed by three to four shallow breaths. I matched his breathing with my own breathing. I timed the slowing pattern with my watch. I made some mental calculations and then looked away. Once again I noted the quiet of the room and the whiteness of the walls. I noted the empty beds, and the ceiling, and the antiseptic smell. Again, I watched the expectant soldier who was oblivious to all of my watching.

I stood at the triage bedside, thinking that if this were my son, I would want soldiers to gather in his room—listen to his breathing. I would want them to break stride from their war routines, perhaps to weep, perhaps to pray. And if he called out for his dad, I would want them to become a father to a son. Simply that: nothing more, nothing less—procedures not in Department of Defense manuals or war-theory classes or triage exercises.

I moved to the head of the bed, placed my right hand on the chest of the patient. And my hand rested there with barely any movement. I turned to the other soldiers, gave them an acknowledgment with a slight upturned purse of my lips, and then looked away. I lifted my hand to the patient's right shoulder and let my weight shift as if trying to gently hold him in place. I half-kneeled, half-bent—closed the distance between our bodies. I noted the weave in the fabric of his skull-cap dressing and the faint show of blood that tainted its white cotton edges. I lingered. I prayed for God to take him in that very instant. I whispered, so only he could hear, "You're a good soldier. You're finished here. It's okay to go home now." I waited. I watched. I saw the faces of my own sons in his, was glad they were not soldiers.

I finished, stood up, and walked to the foot of the bed. One of the soldiers asked me if there wasn't something I could do. I said no. I meant no. I wanted my answer to be yes. I faced the captain and put my hand on his shoulder, told him that we were finished, that the expectant soldier did not feel pain, that he would be gone soon, and that everybody had done everything they could. The tone of my voice was neither comforting nor encouraging, neither sorrowful nor hopeful. It was, as I remember, military and professional.

I think about that expectant soldier so often. I know I would have seen his name in his hospital chart or been told his name by his commander.

I did not take the time to write it down anywhere, and that bothers me. It bothers me because years later he remains nameless—just like so many other soldier-patients I encountered—and I think I equate that namelessness with a form of abandonment for which I feel personally responsible. I do understand, in a professional sense, that the patient was not abandoned, that his triage was purposeful, and that it allowed an ascent to medical efficiency, which, in the end, saved other soldiers' lives. But I also understand that the theoretical basis of triage quickly erodes when confronted with the raw, emotional, human act of sorting through wounded patients and assigning triage categories. In my mind the theoretical and the practical wage a constant battle so that whenever I participate in a triage decision, part of me says *yes*, and part of me says *no*.

I sometimes find myself wanting to speak with the expectant soldier's mother and father. I want to tell them that their son did not die alone in a triage bed—that he was not simply abandoned or left as hopeless in a secluded corner room of a distant combat hospital. I want to assure them that he died in the company of men who stood watch over him as if guarding an entire battalion and that we tried to give everything we could give—that we tried to be more than soldiers or Marines or generals or doctors.

When I tell the story of this particular soldier to my medical colleagues, I always mention that triage is a necessary part of war. I tell them it's a matter of compassionate medical necessity and the entrenched reality of combat—that it's the exercise of a soldier's final duty.

Occasionally, though, I think about telling them how I wished I could have done something—anything. But then I realize I cannot tell them that, because, in fact, I did do something, and I am left with the nameless face of an expectant soldier and countless sheets of history filled with decisions made by doctors at war. I am left with my own understanding that we who are soldiers are all triaged.

I want to remember the expectant soldier as a person with a name, but I have come to accept that I cannot. I remember, instead, the triage room. I recall the general who placed his hand on a young man. And I see the drifting once again—the fading of a soldier back into the womb from which he was born into life. I see him loved. He is a soldier. Wounded. Triaged. Expectant.

# 14

## Lead Weight

MAX "JOE" DALTON
EDITED BY BEVERLY DALTON, HIS WIFE

In March 1944 I was nineteen and received my draft notice, as did several of my West Point, Utah, friends. The induction center was in Salt Lake City. Because gas was rationed because of the war (everyone had to have a gas stamp to get gasoline), we all decided to go to Salt Lake City to the induction center together. My dad had a sedan that he let me use for the day.

We drove down the highway in that big car, and I was full of confidence. I had worked on the family farm all of my life; I knew I was in good physical shape. I passed my physical with flying colors. However, I was turned down by the induction officer because I weighed only 100 pounds. The minimum weight was 110. I didn't see how much a person's weight had to do with being fit and able to fight a war. But I watched all my friends get inducted into military service that day, and I was sent home. I was 4F, a failure. I couldn't believe it. I felt like a real loser.

Soon after, I got a job at Hill Air Force Base, installing heaters in B-24s, so at least I was doing something to help the war effort. However, I was still not satisfied with the noncombat job. Being labeled 4F really hurt my pride.

So I was determined to gain enough weight to join the military. I started eating everything I could get my hands on. My mother was a wonderful cook. For breakfast she started serving me ham or bacon, two fried eggs, and homemade bread with a lot of hand-churned butter and jam. Dinner was fried chicken or some other fried meat, mashed potatoes, and cream gravy. Supper was the lightest meal of day: leftovers, fruit, bread, and milk. But we always had a dish of ice cream before going to bed. We didn't have any scales in our home, but I knew I had to have gained weight from eating all that good food.

Eventually, I wrote the draft board, concocting a story about how I had been sick on my first trip down to the induction center and that I had just now gained back all my weight.

It seems as if I waited a long time before I finally received another draft notice. But when the letter arrived from the draft board, I was so confident that I quit my job at Hill Air Force Base the same day.

Still, I decided I might need a little help in passing the weight requirement, if for some strange reason I hadn't gained enough weight. First, I considered putting rocks in my pockets, until I remembered I would be weighed in my underwear. I knew I needed another plan; just what, I couldn't say.

Finally, the day arrived when I was to report to the Salt Lake City induction center. This time I had to ride the Bamberger, a local electric train because Dad needed his car, and this felt like a bad sign.

The new plan, I had decided, was to cheat my way in, if necessary. A man's got to want something pretty bad to resort to cheating. So in my hand I hid a small pencil with an eraser that could not be seen by anyone. When I stepped on the scales, I watched the weight come up to 100 pounds again and stop. My heart nearly stopped.

The recording agent wrote down 100. But then, luckily, someone walked up to the recording agent to ask a question. When the agent turned to answer, I stepped over to the form, quickly erased the first zero of the 100, and added a one in its place. Now I weighed 110.

The recording agent was so busy, he was none the wiser. He sent me on my way to the next processing station. I was finally able to join, and I was elated.

At the next station the recruiter asked what branch of the military I wanted to join. I knew I didn't want to go in the Army because I had heard horror stories about the Army from my dad, who had been a foot soldier in World War I. So I spoke up loud and clear, declaring I wanted to join the Navy like my brother Darrel and that I planned to make the military my career.

Soon afterward, I caught the Bamberger in Clearfield, Utah, which took me to the Salt Lake City train station. There, I met up with friends who had also decided to join the Navy.

It was May 23, 1944, when we arrived in San Diego. I received the official boot camp haircut (a once-over quickly with a pair of shears). After my hair was cut I was weighed again, and I watched that scale rise to 100 and stop. Fearfully, I asked the officer in charge if he was going to send me home.

"No," he said. "We'll fatten you up."

# 15

# War Games

STEPHEN WILSON

I am seven years old in 1949 and have been living with my mother, father, and two older brothers in an apartment in a remodeled Japanese Air Force barracks since June 1948: white frame buildings forming a U shape around an open rectangle; no trees, only grass; two buildings of four apartments each on three sides of the courtyard, with the runway-now-street forming the fourth side.

On the base are a lot of children as the American occupation of Japan enters its third year. My father is a lieutenant colonel in the Army Quartermaster Corps and has been in Japan since 1946. But for me and my brothers, it's playmates and games. My family and these kids are my world. From a different world, Japanese village kids come over to play. We are all awkward at first, but we quickly warm to each other. We get to know each other. We learn enough of each other's language to play games, mostly war games.

Today, however, I am playing alone in a double sand pile at the corner of two of our apartment buildings. Firecrackers are cheap and available. I have some in my pocket as I take my place on the sand pile. A bucket of water, gathered earlier, sits at my side. I use the water to moisten the sand and make a small town with streets and buildings. I use sticks for trees and sometimes for people.

I move to the next sand pile. I marshal my supplies: marbles, a six-inch-by-half-inch water pipe, and firecrackers, as well as matches. I plan my mortar. I thrust the pipe in the ground with one end sticking up almost vertically. I aim it toward my town. Balancing a firecracker on the edge of the pipe, I light the fuse, shove it down the pipe, and immediately drop a marble in on top of it. A little smoke, but no explosion; the marble goes nowhere. When I've disassembled the mortar, I find the fuse has been snuffed out. Next attempt, delay the marble drop, and it should work.

I reset the mortar, place the firecracker, light the fuse, push it in, and then, after a short wait, drop in the marble. Boom! The marble flies out of the pipe and drops about ten feet beyond the town. I've got to shorten the range. Raising the pipe until it is nearer to vertical, I repeat the load-and-fire operation. The marble is propelled above the town, and then falls directly onto the main street. I have the range, so now I begin systematically blowing up and destroying my little sand town.

March 1969, the twin-engine plane lands at the village of An Thoi on Phú Quôc Island, Vietnam. I deplane and head for a Coast Guard jeep, where a sailor is waiting to take me to my boat. This is my first day on station in wartime Vietnam. The sailor welcomes me and drops me off. I am relieving the executive officer (second in command) of the U.S. Coast Guard Cutter *Point Grace* (WPB 82323). The skipper greets me, helps me stow my gear, and gives me a tour, during which he introduces me to all the crew members on board.

The *Point Grace* is painted battleship gray instead of the bright white of my former ships. Makes sense; white is so easily seen and targeted. She is eighty-two feet long, with an eleven-foot beam. She draws six feet of water when fully loaded and armed. She carries five 50-caliber machine guns, one of which rides piggyback on a deck-mounted 81mm mortar. She depends on a crew of eleven with one added Vietnamese liaison officer. The *Point Grace* is an old but beautiful piece of machinery.

After the tour and introductions, the skipper takes me over to the APL (auxiliary personnel lighter) to report for duty to the CO. We have a quick meeting, during which I sign some papers, hand in my orders, and shake hands around. Then it's off to the O Club (officers' club) for socializing. The skipper introduces me to other officers; we drink, talk, and laugh. Then we all head back to the boat for sleep, since we go on patrol early in the morning.

My first impressions of An Thoi. Being March, the middle of the dry season, it is hot, dry, and sandy. We drive through sand, walk through sand, and drink sand with our whiskey at the O Club. As I look around, I remember how much I enjoyed playing in sand as a child. That was always the first place I looked for when we moved onto a base after a transfer. I loved making things in sand even though they collapsed easily.

I hit the rack. Before drifting off to sleep, I realize that I'm thinking about the mortar and about how exciting it will be to see it firing.

Summertime in Japan. Japanese children have come onto our base to play. We meet behind our apartment houses. We choose a large field for the games of war. This is a common theme of play for us and for the Japanese kids from the village. We have no common language except for the innate understanding of play. A lot of hand signals with some phrases of Japanese and English thrown in. There are about fifty boys ages five to fourteen set to play.

Scattered around our play area are burned-out tanks and antiaircraft guns from the war. The destroyed weapons give us a sense of being in a war. Today, the over-twelves, including my older brother, Bob, face our opposing army of under-twelves. The over-twelves are larger, faster, and more sophisticated than we are, so we will have to use deception to defeat them. The two teams gather at opposite ends of the field. The under-twelve "commanders" are three of the oldest boys—two Americans and one Japanese. The signal to begin the battle comes from the other side—an American shout of "Go!"

The field is large and covered in brush for hiding and ambushing. All weapons are pretend with our hands. Sounds of shooting are made orally. Dirt clods become grenades and are liberally spread across the battle lines. The older kids are the aggressors, and we are the defenders. We hide in groups under and behind the bushes and field weapons. As the attackers approach, we crawl to get behind them and then stand and begin shooting. Sometimes we get a number of kills. Arguments start about fairness, cheating, and who shot whom first. The arguments take place in two mutually unintelligible languages.

Eventually, the battle dies down to nothing. The older kids go back to their side, and we under-twelves return to our home base.

Once the day's battle is over, the girls are allowed to filter in, and we begin to play more normal games, like hide-and-seek, tag, and kick-the-can. Then as suppertime approaches the Japanese children head back to the village. We American kids return to our apartments.

The *Point Grace* is on patrol in an area just off the southern coast of the Mekong Delta. Today is July 4. We've been told to expect a surprise this evening. A U.S. Navy rocket-launching ship is deploying to our area. We are to provide any assistance they need, including forward observing for targeting. They arrive just before sunset. About an hour into darkness, we guide the ship into safe waters near the shore. Their captain orders us to stand down and move out of their area of operation. We comply with these orders.

The captain announces to his crew and by radio to our boat that in celebration of the Fourth of July, he is going to unload a large barrage of rockets into the enemy free-fire zone established by the American command. The free-fire zone is defined as an enemy-controlled area where we are to shoot to kill anything that moves, combatants and noncombatants alike. Of course, we can't see any targets as he is firing over the jungle cover into the local villages, but we know that these are the people we will be inspecting and interacting with tomorrow. The ones who survive will be out in their sampans and junks fishing these very waters.

We are invited to observe and enjoy this display of pyrotechnics. Does he have specified targets? Probably not. We know of no active enemy units in this particular area. Does he need to have specified targets? No. He has the power and the approval of Naval Command to perpetrate this indecency in the name of the United States.

He fires salvo after salvo of rockets into the Mekong Delta for no other reason than it is the Fourth of July and he wants to. After each release cheers come from the ship. There is silence on our boat as we watch this travesty. Sad. This playing at war is no fun. On the *Point Grace* we'd rather play anything but war games right now.

I'm nearly eight years old now, and I'm visiting the historic and sacred city of Kyoto with my family. Mountains and waters surround the many temples and pagodas. Feeding ducks on the lake is a joy for me. My father is rowing our boat, so the rest of us just relax and watch the scene unfold before us. Small cinders tumble from the sky into the lake waters where we paddle. They sizzle when they hit the water. This frightens me and my mother, but my father is unfazed and keeps rowing. He explains to us that he has visited here before and that these little cinder showers happen often. The ducks, equally unfazed, continue to swim and follow our bread-crumb trail.

Onshore we're walking along a street filled with people, mostly Japanese. Many Japanese families are out walking the streets, just as we are. We've been here long enough to know it is polite to greet with a bow. The kids on both sides giggle a lot while bowing, even though the parents try to affect a formal solemn attitude. It's a relaxed place to be.

Before we enter a Buddhist temple, Mother and Father stop us and deliver a short lecture on courtesy in this foreign land. My father says, "We are guests here now, so we must all be courteous to the people here. This temple is a holy place for these people. Therefore, it must be a holy place for us. No talking, running, fighting, or other disruptive behavior will be allowed. Also, no more giggling. Understood?"

"Yes," my brothers and I respond halfheartedly, wishing for some fun and frolic instead of this solemnity. Or maybe we could engage these Japanese kids in some war games like at home. One look at our mother's face tells us to settle down.

We enter. Monks are sitting on cushions in quiet meditation around the great hall. The place is both dark and light. The walls are a flat white and barren of decoration. There are no seats or pews as one would find in a church or synagogue back home. Incense imbues the air with a fresh scent, which is exciting and quieting. Dark and light, exciting and quieting, welcoming and distant. The seated Buddha dominates the great hall. He is smiling gently. What an honor to be here. I'm thinking, *Thank you, Buddha. Thank you, Japan. Thank you, Army. Thank you, War, for bringing me to this place of peace.*

Today, the *Point Grace* is running courier duty, meaning we're hauling water and supplies from Phú Quốc Island to Hà Tiên on the west coast of the Mekong Delta of Vietnam. The town lies almost on the border with Cambodia. Hà Tiên is a small town of about ten thousand souls. The harbor is excellent, but is a little difficult to enter for a boat with our six-foot draft. With the extra water and supplies on board, we're down another half foot, so our functional draft is six and a half feet.

The harbor entrance has a sand bar that must be crossed. At high tide the depth of the water over the bar is just about six feet. Our method of entry is to use the boat as a sort of dredge. Because I'm the primary boat driver or pilot, I'm charged with getting her across the bar without hanging her up. Should I hang her on the bar, we could be vulnerable to attack from the shore about fifty meters away. We would not be able to move until the next high tide, approximately twelve hours from now. A sitting duck.

This is serious, so we calculate high tide as carefully as we can. We wait in the approach channel for the stillness that marks maximum flood tide. Then we go. We must move slowly but steadily. Too quickly and we damage the hull. Too slowly and we lose the advantage of high tide and hang her up on the bar.

When the moment arrives, I put her engines ahead one-third, which will give us about three knots. We feel the initial resistance of the sand and hear the scraping of the hull from below. She hesitates for a few seconds and then begins to move into the sandbar. We guess the bar to be about fifty meters wide. She makes way slowly. As she rides higher on the bar, we begin to hear and feel the twin screws begin to dig into the sand. I increase RPMs to nearly half speed, and she keeps moving steadily, noisily, and roughly through the sand and water. Soon we begin to hear the scraping ease. Eventually, thankfully, the screws become less agitated, and we are over the bar.

We all breathe easier and begin to relax. Hà Tiên is a relatively safe place. The Viet Cong like their R&R spots as much as the Americans, so they don't do much fighting in this town. But we all remember what happened a little more than a year ago, when many of these small peaceful towns were attacked during the first night of Tet 1968.

The waterfront is a simple wooden pier. The Navy folks meet our boat and help us unload the supplies. They drive the supplies to their base on the edge of town, but we know they will join us later for beer, food, and fun. We secure our boat to the pier and leave three men and the skipper on board to protect the boat from any possible enemies.

The rest of us walk up the dusty street to the nearest bar. The bar is very different from those in the larger cities like Saigon. There are no bar girls hustling drinks for themselves and us. In fact, there don't seem to be any women in the bar, except for a couple of waitresses delivering food and drink to the men. The crowd is predominantly Vietnamese, but there are a few other Americans here. We also know that the Navy will be back soon from their supply run.

Most of the men are sitting at the tables drinking Ba Muoi Ba beer or Black Cat Cambodian whiskey. The beer is served warm with ice in it, and the whiskey is served straight. The beer is good; the whiskey is awful. Some of our crew are here, but as the only Coast Guard officer, I sit alone at the bar. The owner-bartender is a distinguished, elderly Vietnamese man. He has the traditional white beard, almost like a goatee but much longer—something the elderly cultivate in Vietnam.

"Papa-san, bring us some Ba Mi Ba . . . ," shouts one of the young sailors.

"Papa-san, bring us some food . . ."

"Papa-san, where is your daughter? Bring her to us. We want to get laid . . ."

On and on the insults fly from these young Americans. The old one brings the food and drink silently and scuttles back to the bar. I shoot them warning looks, but they are drunk, not under my command, and are Navy to boot. Anything I say would be useless in this situation. Looking over at the table where the guys from my boat are drinking beer and talking quietly, I feel pride. When they need something, they ask politely and are grateful for what they get.

The owner comes back to the bar and continues serving other customers. Most of his customers, American and Vietnamese, are friendly and courteous like my crew. Only a few of the young American servicemen are discourteous. They call him "Papa-san," a Japanese term of familiarity and family. Calling him this is a deep insult. One only needs to know that the Vietnamese lost at least two million people because of the Japanese occupation of their land. The Japanese army took most of the rice, including much of the seed rice, leaving famine to savage the land.

Finally, one of the naval officers arrives and orders his swabbies out of the bar and back to the base. Things quiet down. The games are over. I go back to my boat to sleep. I feel a deep sense of shame at the insults hurled at this old Vietnamese gentleman. This is his country, after all, and we are his guests. Memories of my father and mother in Japan flood my soul. What would they make of this war I'm fighting in? Would that they were still alive so I could discuss it with them.

I'm now eight and a half years old and standing on the deck of the *General E. D. Patrick* with my family. Father, mother, my brothers, and me. With red and puffy eyes my father points across the sea to the east. We see the Golden Gate Bridge rising out of the fog. What we can't see is the future. Will my brothers and I have to fight a war someday? If we do, I hope I get to drive a boat with a mortar on it.

Still a small child, I don't understand my parents' excitement about returning to the United States. I'll go wherever the family goes, but I'm not happy about leaving Japan and all my Japanese and American friends.

Whining, I beg to go sit below in the warm cabin. The air on the deck is chilly in the early morning, and I'm cold and tired of standing. But my parents insist that I stay with the family to witness our homecoming. I'm thinking, *Homecoming? We just left our home, a wonderful home, in Tokyo.*

# 16

# False Positive

ALEJANDRO MUJICA

It's taken two years of being "normal" to return to the VA Medical Center. "Normal" is what the psychotherapist told me in '05, the year I left the Corps. First year out of the military, treatment felt like a healthy choice. Two years later, it feels like a necessity.

The automatic doors to the VA lobby slide open, and the shower of cold air chills my skin. But it's the hallways that hold my attention, like vanishing points where white lab coats and wheelchairs appear and vanish in an off-white hue. And the smell, stale and lifeless as potted silk. The intercom, clear as a bell, however, calls for a doctor's attention.

This time the patients look even younger, more veterans in their thirties and twenties, fresh from discharge, some still in high-and-tight haircuts, reviewing their paperwork, ready to take advantage of two years of free VA health care. With constant deployments and such long occupations in Afghanistan and Iraq, it feels as if the number of young veterans seeking affordable medical care is becoming too difficult to handle well.

The clinic handles patients by appointments, and sometimes they also take emergencies, but I never see where they take them. I see the EMTs racing through Baldwin Park on the way to the clinic, but I never see where they send their patients, and I never see the stretchers roll by. It's as if they warm their sirens and do laps around the clinic for fun.

I follow the signs leading to each clinic. Along the way Cardiology, Surgery, Prosthetics, Mental Health. It's on the second floor. I find the elevators nearby, large enough to move bed-bound patients from floor to floor.

The doors of Mental Health slide open, and I find my way to the waiting area, which has two dozen stuffed chairs crammed into the middle of two hallways and a lemonade stand for a reception desk. Veterans pack the seats. Most are in various stages of filling out packets of paperwork clipped to metallic boards. The rest rock in their seats or sit on their hands until someone tells them what to do.

At the desk a nurse with wide-framed glasses scribbles on her own clipboard, busy enough not to notice me standing in front of her, or pretending not to notice. She's middle-aged, I'm guessing, by the silver hair that swirls throughout her receding brown dye job. Her name tag says Maureen. She looks like a Maureen.

"Hi there," I finally say. "Is this where—"

"Stand behind the line, please." Maureen doesn't lift her head from the clipboard when she says this—just points to the floor and a black line of electrical tape that surrounds the kiosk. I am the only person in line, but I take a step back and point my feet behind the line anyway. Military training kicks in.

Now she lifts her head. "You'd like an assessment?" she says.

I don't know what that means for sure. "Yes, I think so."

"It's a PTSD assessment, right?" she says. "Do you have insurance? Your VA identification card?"

"No, I—"

"Just your driver's license, please."

I hand her my license, and she scribbles my information down on her pad and then riffles through her folders and hands me another clipboard with a stack of paperwork attached to it. "You'll need to read and fill these out before seeing the therapist," she says. "Give it back to me once you're done."

I nod and find a seat next to another man in a black T-shirt and jeans. His arms are folded, and the rest of his body is propped like a plank across the seat. I flip through the pages: basic waivers, permissions, acknowledgments, and three pages of checklists and charts. Many questions I answered the first time I came looking for help, but the paperwork now is lengthier. Last time it was a simple consultation with a psychiatrist in his office, a mental checkup and well-wishing. Now I have to talk to a clipboard first. Drug-related questions, reoccurring-memories questions:

*How many drinks do you have a month?*

Drinking isn't an issue, I want to say, because I know plenty who drink more than I do and function on both feet. No, I've had drinking binges, but those are miles apart. I've broken up enough club fights, detained enough violent drunks, and fished enough Marines out of gutters who were paralyzed by drinking of their own. I don't need to join them, but a dozen or so drinks is more than enough to sustain me for the month. So, I write in 15.

*Do you have thoughts about harming yourself and/or others?*

There'd been fits, momentary irrational, self-inflicted rages and on objects in my room, holes through walls, through doors; I have the scars on my hands to prove them. And thoughts of slamming complete strangers into traffic, beating them senseless. An hour won't go by without such a thought. *Yes*, I write.

*Do you have reoccurring dreams of a service-related experience?*

They mean nightmares, flashbacks, and no, the dreams don't come on their own, not shocked to life, not in the way this question hopes I'll answer. But fantasies and memories, yes, and not a jump into them, but the sharp stab of instinct, being in the moment, a pedestrian world burned away to reveal a flaming desert underneath. Fear and anger can control posture, but not what I see, and not what I hear. Only what I feel—the compression of fluids through my body, waves of pressure collapsing my chest into bone chips, punctured by white sparks burning through my limbs. Where torches blast at a concert's first song, where crowds bury the exits, where families celebrate their freedom by bombing the sky, that's where it lives, and I am grateful it's left my dreams years ago. *No*, I answer.

*Do you sometimes fantasize about suicide?*

Not exactly. Not until traffic stops and cars limp in feet and yards do I consider getting out of the car to find him—the lynchpin holding back the rest of the rush-hour crowd—so I can mash his mouth into the curb. And when the cops come, you know, you've been trained to know, that if their guns aren't ready when you cross that line and become a threat, they won't be by the time you get there. No, there has to be another name for this. Not suicide. Self-detonation. But still, a *No*.

The rest of the questions are even lengthier than they are difficult. Maureen sits where I left her. She is wading through her sea of papers. I stand on the line until she waves me closer, and I hand her the list.

"Please have a seat, and we'll call you once the therapist is ready to see you."

A half hour rolls by before another lady in white, glasses, and fading brown hair visits me at my seat.

"Hi . . . Alejandro?" She pronounces it with an English *j*, like *January*. "My name is Dr. Patterson." She offers her hand; we shake. "Could you come with me, please?"

I follow Dr. Patterson to an office a few yards away: marble-style linoleum, a collection of diplomas in a huddle on one of the mint-green walls. There are two puffy chairs on my side of her desk. Group counseling must be one of her responsibilities, too.

"Please, have a seat." She looks over the papers in her hand. Frowns. After a moment, "So, you've been out for three years?"

I nod. "That's right."

"And when were you deployed? Iraq? Afghanistan?"

"Yeah, Iraq in 2003, February to September."

She sucks in her teeth and flips back and forth between the pages. I wonder how the usual evaluations work and if the human plank in the waiting room will be judged in the same way. Or maybe he's already been judged and is standing by for the next leg of treatment. Does every veteran have to go through this type of questioning, or do some of us look so at risk on paper that we go straight to counseling?

"Good, so one tour to Iraq?"

"Yes, that's right." And thank goodness. Along with base patrol back in the States, one tour was enough.

"Do you get along with your family?"

"Yeah, pretty well," I say. "We spend Sundays together. My parents are separated, but they live nearby and my brother and I visit them every weekend or so. My brother and I live together."

"That's very good. So, how do you feel about your drinking? It says fifteen for the month. Does that seem like a lot to you?"

This feels like a trick question. It's not a lot to me, but to her that might be pushing it. There's a margin of relativity to it, right? Does she know that it's not a lot for me? Never mind. I'll just answer honestly. "No, it doesn't seem like a lot. Sometimes I might even have more." Now I've done it. Did I just brag to a doctor about how much I can drink and then tell her I can drink *more*?

"I see." She's scribbling. What is she scribbling? Defining mental illnesses? Future prescriptions for Paxil?

After a few more basic questions she sets down the paperwork, removes her glasses, squeezes the bridge of her nose, and then puts her glasses back on.

"From what we have on here, and what we've been discussing, it doesn't look like you have PTSD, not *really*."

This doesn't make sense, not the complete prognosis I was ready for. *Not really*, like a pseudosyndrome, almost treatable. Sorry, but your symptoms fall outside of our psychotherapeutic jurisdiction.

"You might have related symptoms, but not the major concerns to consider for extensive treatment. You're not suffering from flashbacks or hallucinations, for example. Again, it might be adjustment disorder. We do offer scheduled one-on-one therapy sessions and group sessions. I wouldn't recommend those, but you could visit the group sessions, if you feel they'd be helpful. Do you really feel like that's something you'd like to do?"

It's not so much what she said but how she said it—her tone, as if I were inconveniencing her, like a professor eager to go home early, but there's still that one student in the front row with a hand in the air. And her eyes, the way she tilts her head when she asks . . . as if I shit in her chair. Should I join group sessions, or should I wait and improve on my own? From her tone I know I am not a solid fit.

I remember one Vietnam veteran confessing to me that he needed to pull the bottle from his hand and the gun from his mouth. Men like him need these group sessions. But me, I feel too young, too connected to the people who matter most in my life. There are veterans with deeper, darker wells than mine.

"No, that's all right," I say. "I'll be okay." It's all I can say, and what she wants me to say.

I walk out of the office, into the hallway, and back through the lobby. The only relief is that I am better off than most, it appears. Yet I'm leaving with so many unanswered questions about how to deal with what and who I am, and worse . . . now I don't even know who to ask.

# 17

## Prisoners of War

LEILA LEVINSON

"We have an old documentary showing how people with mental illness used to be treated . . . Are y'all interested in seeing it?" asked the psychologist leading the intensive five-day training at the Veterans Administration in Austin.

The training was to qualify us to become peer-to-peer specialists who would lead support groups for veterans and their family members. Some of the trainees were veterans, some of us—like me—children of veterans, all of us committed to helping veterans with mental health challenges.

My fellow trainees and I looked at one another, their faces mirroring my uncertainty about seeing this documentary.

"Sure," a Vietnam veteran said. "Why not?"

A chorus line of men suddenly appeared in black and white on the screen in front of us. To the tune of "Strike Up the Band," the gaunt men with closely cropped heads kicked their feet and waved batons in unison, their eyes darting to one another to make sure they were staying in step. The documentary, *Titicut Follies*, is about the conditions at the Bridgewater state mental hospital in Massachusetts.

With no voice-over, the scene changed to that of men undressing before armed men, their uniforms and hats reminding me of those police wore during my early childhood in the 1960s. But this couldn't be from that time, I assured myself. State hospitals must have been more humane by the 1960s.

The naked men stood in line to receive uniforms before being led down a hallway. Some were placed in jail-like cells. Some were led into rooms and interrogated. "Do you know why you are here? Can you explain your behavior?" The men shook their heads, their faces dazed, vacant. One man began to babble, his voice a rushing stream of words, about Jesus, JFK, President Johnson.

JFK? President Johnson? My body knew before my mind would accept that this movie was shot during the mid-1960s. I stood up and left the room. In my car I froze. One thought coursed through me: That was the kind of place my mother had been sent to. That was what happened to my mother.

A few days after my fifth birthday, my mother took me shopping for sneakers to go with the turquoise poodle-dog skirt I hadn't taken off since unwrapping it.

I didn't want to go shopping. Stores were dangerous places: sometimes my mother stole things when she went into stores. But I also didn't want to say no, because her anger was dangerous, too.

Instead of bringing us the sneakers, the salesclerk appeared with a policeman who arrested my mother and directed us into a black-and-white car with a large red light on top. All the way to the station, my mother squeezed my arm. "Don't let them take you from me. If they take you, I'll never see you again."

At the station they took me from her, her screams following me down the stairs to where my father was waiting. Without saying a word, he drove me home. Over the next few weeks I pleaded, "Where's Mommy? When's Mommy coming home?" My father didn't get angry. He didn't yell. He responded with total silence.

It was my oldest brother who talked. He put his face right up against mine and said, "She's in an in-sti-tu-tion. She's a loony bird. Do you want to be a loony bird, too?"

At dinner my father played records: Barbra Streisand or the Yale Whiffenpoofs—my father's tribute to his beloved alma mater. The refrain of one song felt like the needle of a sewing machine piercing my brain: *Sometimes I feel like a motherless child, a long way from home.*

I became the good daughter, the perfect student. My only dissent was a perpetual pout. I pouted despite my coarse housekeeper's frequent admonishment, "Someday your face is going to freeze like that, and then you'll be sorry." But even though I pouted, I believed what my father, who had been an Army doctor during World War II, believed: that I was unscathed, that I was *strong*. I kept, as he put it, "the flag flying."

But all this collapsed in on me when I attended law school. In the middle of the second semester, all semblance of mental and emotional cohesion disintegrated as a nightmare came to visit and refused to leave.

I'm in a canoe on a lake. A breeze cools my skin, and I lean back against the gunwale and close my eyes. Cold wind smacks my face, flips the canoe, hurls me into the water. I sink and sink, falling onto a rock shelf where she sits, her hair floating before her face like Medusa's snakes; an anchor is tied to her neck.

Something (morbid curiosity? concern?) pulls me closer. Her hand snaps out, seizes my hand. Her other hand snaps out, encircles my neck. She lifts her head. My God, my God, she is as white as the moon. She is wax. Her eyes are pearls. Jagged teeth line her mouth.

From these nightmares, I woke up screaming, my chest heaving as I tried to find air.

After the third night I lost the ability to sleep. I couldn't focus on legal opinions. I couldn't answer the phone or leave my house. A classmate came by, concerned by my disappearance. "Why not go to the university counseling center? It's free." As she looked at my face, she whispered, "I'll go with you. It will be okay."

As I entered the therapist's office, I was reminded of the day my father had taken me to Grand Central Station to put me on a train to summer camp. A month shy of six, I had pushed past my fear and gotten on the train that took me to camp, which turned out to be a paradise of woods, mountains, a lake, and kind women counselors.

"You're terrified you'll disappear like your mother did, that you'll go crazy, become an alcoholic," the kind university therapist told me. "You need to find out what happened to her. You need to learn her story, so you can create your own. I suspect she didn't deserve to be cast off as a crazy alcoholic. I suspect she gave you many gifts, or you wouldn't have done as well as you have."

All that I knew about my mother was that she had died during my junior year of college, a fact I learned from my oldest brother only months after her death. The where, the why, the how he did not tell me. (As I was sobbing upon hearing the news, my father came into the room and told me, "This is how it had to be, Leila. Your mother was weak. But we're not. And now you can do her name good." But I was not even sure of her name.)

After my meeting with the therapist, I went back to New Jersey and visited my father at his office, timing my arrival to coincide with his lunch break.

"Leila!" His eyes lit up, and his voice rang like a bell. In moments such as these, I believed he did love me. "Come, have a sandwich with me."

We ate at a red linoleum-topped table in the little kitchen of his office and worked through our usual conversation about his certainty that I would make a great constitutional scholar. As we washed off the dishes, I took a deep breath. "Dad, I need to know what happened—to my mother."

His hands squeezed the sponge. "I . . . I can't talk about it. Not yet. Maybe someday." And then he was suddenly crying, tears flowing down his cheeks. I wrapped my arms around him, but he pulled away. "We have to be strong, Leila. We've been strong all this time. We can't stop now."

I stayed strong. I mustered my way through the next two and a half years of law school. I kept the flag flying.

My father maintained his strength of resistance for another five years, when he died of a massive coronary. Upon learning of his death, I fell to the floor, sobs breaking from my throat, because now I would never know the truth about my mother.

Three days after my father's funeral, I found photographs he had taken during his time as an Army doctor in the European theater of World War II. They revealed my father's untold war stories. And in so doing they also revealed what had happened to my mother.

Inside my father's Army trunk in the basement of his office was a Nazi helmet standing guard on top. While that helmet had kept me out of the trunk throughout my childhood, I now moved it to the floor and opened the trunk. Next to my father's captain jacket was a shoe box. As I lifted the lid photographs spilled out, hundreds of photographs of my father's war.

One showed a sea, lit by a cloud-shrouded moon. My father's seismographic handwriting on the back noted: *The English Channel, June 5/44. Prelude to the Invasion.* The next, labeled *Clearing Station on "Utah"*

*Beach, Normandy, June 8/44,* showed GIs lying on the ground, white bandages on their heads, their arms, their thighs. In other photographs I saw circus-size tents, adorned with red crosses. Children wearing berets and shorts nestled under arms of a GI: *The magic of chocolate.* Then photos of ruined towns, devastated homes and churches. Photographs of fields of snow, tanks covered in snow, bodies covered with snow. Fields covered with white crosses and sporadic Stars of David: *The boys who died in the Ardennes.*

I flipped through the photos, repetitive with war's destruction, until at the bottom, blurred stripes seized my attention—rows and rows of blurred stripes swelling into a wave that upended the ground. A foot emerged from the wave, and then faces. I turned the photo over. *Nordhausen, Germany. April 12, 1945.*

Nordhausen—what was Nordhausen?

Another photo, in focus, revealed an endless canal-shaped ditch lined with bodies. Civilians stood alongside the ditches, their faces looking straight ahead. On the back, my father had written: *The burial of the concentration camps victims. April 15, 1945.*

I locked the photos back inside the trunk.

I married a year later. The year after that I gave birth to a son, and three years later I had another. Life swept me away from thoughts of those photos, until twelve years later when I began teaching freshman composition at St. Edward's University. I noticed there was no course offered on the Holocaust, so I requested to teach one. I assigned *Night* by Elie Weisel, *Auschwitz and After* by Charlotte Delbo, and books by children of survivors: *Maus I* and *Maus II* by Art Spiegelman, *The Holocaust Kid* by Sonia Pilcer, and *Secondhand Smoke* by Thane Rosenbaum. Because the grandfathers of many of my students were World War II veterans, we read a number of oral histories of GI liberators. Amazing as it is to me now, I wasn't conscious of my personal reasons for including the oral histories in the curriculum.

*Night* and *Auschwitz and After* reveal how the psychological and physical brutality, the constant presence of death in the camps, claimed the spirits of all the prisoners—survivors as well as the dead. "None of us should have returned," Delbo observes, because the price of their survival was their "deep memory" of the horrors that no amount of time could erase. Delbo describes a membrane-thin wall encapsulating the annihilating memories of the camp, the memories seeping out unpredictably, hurling the survivors back into the hell of the camps.

And so, despite the survivors' intentions, they exposed their children to traumatic memories. The literature by the children expresses how the single most defining moment of their lives occurred before they were born, because the Holocaust—Auschwitz in particular—imprisoned their own lives. Even if the parents remained silent about their experiences, melancholy and anger saturated the children's lives. As well as feeling compassion and love for their parents, the children felt resentment and rage, as well as guilt and inadequacy for not having suffered like their parents did.

"Trauma is contagious," my students insisted.

I could find only one book about the experiences of the GI liberators. *In Evidence* by Barbara Helfgott Hyatt arranges portions of liberators' oral histories into poetic form. I read a few of the passages to my students:

"When I walked through the gate of Dachau, my mind somersaulted and froze."

"Our men cried. We were a combat unit. We'd been to Anzio, to southern France, Sicily, Salerno, the Battle of the Bulge, and we'd never, ever seen anything like this."

A student raised her hand. "Did the trauma of the GIs affect their children like the trauma of the survivors affected theirs?"

Facing my students' wide-open eyes, their minds moving to the edge of insight, the air parted before me.

"That's a question worth pursuing," I managed to say.

At home that evening I went out to the garage where I had stored my father's trunk and took out the shoe box. I carried it up to my bedroom, away from the curious eyes of my eleven- and seven-year-old sons. As I lay the photographs on my bed, I kept looking away from the twisted corpses. "Look," I commanded myself. "See a mere fraction of what Dad saw."

Yes. Of course. Trauma. Utter and infinite. There it was. Even after D-day, even after the Battle of the Bulge, walking into Nordhausen must have been traumatic beyond my ability to imagine. What had happened to the men and women who opened the gates of Buchenwald, Dachau, Mauthausen? Nothing had been written about their trauma. Nothing. Not to mention anything about the consequences for the families of these veterans. How did the wives of these men—women like my mother—respond to the news of what their husbands had witnessed, to their memories, their photographs?

Feeling as though I hadn't a moment to lose, I began researching what divisions liberated camps, began finding names and addresses, wrote grant proposals for travel funds. And six months after my student asked me how the trauma of the liberators shaped their children, I was on my way to meet liberators and ask them questions no one had ever asked them: How did witnessing the camp change you? What relationship do you have with your memories of the camp you liberated? What have you shared with your wife, your children?

"The shock was complete and total," George Kaiser told me as we sat in his living room in the seaside town of Winthrop, Massachusetts. "You just couldn't believe it—you just couldn't believe it. I just lost it when I saw bodies stacked up, the killing. It hurts, it hurts, it brings back memories that just don't go away. Every once in a while they just appear . . ."

His eyes revealed he was back in Dachau, April 1945.

After endless minutes of polite silence, I asked what he remembered.

"When I walked into the courtyard, I couldn't move. My mind froze. Especially when we saw the crematoria, still hot with these piles of bodies, stacked five bodies high . . ."

His voice broke off, his mouth hanging open. He put his head down into the cup of his palms, his shoulders shaking. Excusing himself, he left the room.

Cyma, his wife, appeared. She was a tall, graceful woman. "How's he doing?"

"I'm afraid I've stirred up a lot of pain."

"It was his decision to talk with you," she said. "It's not like his silence all these years has helped him. So maybe talking will."

"Has he talked about it with your children?"

"No," she said. "He's never told them anything. I only learned a few years ago after he decided to speak to a church group, and I went to hear the talk. He speaks to strangers more readily than to us. For my children, it's all reading between the lines. What they know they read in a newspaper interview of him. I try to help them understand what's behind his silence, his tendency to withdraw, to erupt."

*Silent* and *withdrawn*: words that had been used to describe my father. And, yes, the flares of anger, out of nowhere. Anger I hadn't wanted to remember, like the time we had gone for a Sunday drive—my stepmother, stepbrother, and I—and we passed a Modess plant (a company that made sanitary napkins) on Route 1. Strung along the huge lawn of the plant were these huge words: "Modess, because . . ." And my stepbrother asked, "Because why?" My father whipped around, his face engorged with rage. "You shut your mouth, do you hear me!" My nine-year-old stepbrother shriveled into himself, but that wasn't the end of it. Once home my father followed him into his room, and through the walls I heard, "Don't you ever embarrass your sister again, do you hear me?"

"No words could convey," another liberator, Dr. George Tievsky, told me. Like Mr. Kaiser, after receiving my letter, he agreed to speak with me and told me that, like my father, he had tended to survivors, though he was able to save few from death. "Nobody knew what I had witnessed. I couldn't talk about it because words could not convey the horror." Tievsky's division liberated Dachau. His photographs sat before us, tied with yellow ribbon along with the many letters he had written his wife, his "best friend," Priscilla, the one person to whom he spoke, the person who kept him grounded. "Only with Priscilla could I talk, and that was such a relief, not to be alone with those images."

When Priscilla came into the room to ask if we would like some iced tea, she gently reminded her husband that he had shown the photographs to their children.

"When they were older, yes."

"How did they respond?" I said.

"Well, they didn't verbalize much. They internalized it, I guess. I haven't pushed it. I knew that if I had to speak, I wouldn't sleep well the night after. Just remembering all this brings bad dreams. I won't sleep well tonight."

I winced. Who was I to break the silence?

I thought of Priscilla, of Cyma. How might these women have differed from my mother? What had enabled them to become their husbands' means of salvation rather than the albatross my mother seemed to have been for my father? Had my parents been all too similar, all too sensitive to life's darkness?

· · ·

"To this day I'm not prepared for Mauthausen," Edgar Edelsack said, wiping tears from his cheeks. His wife, Charlotte, held his hand. "The pictures I took were so emotionally disturbing that I gave them away. I couldn't face looking at them. The whole subject is one that I have subjugated, because it always brings tears."

Tears. The only time I saw my father cry was when I asked him what had happened to my mother. And he had acted as if crying were shameful. I had always known, without a word being said, that crying, grieving in any visible way, was impermissible in my father's home. But why? What was it about my mother and father's marriage that had been so untenable?

Perhaps if I met a women liberator, I might gain this missing piece. Perhaps a woman's response to witnessing the Holocaust would help me understand why terror paralyzed the ability to grieve.

"I don't like to go back to these memories," Kay Bonner Nee said as I packed up my tape recorder. A uso entertainer during the war, she had joined troops on their way to Buchenwald shortly after its liberation.

"Why?"

"Because I am certain they will destroy me."

And those were the words that completed the final piece of the puzzle surrounding the mystery of my parents' marriage and my mother's emotional breakdown. The extreme trauma from encountering the last gasp of a Nazi concentration camp created a terror that did not fade with time, a terror that the horror would devour the witness along with the victims. And the witnesses knew no other strategy of self-defense than suppression of the memories. The memories themselves became the threat. And so grief was impossible, and the exile of grief took all other emotions with it.

It became the job of the veteran's spouse to fill in the vacuum around her veteran husband. To support everyone in the household, including the veteran. To work around the husband's emotional absence.

What was untenable in my parents' marriage, I later came to understand, was that unlike Priscilla and Cyma, my mother came into the marriage insecure and emotionally fragile. She needed support herself, and like so many brides of returning World War II veterans, she was clueless about what she was up against. My parents had eloped days before my father shipped off to Europe. Their cohabitation began only after my father returned, and by then a shattered man who could not speak of what had shattered him, or admit even that he was shattered.

I began to see the miraculous triumph in my acknowledging that I needed help, in my unwillingness to raise my sons in the shadow of my depression, in my marrying a man who was willing to go to therapy with me. My therapy took on new focus, as did my parenting and teaching. I brought veteran liberators to St. Edwards so my students and the Austin public could meet them, so the liberators could have an opportunity to speak their truths. In meeting them my sons gained understanding, of their own history and of their mother.

But it was only a year afterward that I met a veteran who had, like my father, been a liberator of Nordhausen. At that Nazi weapons factory, prisoners carved tunnels out of mountains using only pick axes. Inside those tunnels they manufactured the v-1 and v-2 rockets that firebombed England. Mort Weinstein sat alongside his wife of sixty-one years as he shared these memories with me. Near the end of our conversation, he turned to her. "I have struggled to stay alive every day since." Her eyes glistened with love.

And I finally understood my father.

My father could not see that I needed to grieve for my mother because he could not acknowledge his own trauma. His survival depended on not seeing it. And as he could not see it, how could he have seen that it isolated his wife and cut off intimacy between them? Alone, she turned to drinking with a neighbor, and my father, the doctor, could not see that she was depressed, that she was drinking too much, that she was an alcoholic. He withdrew into his work, and after her arrest and institutionalization, he could not see that his children were depressed and despairing. His survival depended on keeping his enormous grief locked up so tight he might have a chance of being safe. I think he told himself he was providing us with security, the one kind he was able to provide—financial.

Learning about the struggles of these World War II veterans, I began thinking about the challenges facing veterans returning from Iraq and Afghanistan and posted a comment on Facebook. A friend who is a veteran of Vietnam messaged me. "Workaholism was my drug of choice. It sure beat alcoholism."

When I asked Mike whether he went silent about his memories, he wrote, "I know you don't understand. You can't. Don't say you 'understand' when you cannot possibly do that. And know that anger is central to PTSD and applies to all wars."

One of the photographs in my father's shoe box shows him sitting on a beach, his face twisted with a blank stare, his officer's jacket unbuttoned, hanging loose, and the only visible clothing. The writing on the back says *Cannes, France, May 3, 1945. "R & R."* When I asked his sister if she had ever heard of Nordhausen, she said, "Yes, your father's division liberated that camp. Because he was a doctor, he stayed to treat survivors, until he had a mental breakdown."

When my father returned from World War II, society did not acknowledge war's aftermath. Families did not want to hear what the veterans had experienced and witnessed. Society told veterans to get on with their lives. To keep the flag flying. To be strong. A veteran suffering from "battle fatigue," as it was called then, had few options. The Veterans Administration prescribed Thorazine, placed people in mental institutions, and even performed lobotomies.

And though we like to believe we have made tremendous progress in understanding what we now call post-traumatic stress disorder, many veterans of our wars in Iraq and Afghanistan still face tremendous difficulty in receiving help. The number of veterans needing help is overwhelming the VA. According to Veterans for Common Sense, which obtained this information through the Freedom of Information Act, as of the spring of 2013, the number of U.S. veterans waiting for a decision on their disability claims is almost 900,000 and was expected to reach 1 million by the end of 2013. The average time to process a claim is 325 days, but in major cities such as New York and Chicago, the wait is nearly twice that long.

In addition, 251,000 veterans have pending appeals of claims, the average time for resolution being four years. Veterans are committing suicide at a rate of 22 a day. Studies show a significant link between PTSD and getting caught up in the justice system. Prisons are the biggest provider of mental health services in our country, and veterans often end up in prison for decades.

But veterans are not alone in the suffering. Suffering spills over from veteran to spouse to children. Yet we do not keep tallies of the suicide rate among spouses, among children, or of their fates years later. The VA provides services to a veteran's spouse and children only if the veteran is ruled 100 percent disabled.

"For many families, help for the spouse comes way too late," Mike Mullins said.

After seeing *Titicut Follies* at the VA training session, I drove straight home and looked up Marlboro Psychiatric Hospital. It had a long history of problems. Between 1978 and 1988 there were eight probes into patient deaths from inadequate medical supervision—strapping to beds, neglect. In 1998 the *New York Times* covered the closing of the hospital after a finding of rampant patient abuse. The article quotes the hospital director: "This is the kind of place people were talking about when they said someone had been 'put away.' For a long time, that's what happened—people were put here and all but forgotten."

I ran into the bathroom and threw up. As I sat on the cold tile floor, clutching my knees to my chest, I was struck by a wave of knowledge: my mother had been erased. A tsunami of grief came barreling down on me; I had no strength left to run.

Today, at the end of every talk I give on the trauma of the GI liberators and the children's secondary trauma, someone in the audience inevitably asks, "What happened to your mother?"

"I don't know," I answer. "I don't know what happened to her after she was institutionalized."

But I do know. One of her sisters got in touch with me after my father died and told me that while my mother was in the institution, my father filed for divorce and won custody. Thirteen years later my mother died, alone and penniless in a tenement in New York.

I needed to know more. I found a phone number for a cousin.

"No," she said, "your mother wasn't bipolar. She was a sweet, generous person who became very depressed. And despairing."

"But why did she never come to see us?"

"Have you considered that maybe your father kept her away from you?"

"How could he have done that?"

"He was a respected physician in the community, Leila. All he needed was to get two lawyers and a doctor to agree to commit her. Then she would never have gotten out."

Years before, when I learned of my mother's death, my father said, "It had to be this way." Perhaps, in his mind, keeping her away was the only way my brothers and I would have healthy childhoods. But it was also his best chance of staying safe. His memories of Nordhausen, his struggle to survive those memories, so imprisoned him that he could not bear to take into account how his trauma and anger and nightmares affected her. Her departure must have made his struggle to survive much easier.

Some veterans return to spouses able to contain, even heal, the wounds of war. Some veterans are not so lucky; their wounds infect their homes. Often, the veteran is the silent carrier and the spouse the one who manifests the illness.

"Your mother was weak, Leila," my father told me. I hear my brother taunt me throughout our childhood, "Do you want to be a loony bird, too?" Thirty-seven years later, when we were arguing, he said, "You're crazy, just like our mother."

Am I the crazy one? Or is my brother? Who's to say?

Here's what I've come to know now after years of research and training: My mother was not weak. She was defenseless. Defenseless against the war that came home with the husband she hardly knew.

His war led to hers. His war trauma infected our entire family. And for years, too many years, I feared I would also go crazy one day. "Because that's what women do when they are weak," my father, the doctor, had said.

If countless male veterans stay away from the VA for fear of stigma, imagine how many women do. Women veterans are seeking help for their trauma in far fewer percentages than are their male counterparts, yet we are paying little attention to their devastation.

Yet, in my dreams, my mother calls me to open my eyes, to see the lady in the lake and to carry her to the surface.

# 18

# Memory Sky

AMBER JENSEN

"I *saw* him today," I said.

I directed my words at my husband, Blake, who was driving, his eyes fixated on the road ahead. It was small talk. Sound to fill our forty-five-minute drive home. But really, I talked for my own benefit, like a child repeating new words. Processing information through recreation. As we drove I had been examining an image of my grandpa Dayton, etched in my mind since my grandma Evie's eightieth birthday party earlier in the day. Dayton's sharp features and the recesses of his deep, narrow eyes were shadows in my line of vision, like a photo negative held up to the light.

"He was alive and smiling," I explained. "Something I never thought I'd see."

When I shifted in the passenger seat to face Blake, I saw him through that image: saw the past layered over the present, the face of the grandfather I never met cast over the husband I've known since childhood. The two men had been connected in my mind for years, as soldiers, as husbands and fathers, as significant men in my life. I wanted Blake to understand that connection and to understand the significance of the new image of Grandpa Dayton I'd acquired that day, but I wasn't sure he could. It was only beginning to make sense to me. Blake glanced at me from the driver's seat, lifting his chin, and then looking back at the tar-veined hills of the highway, his way of inviting me to continue.

Blake had been home from Iraq for almost two years, but every time I received this invitation to communicate—this sideways glance of his with the inquisitive lift of his eyebrows and chin—I felt grateful. Grateful for the expressions that had been missing during awkward international phone calls: the tucked chin that signals Blake's serious disagreement, the slight curl of lips that shows he's preparing for a playful debate. But grateful, too, for the reassurance of his physical presence: the fingers I could intertwine with mine, the sound of his steady breathing, and the beating of his heart when I leaned against his chest. As we drove I was anxious to accept Blake's invitation. But I was hesitant, too, afraid Blake might not understand.

Grandpa Dayton had always been a source of questions for me. I knew him from black-and-white photos and fragments of stories sprinkled here and there at holiday meals and afternoon coffee like powdered sugar over brownies; Blake knew Grandpa Dayton only from my versions of those stories. Yet Blake understood Dayton in ways I could not. Once, noticing a small black-and-white photo tucked in a china closet, Blake said, "Dayton was a first sergeant? You never told me that." I'd never told him because I hadn't known. "The patch on his uniform," Blake explained. "First sergeant. That really meant something, especially in those days." I had studied that photo for years, hoping to gain some understanding of the mysterious man who died so young, so long before I was born. I had memorized the slope of Grandpa Dayton's nose, the droop of his eyes, and his faint smile lines. But in a glance Blake had made meaning from the photo and established a connection. To Blake it was a simple, objective interpretation.

That strange combination of detachment and connection made me hesitate. Blake wasn't especially close to my mom's side of the family. Grandma's memory had begun to fade even before we were married, so the family connection had started to loosen for all of us, but especially for Blake, who wasn't anchored by memories of sleepovers at Grandma's house, games of croquet in her hilly yard, or her chocolate sheet cake. As we drove in a moment of silence, I looked past Blake into the clear, spring sky—the waves of light, split and scattered, made perceptible by dust particles and water droplets—and decided to take a chance.

"It was after you left the party today, when Martha showed Grandma her birthday present," I said. "It was a video their old neighbors found and put on DVD. Martha just told Grandma to watch the TV, and there he was. Grandpa Dayton. It was amazing."

The car hummed, tires dragging over pavement. In the back our son, George, slumped against the side of his car seat, sound asleep, so instead of naming the farm places as we went by—Grandpa Jensen's, Cliff Corey's, John T.'s—I let my eyes drift along with clouds, re-creating

Grandpa's image: eyelashes fluttering, lips moving. "It wasn't even black-and-white," I said. "He had color in his cheeks. He was standing there with Grandma and all the kids, just grinning." I closed my eyes to examine the memory. It seemed like a dream now. "I just never thought I'd see him so . . . happy. I never imagined him that way, you know. All the stories about him came from Grandma Evie, and they were all sad, so I guess I just pictured him that way." As I explained, I remembered the look on Grandma's face when she saw Dayton. She'd been smiling and shaking her head at her great-grandkids, who toddled and giggled around her, when she glanced up to find the image of the husband she'd lost more than forty years before glowing on a flat-screen TV. "When she saw him, she gasped, raised her fingers to her lips, and said, '*Oh, Dayt.*'"

She'd whispered the words so quietly I couldn't be sure I'd even heard them, but her expression was one I understood, one I'd imagined myself wearing. When Blake was in Iraq, I worried that he might not come home and that someday his memory would catch me by surprise, leave me shaking my head in that sad, slow way, like I couldn't believe such a tragedy could become distant memory. I understood Grandma's response, but I wasn't sure if Blake did. I reached toward him, resting my hand on his thigh, my fingers circling his knee.

"Grandma used to say how hard it was when she married Baine. How she was Baine's first love, but she still loved Dayton, too. She never fell out of love with him, you know; he just died." My voice trailed off as, for a moment, Blake and I, in our tan Impala, were swallowed up by a shimmering shelterbelt of cottonwood trees. I'd passed through that corridor of green thousands of times, a mile from the farm where I bottle-fed Holstein calves as a kid. The covering of trees was familiar and comforting, but that day, as Blake and I passed through its thick shade, it felt as though our story was merging with that of Grandpa Dayton and Grandma Evie. The past hovered like low clouds—floating mist thin enough to see through, but still visible, thick enough to be felt on the skin—and I experienced the weight of their steel-gray tragedy, how when Blake was a soldier in Iraq, Grandma's story of loss had shadowed the possibility of my own.

"Grandma spent her life wishing Dayton weren't gone," I said, "but loving Baine at the same time." I slid my fingers over the back of Blake's hand and tucked them against his palm. "I'm just glad I didn't have to find out what it's like. Because while you were in Iraq, I guess I imagined the possibility." I turned to the blur of green and blue outside my window, unable to face Blake as I confessed. "I was afraid, you know, that maybe you wouldn't come home."

My fingers were still linked with Blake's, but I felt far away from him, separated by an emotion I feared he wouldn't understand, as if my arm stretched across an ocean that divided continents, not a console that divided the driver and passenger seats of a car. I didn't exhale until Blake spoke.

"I was, too," he said. "I thought about it. But I guess I always believed if it happened—you know, if I didn't make it home—we'd be like them. That if you had to, you'd move on, get remarried. But I pictured it like that. That I'd be your Dayton. That it would always be me."

Dayton was just over twenty when he came home from the war. From Japan, however, he had written home to his parents, dull lead pressed over thin paper in even cursive, outlining his plans for protective shelterbelts, fields of corn and soybeans. Once home he met and married Evie, a twenty-seven-year-old nurse anesthetist, and they started a family—six kids in nine years. They treasured their children and felt blessed, but life was a struggle with a large family and income from only a few pigs and sheep, the milk of thirteen cows, the eggs laid by their barn full of chickens. But those struggles weren't part of the stories Grandma told me. She talked about the fact that Dayton always believed he would die young.

She told the story so many times that it feels familiar now, plays in fuzzy gray tones in my mind, like an old eight-millimeter movie: two young wives in belted dresses with full skirts; two husbands wearing suspenders and plaid; sweet clouds of pipe smoke; Dayton shuffling pinochle cards, silence punctuated by their crisp flip and snap.

"Life insurance? Seems like a waste. Why now?" asks a young man, a pipe dangling from his lip.

"Because a man needs to take care of his family," Dayton replies. "Even if—especially if—something happens to him." His slender fingers spin cards across smooth-finished maple.

I envision Evie fluttering from the kitchen, where flower-etched glasses clank in a stainless steel sink. She laughs, skirt lifting as she spins toward him. Flannel crackles under the friction of skin as she slides hands over shoulders, crosses them in front of his chest, and says, "Oh, Dayt, you're not going to die."

In the time line of Grandma's stories, only a few weeks passed before Dayton made a trip to town. Piecing together shards of stories, mining details from photos I've seen and newspaper clippings I've read, I imagine that he emerged from the bedroom, having changed from worn denim overalls to fresh jeans. Just a few errands, he said. He'd be home soon. His sharp elbows jutted out from below crisp, rolled cotton sleeves. His boots plodded down the hallway, past the kitchen to the front door of the farmhouse, and his narrow wrist flipped in a casual wave. Evie turned from a sink full of dishes, a boiling pot of potatoes, or a crying child to look over the half wall of the kitchen as he passed. She considered offering coffee, but it was too soon after lunch, so she lifted her chin with a warm, see-you-soon smile. And then he disappeared out the door, into his black Ford, and down the road.

According to Grandma, when Dayton neared the train tracks a half mile south of the house, he remembered the previous day, when the calves got out and into the neighbors' corn. Grandma has always been sure of this detail. She knew Dayton, his tendency to worry, the care he took with his farm. He glanced to the fence line, thick with crab- and snake grasses and fat-stemmed weeds, and he shielded his eyes from midday sun. He squinted, searching for a thin line of barbed wire against overgrown green. When the train emerged from the grove of trees along the track, he was thirty feet away. He hit the brakes.

That night, when Grandma Evie learned of the accident, Dayton was already dead.

Years after the accident Grandma wrote about Dayton's death, how when she saw his body in the morgue at the hospital where she used to work, she thought he could have been sleeping. His forehead was bruised, nothing more. She told herself he couldn't wrap his arms around her, but she could wrap hers around him; she slipped her hand behind Dayton's head as the coroner gasped. Her husband was cold and stiff. She lay him back against steel, felt blood streak across the back of her hand.

Later, when she read his death certificate, listing "obstruction of airway" as cause of death, Evie would say, "I could have saved him. I'm a nurse. I was only a half mile away. I could have cleared his airway." And she would state this possibility over and over again—to her friends, children, and grandchildren—as if repeating it might make the wish a reality.

"If only they had called . . . ," she would say, her voice hollow, eyes vacant and tired. She nodded a faint no. "He was only going to be gone a few minutes . . . I was busy with one of the kids, with something. *Why* didn't I go to him? *Why* didn't I kiss him good-bye?"

She repeated these stories to me many times, but I misunderstood for years, thinking that what she regretted was not telling Dayton she loved him one last time. I was young and had probably seen too many romantic movies. But eventually, when I came to know the threat of dying young, when my husband was at war, Grandma's stories became part of my own, and I realized that she wanted more than a good-bye. If she had stopped him, said good-bye, the train would have passed. If she had just given him a kiss, he wouldn't have died.

She wanted to save him, change fate, prove Dayton wrong. She wanted to be the something that kept him alive.

I thought I had seen Grandpa once before.

It was the summer after my sophomore year of college, after Blake's three months at basic and advanced individual training. It was the first summer that Blake and I spent isolating ourselves in the corner of the dugout after baseball games, accidentally brushing our arms against each other as we drank beer and talked quietly about books like *The Things They Carried*, *Catch 22*, and *Closing Time*. I thought we were going somewhere. Making some progress. Becoming something. And I thought a night at the movie theater, seeing *Saving Private Ryan*, would be the perfect way for Blake and me to connect at home, face-to-face, like we had in the letters we sent to each other during his Army training. Those letters had made it seem like Blake was my soldier and I was his something to come home to.

But Blake didn't come to the movie, and by the time my friends and I made our way inside, the movie had already started. The handheld cinematography of the opening sequence dizzied me, and when I fell into a fraying red seat, I landed in the middle of a nauseating war scene: the stuttering staccato of gunfire, a chorus of screams, soldiers collapsing midstride, limbs blown from bodies. As the movie progressed, the story of three brothers dead, one still alive and serving somewhere in Normandy, kept me thinking about my soldier and his two brothers who also served in the military.

Halfway through the film I watched Tom Hanks as Captain Miller, standing among dusty ruins with a German POW who was trembling and mumbling at the captain's feet. The captain wants to let the man go. His soldiers resist. So he explains his fear, that every man he kills makes him feel further from home, that maybe he will be a stranger to his family when he returns from war. As I watched, the one-dimensional character and his words leaped from the screen and morphed into my memory. His face faded to black and white. His dusty fatigues stiffened into a crisp dress uniform. His eyes darkened, his nose sharpened, his shoulders turned slightly, and I found myself studying the black-and-white photo of a soldier—the one my mother framed and displayed in her china cabinet. I remembered Grandma Evie's words— "Dayt was afraid he wouldn't know how to be a father after the things he had seen and done in war." Only I heard them in first person coming from the mouth of the young man in the photo, the image on the screen, transformed. "I don't know if I can be a father after what I've seen and done at war."

I closed my eyes to examine my memory of the photo, remembered Dayton's face, the pulling back of his cheeks into something short of a smile, and I interpreted the expression in a new way, as something like regret. I'd heard my grandfather's voice for the first time, I'd seen him come alive, and for the moment I felt satisfied. As if I understood.

Blake had been in Iraq for less than two months when a muffled trill from deep inside my black knock-off Prada purse interrupted my shopping trip. I dug into the purse and found my phone, which flashed "o-unknown." As I flipped my hair back, making room for the phone against my cheek, I leaned into my shopping cart and pictured Blake in digital camo, leaning into the frame of a payphone. I grinned, anticipating the deep scratch of his voice, and answered with an intimate, lilted, "Hi."

He must have responded because I heard myself asking the usual, "How are you?" But then he hesitated, exhaling into the phone. I drew the heavy pause into my lungs and panicked as my voice echoed back to me. Finally, Blake spoke, his words giving the moment sudden significance.

"I'm okay," he said, "but something's happened; some guys were hurt."

Unable to comprehend the full meaning of his words, I absorbed insignificant details, instead. Steel beams glaring with a fluorescent-white glow. Blue honeycomb cart blurring before me. A bright waterfall of women's clothes. Towels of blue, green, burgundy, and gold, folded neatly, stacked in fours. I choked on dust particles suspended in the air as I tried to find words to say, something appropriate to feel.

"I'm so sorry, Blake. Are you . . . ?" I couldn't finish the question.

"I wasn't there, on that mission. I'm okay."

I stood, stunned, unable to recognize his voice, to imagine his face. My thumb scratched the leather seam of my cell phone case.

Finally, Blake broke the silence. "I just wanted to call before you heard it somewhere else. I wanted you to know I was okay."

"Of course, yeah . . . Blake, I'm so sorry. I don't know what to say."

"I know. There really isn't anything to say."

George must have been snuggled in the navy-and-gold plaid of his car seat right there in front of me as I searched for something to say to the father he hadn't yet met, but I can't picture him there. I can only remember my hollow throat, the feeling of having no words. And I remember thinking of Grandpa Dayton, how he worried about becoming a father after having experienced war. I wondered if Blake would feel the same way. This wondering was a conscious decision and an effort made to quiet the scream of a larger fear: What if Blake never got the chance to worry? What if Blake never came home? My eyes followed dingy floor tiles, hoping they would lead me somewhere—backward in time, maybe, to a dugout on a summer night, where I could lean into Blake's warmth, hear the echo of his laugh, or maybe forward to an airport embrace, to a moment when I could feel Blake's arms locked behind my back, his breath on my neck. Instead, my eyes crossed, blurring the grid of grout lines into a fuzzy, floating checkerboard. Eventually, Blake said, "Well, I really need to get off the phone. Other guys need to call home."

I'm sure we said good-bye, but all I remember are numbness and then a slow return to life. I studied the surface of my phone. I breathed and then blinked as I lifted my eyes. My features felt bloated and heavy, as they do after a deep sleep sometimes. My nose blurred my line of vision; lips felt fat and numb. My chin seemed to spill down over my neck; fingers anchored me to the floor. I moved mechanically—lifting, reaching, lowering—abandoning a package of onesies I had planned to buy for George. Then I started to walk, letting the worn wheels of the cart pull me through aisles.

When I made it home somehow, I lifted George from his car seat and paced the living room with him snuggled in my arms. *What if that was our last conversation? "I'm sorry" was all I could say. What if he comes home and that's still all I have to say?* The questions echoed like voices from the hallway, like memories of someone else's life. I thought of Grandma and her regrets. *What if I never talk to him again? What if this is the conversation I spend the rest of my life reliving?*

Sometime later I drove down a corridor of snow-covered cornfields with Grandma Evie, wondering if she'd forgotten Grandpa Dayton. It seemed she hadn't spoken of him in years, but after Blake's going to and returning from war, our stories had crisscrossed somehow, and I needed those stories, as if they might help me make sense of my own. Grandma fidgeted beside me, sliding the fingers of one blue-streaked hand over the thin, waxy skin of the other. She looked out the window, pressed her lips together, and sighed. I wanted to ask about Dayton but knew I shouldn't. We were on our way to the hospital to see Baine—Grandma's second husband, the grandpa who gave me whisker burns when I was young. He was the only grandpa I'd known, so it seemed awful to be wondering about Dayton while Baine suffered in the hospital, but I was.

Threads dangled from incomplete vines and blossoms that swirled over Grandma's black cotton dress, unraveling like her mind. But she seemed alert that day, her eyes narrow and focused, not wide and darting with confusion like they did sometimes. So I told myself maybe she would remember. I hoped that crossing the train tracks would trigger a memory and a story, but she didn't notice the snow-covered tracks. So finally I asked, "Grandma, how did you meet Grandpa Dayton?"

She looked down at her lap and said, "You know, I guess I don't remember." She fell silent.

I gave her time to think as wheels buzzed over the highway and spun by green mile-marker signs. After straightening her bracelets, she lifted her left hand and tucked her thumb under to spin her gold wedding band, twisting, until the diamond stood at center. Studying the square-set gem, she said, "It's awful, all the things you wish you could remember, wish you could understand, but you just can't."

I had turned back to the ribbon of road ahead, feeling bad for mentioning a difficult subject, when I realized I had seen only one wedding ring on Grandma's hand.

As a child I loved to sit on Grandma's lap and trace the delicate two-toned leaves of Black Hills gold, slide my fingertips over the smooth shimmer of herringbone, and imagine the sharp edges of cut stones. One by one I pointed to the nine gemstones of her mother's ring—ruby, amethyst, peridot, aquamarine—as she recited the names and birthdates of each of her kids. And I always asked Grandma why she wore two diamond rings. I knew the answer, but I liked to hear her say, "Because even after I married your Grandpa Baine, I never stopped loving Dayton. He was my first love. Your mom's daddy."

My eyes back on the road, I told myself she had to be wearing both rings. She always did. I glanced from the road to her lap every few seconds, trying to catch another glimpse, but she had curled her thin-skinned hands together. While I waited for a clear view, I reasoned. It had probably been years since I paid attention to Grandma's rings. Maybe she had stopped wearing it years ago and I had failed to notice. Still, my heart pounded with panicked sadness at the possibility.

When Grandma lifted her head, piled with white curls showing a hint of gray, and stared silently out the window, I reprimanded myself. *No more questions. No more confusion. Let her rest.*

Then I heard her voice again, this time amazed, like a child. "Look at those clouds, so big and white against such a perfect blue sky. I wonder if I've ever seen any so beautiful in my life."

"I have," I said, bringing the car to a stop at a red light a few blocks from the hospital. "On my wedding day. We took pictures outside. In the background are the same puffy white clouds, the same blue sky."

While I waited for the light to turn, I let my eyes and words wander, follow billowing white across an otherwise clear sky. "But I remember those clouds from another day, too . . . the day I took Blake to Sioux Falls . . . when he left for Iraq."

I paused, thinking that Grandma probably didn't even know who I was talking about. Her memory had started to fade before Blake and I married, so I wasn't sure she even knew his name. Still, I continued.

"That day when I hugged Blake good-bye, this is what I saw over his shoulder, this beautiful blue and white. It's silly I'd remember that. I don't know why . . ."

From the corner of my eye, I saw Grandma lower her head as she returned to studying her wedding ring. I could still see only one ring, but I let myself imagine the other diamond dangling below her hand, close to her palm, maybe not visible, maybe only a memory, even, but still tangible enough to be felt against callused skin. She spun it around her finger and said, "Those were hard days. That's why we remember them. Why we can't forget."

# 19

# Breathe through Your Mouth

BROOKE KING

Sitting there, outside the San Diego Mission Valley PTSD clinic, I stared at my hands, turning them over and over again, as if to study each time why they looked as though they belonged to a distant person walking in the shadow of my life. As the minutes faded into hours, I soothed my pregnant belly, caressing the skin that separated me from the two children that grew inside. I watched as their feet poked from within and smiled at the two small miracles that James, my fiancé, and I had created. Though they were conceived in the middle of a war zone, I sat there marveling that there was something inherently beautiful about creating life where only death should have been.

I sat in a long line of plastic chairs that were badly stick-welded together—like something you'd expect at a psych ward to discourage the patients from throwing them. I looked at the eggshell-white linoleum tiles on the floor of the PTSD clinic and thought about the concrete memories that I carried with me from my first deployment to Iraq in 2006. I had been stationed then in Baghdad with 1st Infantry Division in 299th Forward Support Battalion as a wheel vehicle mechanic, just one of two females in a squad with four men. I had acquired additional skills in vehicle recovery while in the field training for deployment, and I had no idea what I was doing when it came to recovering a vehicle. But recovering blown-up, broken-down, and even burned-up vehicles was my job when my boots hit ground zero in Baghdad. After my first recovery mission, I transferred from Bravo to Alpha Company and rode out the rest of my deployment as a mechanic or convoy support.

My first recovery mission had been simple. On a desolate street somewhere outside of Camp Liberty, a Stryker had hit an improvised explosive device. Its rubber wheels had caught fire and disintegrated from the heat of the blast, and its armored hatch had been blown open from the force of the explosion. My recovery team arrived an hour later and hauled the Stryker onto our heavy equipment transporter trailer and brought it back to base. With no experience to draw on, I did the best I could to help extract the vehicle from the side of the road where it had lain a couple of hours earlier in a flaming ruin. Despite my blackened, mangled uniform from grappling with the chains on top of the Stryker and the less-than-adequate ability to assist my section sergeant during the mission, and even though my first recovery mission had been my only recovery mission, I still could not recall it in any length of detail as I sat outside the Mission Valley PTSD clinic.

Though it had been less than a year after that first mission, the events of that day were beginning to creep back into my life, forcing me to remember that day in the most horrific way by turning my dreams into nightmares.

Becoming pregnant while deployed was a female soldier no-no rule that I, of course, being stupid in my youth, broke. I left Iraq, and subsequently the Army, so that I could go home to my grandparents' house in California, wait for James to leave the service, and then give birth to our twin boys. When I returned home my grandparents rejoiced at the fact that not only had I come back from Iraq alive, but I had left the service to start a family. However, I was off to a rough start as a mother, suffering through a complicated pregnancy that left me on bed rest for the last five months, as well as a handful of problems that surrounded James's court-martial for knocking me up, and the beginning stages of what the VA called PTSD. I could not comprehend what post-traumatic stress disorder was because I had not really been in combat, at least nothing that I considered traumatic. Yet the PTSD specialist that I saw only once insisted that the nightmares I was experiencing were suppressed events that my mind had blocked out. Though the PTSD specialist was probably right, the treatment they were offering me as a female veteran seemed to make the nightmares only more vivid and real, rather than making them go away or manageable, so I never returned to the VA PTSD clinic. Yet I think I really left the VA and never went back because I was afraid to admit that I had a problem. I was in denial that the war had affected me. Instead of returning to the VA for help, I did the only normal thing an irrational postdeployment soldier in denial would do: I ignored the VA's suggestions and, in turn, ignored my problem, forcing it deep within me. Unfortunately, repressing it that deeply only made it worse. Soon my everyday life started to become a struggle between living and hating myself.

"Brookie, honey, is everything okay?" my grandmother wanted to know.

Sitting in the living room recliner of my grandparents' house, I glanced up from staring at the blue carpeted floor and let the numbing pain in my chest subside before I said, "Yeah, Nana."

By this point I had been back from Iraq for a month, and it had become easier each time my grandparents asked about my state of mind to just admit that I was fine. The endless maniacal questions that followed any other response to them would be followed by my futile attempt at trying to convince them that I was "better" and that I didn't need a babysitter, at least not until the boys were born. To them I was still their eldest granddaughter, the one they had invested their love in first, and so it was hard for them to watch as I slowly mentally disintegrated from the inside out.

Each time I refused to talk about Iraq or go back to the VA, Grandpa would pull out his newspaper clippings from the *San Diego Tribune* and magazine articles from *Newsweek*, in an endeavor to comfort me. "Look here, Brookie, this guy's got the same thing as you, except they gave him one of those service dogs for his PTSD."

"Grandpa, I'm not even close to being as bad as he is. Besides, I don't have PTSD. Okay?"

"All right, Brooke," he would say as he set the clippings on the kitchen table and walked out of the living room. "I'll just leave these here for you."

I watched as he walked into the kitchen, poured himself a cup of black coffee, and, without raising his head or saying a word, disappeared to the den. I sat there in the recliner in the living room, and though Nana sat in the other recliner next to me, I felt utterly alone.

Grandpa was right most of the time, but his valiant efforts at helping me seemed to pull me only closer and closer to loneliness, a dark place I created inside myself where I could cope on my own or wallow in my self-induced misery. I had dodged yet another bullet by deflecting Grandpa's conversation, one that surely would have ended up with everyone in tears. I was not ready to talk about Iraq because I still was not sure how I had made it out alive when so many others had not.

Before I was processed out of the Army for pregnancy, I was put on funeral detail at my duty station in Schweinfurt, Germany. Almost every day I stood there in a crowded chapel that smelled of death, saluting yet another casket or picture of a soldier with a pair of combat boots below it and an upside-down rifle adorned with a Kevlar helmet next to it. Each time I saluted another dead soldier and heard the twenty-one-gun salute from inside the open doors of the chapel, a little piece of me died. It was as if each salute and each bullet punctured my heart.

I started to regret getting pregnant. I hated myself for not being there for my fellow soldiers. After a solid month of saluting slowly at dead friends, I asked to be taken off funeral detail because I was tired of watching time and again as people I knew were carted in, closed up, hauled off, and then buried, as if by burying them, the Army (or the rest of us) could forget that they had ever existed.

Though I didn't expect my family to understand all of what I went through in Iraq, when I first returned home to the States, I had asked for some distance until I could cope and fully comprehended the extent of how much I had suffered. My grandparents, for the most part, left me alone. Grandpa gave me what he called "my own space," and Nana fussed at me only when I cursed in front of her.

"Brookie! You're going to be a mother soon. You can't curse in front of your children." Pointing at my pregnant belly, she said, "You need to set a good example for those boys."

Having my grandparents there during my first month home while still adjusting to civilian life was a comforting reassurance that if I did decide to talk, I would have two sets of ears ready to listen. However, "my own space" lasted only a month before Nana was pestering Grandpa into talking to me.

Grandpa seemed to be more attuned to what I wanted and, for the most part, kept his word and left me alone. But Nana felt it was her job to chime in when it came to my health. She was slightly less oblivious to the fact that my repetitive monotone two-word responses had not changed in a month.

"Brookie, you know you can tell me and Grandpa what's going on. I heard that a lot of soldiers that come back from Iraq have this PTSD thing."

"Grandma's right, you know, Brookie," Grandpa said. "If you want to talk, we're here."

Glancing up from the mechanical drowning of my sugar into my decaf Earl Grey tea, I said, "I don't have PTSD, so can we drop it?"

"Brookie," Nana said, "someday you're going to have to talk about this . . ."

I interrupted her. "Yeah, but today is not that day!"

Breakfast had slowly turned into another one of their ploys to get me to open up, but growing up with them under the same roof almost all my life, I knew the best way to avoid a conversation was just to walk away. Getting up from the table, I grabbed my teacup and said, "I've had enough of this."

Their longing stares of concern left a burning sensation in my heart, filling me with the awful sense that by not telling them, I was somehow making *them* suffer. "I'm just going to lie down," I said, an apology, I think, in there somewhere. "My back is killing me from carrying these two so low."

Like a fat Mother Goose, I waddled side to side away from the kitchen table. As I walked toward the blue floral print couch in the den, I allowed myself to remember a traumatic event of time in Iraq when I was blown ten feet backward by a mortar round that had landed inside the motor pool, while I had been trying to fix a forklift. I had blocked out most of the memories, but the nightmares added to the sense of frustration and anxiety.

And the nightmares had worsened. Seven months pregnant, I was fed up with not having James there, and I was worn out from being pregnant. Every physical demand that my body endured left me feeling overworked.

My family was growing more and more frustrated, too, over my unwillingness to talk about Iraq. I may have left behind the war in Iraq, but I was fighting another battle at home.

"Brookie, honey," my grandmother would start at least once a week, "you really need to go back to the va. They can help you with what's going on. Do you want James to see you like this? He's going to come back from Germany and find you a wreck. You haven't been yourself lately, Brookie . . . I'm starting to worry."

"Leave me the fuck alone!" I'd shout and slam my bedroom door until it began to splinter. Each slam of my door felt as though I were shutting out the girl I used to be. Each time I slammed my bedroom door, thinking to protect my grandparents from the monster I had become, only led to Nana's quiet sobs I could hear emanate from the kitchen.

Gone was her granddaughter who used to help form small round meatballs for Great-Grandma Romanolo's famous spaghetti or who used to help shred Swiss cheese for the quiche lorraine we had every Tuesday.

I could also hear Grandpa's comforting words to her as she sobbed in the kitchen. "She's got to figure it out on her own, Jackie," he'd say. "You just can't keep reminding her like that. When she's ready, she'll talk to us." I think Grandpa knew from the beginning that I would never be the same; I think it took Grandma a lot longer to reach that realization.

After every nightmare I'd be slouched over on the floor, kneeling in the middle of my bedroom, rocking back and forth, sobbing, smothering my screams with both hands, and shutting my eyes tight to prevent the tears. I hated myself, the person I had become. I tormented myself with guilt until my brain felt as though it would crack open and bleed onto the floor. And each time the nightmares came, I tried to piece together a little more and more about what had really happened during my deployment. Sometimes the pain in my chest would be so unbearable that I thought about killing myself. In a sense I was killing everyone around me; Nana and Grandpa no doubt heard my two-in-the-morning screams of terror. I tried smothering the screams in a pillow, muffling them with hands, anything and everything to keep from hurting them the way I was hurting.

The effects of my time in Iraq had spilled over into my civilian life and were ripping it apart like a frayed, loosened seam on a worn-out shirt that was slowly coming unstitched. The only thing I knew for certain was that the nightmares I was having were fragmented, a distortion of the truth, or so I think, and this scares me shitless.

In the actual clear memories, I am dragging heavy chains to latch down the Stryker, and my uniform is stained with black char smudges and sweat, not the blood and fragments of bodies that show up on my uniform during my nightmare of that event. So which of the two should I believe?

In my nightmare on that recovery mission, I am climbing through the blown-out compartment of the Stryker. My nostrils are filling with a putrid smell of iron—that taste you get after licking the end of a battery. I am trying to breathe through my mouth, but I can already feel vomit rising in my throat. I just make it back outside and into the early-evening light before puking beside the Stryker. And then I head back in to do my job.

Making my way toward the front of the vehicle, something stops me. My right hand strikes something. I stop and sweep the light onto the object. There he is, slumped over. His uniform is blood soaked and shredded from shrapnel as if he crawled through barbed wire. Where his left leg should be is only a thin pool of blood. A week of combat life-saver training, and the only thing I retained was how to give an IV and how to check a pulse.

But there isn't one.

For the first time I point the light toward his head and wish I hadn't, because what I see causes me to stumble backward and slam into the compartment wall behind me. His face is half ripped off his skull and dangles from his neck, weighted down by his helmet. A gash on the left side of his face is still dripping blood onto his trousers. He is contorted, mangled, and burned alive, and this is his death.

In this nightmare there are two other bodies to account for. I inch farther into the vehicle. I approach the gunner's hatch and find it closed. I turn the handle and open the hatch to get some fresh air circulating into the cabin of the vehicle. I approach the driver's side.

The driver is burned alive to his seat. All I can see are both of his black hands, dangling with chunks of flesh, both lying limply, palm up in his lap, turned in as if he had been praying to die quickly. I turn away from the smell of burned rubber and soured blood.

In the passenger seat there is nothing left of the officer, only half a torso. His entrails lay scattered about the seat and on the floor. I try to find something, anything, that will give anyone back home comfort in knowing he came back in one piece. I can find nothing.

Yet all bodies are accounted for, and that is my mission. And as I turn to leave and walk back into the light of the day, I awake.

Throughout the years after my deployment, each time the nightmare revisited, it changed slightly, contorting the truth of what happened on my first mission. Even three years later the truth of what happened on that first mission has been lost forever, supplanted by the latest nightmare version. I am left with horrifying reality that I can't and probably shouldn't recall what really happened that day. Sometimes I even pretend that day never happened.

After the mission I remember walking past the company building, ignoring everyone who walked in my direction. I staggered to my hooch. All I wanted to do was get all that gear off and go to sleep. Fumbling to get the keys out of my pocket, I managed to drop them onto the graveled ground.

"Fuck!"

I yelled it loud enough for everyone in a three-hundred-yard radius to hear. Too tired to bend down, I peeled off my combat flack vest, helmet, and knee and elbow pads and let each one drop to the ground with a haunting thud. I sat down on the stoop in front of my door. I pulled out my crunched pack of Lucky Strikes and lit my last one. After a couple of long drags, I sniffed myself to see if I needed a shower, and the stench caused me to reel backward. When I opened the door to the head, every single female soldier stopped what they were doing and stared. I looked into the mirror and saw a face so weathered and beaten, as if this woman, me, had been fighting life itself. My face was covered with charred traces of flesh and black smudges. My hair was tangled and matted with blood. On my face was expression unhinged and lost. The uniform top and bottoms were covered in charred fragments and battered and ripped. There were huge voids of cleanliness on my uniform from where my gear had been worn, but everywhere else was spattered and soaked with someone else's lifeline.

"Brooke, you awake?"

I turned in bed toward my husband, James. He's home now, finally, and was plugging his iPhone into the charger on the wall. "I took the trash out and checked on the boys," he said. "They're sound asleep."

Sitting there in bed, I must have looked off because James shot me a look of concern, his cobalt-blue eyes staring inquisitively as if to judge the appropriate level of concern. "What's that look for?" he said.

"What look?"

"That look you just gave me. You okay?"

I hesitate to tell him when I've had a nightmare. "I'm fine. What about the boys?"

"You look like you're about to cry . . . What's going on?"

*Breathe through Your Mouth* . . 159

I'm thinking to myself, *Why did I have to marry the one guy who actually gives a shit? Wouldn't it be easier if he didn't?*

You see, when James got back from Iraq, he didn't have PTSD or anything resembling it. He had been an ordnance officer, and while he did go out the gate a lot during his first deployment in 2004, his last deployment had been a desk job. Though we had shared a deployment together in the same battalion, living only five hooches away from each other, we did not share the same experience.

Yet even though he supported me through the tough times during our deployment, bringing me dinner and spending nights in my hooch, holding me after a hard day, his hardest challenge was helping me now. There had been times in the beginning when he first came to California that I woke up hyperventilating from a nightmare and wished that he could have shared my pain, but I know now that I would not wish this struggle on anyone else. To have done so would have been to witness a wreck on a wreck. I could not imagine a family where both parents suffered from PTSD. For our family it would have been like living in a house where no one survived. The children would have been used as collateral damage to the horrific pain of a marriage forced apart by war and words unspoken.

"I had a nightmare," I finally admitted.

With one eyebrow raised he said, "I thought those stopped a while after the boys were born. How long has it been since your last one?"

"A couple of months."

"A couple of months? How come you didn't tell me?"

"You've been so busy with work, I didn't think to bother you with it. Besides, they haven't been bad enough that I've needed to talk, and to be honest, I'm not really sure why I just had one."

"You going to be okay?"

"Yeah," I said, as though I believed it. This one had felt more real than the others over the past three years. "This one was different. It was less graphic, less scary in a way."

"Hmmm . . . Maybe that means you're getting better."

"I don't know. It could've just been a fluke."

"So you're sure you're okay?"

"Yeah, I'll be fine."

James had processed out of the Army in Germany and had come to California for the boys' birth, but I had made Nana and Grandpa promise not to tell him about what was going on with me at the time because I wanted him to focus on the babies. They had kept their promise because it wasn't until after the boys were three months old and we had already moved to Florida to be closer to his family that I woke up one night screaming.

After several long conversations and several futile attempts by him to make me go to the VA, we made it a point to avoid the words that could trigger my nightmares. We thought of them as a silently understood struggle that most of the time I blocked out as if they didn't exist. It was just as well because I never *really* wanted to talk about them, and he never *really* wanted to listen, a match made in denial heaven. Most of the time I didn't tell James because he had a habit of ruining moments, moments where we could connect as a normal couple, but James and I weren't a normal couple. We never talked about politics or war. Instead, we exchanged stories and laughed at how ridiculous our day had been, and somehow by laughing and joking our lives away, it kept both of us from crying about the pain.

And on this night, with his usual goofiness that helped ease my tension, he shot back, on his way toward the bathroom, "You're not going to start crying when I leave the room, are you?"

"No, jackass, I'm not, but if you don't leave," I said jokingly, picking up a nearby decorative pillow on the bed, "I'm going throw this at you."

"So, I can go take a shower?"

I threw the pillow at him. Catching it, he jumped onto the bed, wrestled with me, and then paused to kiss me before he crawled off the bed and walked into the bathroom, leaving the door cracked slightly. Over the years James had learned how to tell when I needed him and when I just needed to be left alone. Most of the time, though, I had to give him some sort of an emotional cue to let him know I needed him, but tonight he could tell that I just wanted to be left alone.

After the boys were born in 2007, the nightmares had become less severe and less frequent. I had come to the conclusion that it was my pregnancy that had heightened their severity, but even now, three years later, they were still happening. Yet they had changed slightly. Instead of being morbidly graphic, like a battle scene from *Saving Private Ryan*, they had become emotionally jarring.

I had become a more emotional creature because I was a mother, but the added stress of being a full-time student in my junior year at Saint

Leo University and part-time worker made the emotionally charged nightmares just as gruesome and painful. The stress of all my obligations left me stretched thin and worn out again, and it seemed that when my stress level went up, the nightmares became more prevalent. But sometimes I also had flashbacks that came without warning and were triggered by my daily life.

A month prior to the last nightmare, I had just come home from picking up the boys from day care and from a long, exhausting day at school. The end-of-the-day ritual began with the boys unpacking their backpacks and tossing off their shoes, letting each one remain wherever it had landed. In the kitchen I had started dinner, frying potatoes in a skillet. The sizzle of the bacon grease hissed in the pan and wafted the smell into the air.

My kitchen was small and modest, befitting a house that James secretly bought for me as a peace offering for dragging me from my family in California to his family in Florida. After we moved in I made the house my own, but could never get over the vaulted ceilings in the kitchen and living room that made the house echo like a cave, vast and deep. The living room was more like a great room, which I nicknamed my "lovely room of death" because it was where James hung the mounted kills from his hunting excursions. In the living room a large wood entertainment center housed the flat-screen plasma TV that the boys flipped on every day when they came home from day care.

When I heard loud suppressive gunfire from the living room, I instinctually slammed my body to the floor. While I sprawled in a low prone position on the wood floor, my heart thumped hard, like a loud drumming in my chest. As I crawled to my feet and walked toward the living room, a swell of anxiety rose in my body and quickened my pulse. I had hit the floor with my black plastic spatula in hand and still had a death grip on it when I walked around the corner past the fringe and into the living room, where my three-year-olds were watching the movie *Iron Man*.

I snatched the remote from the coffee table with my free hand and turned the channel to *Nick Jr*. Doing an about-face, I walked back into the kitchen. I could hear my kids complaining about how I had changed the channel away from the superhero movie, but I tuned it out.

Back at the stove I gave in to the overwhelming sensation of sadness that had swelled inside me. The stress of the day coupled with a flash-back of being in Iraq brought me to tears. Setting the spatula down, I gripped the rounded edges of the stove, bent over at the waist, closed my eyes, and pointed my head at the floor. The swell of sadness crept over me like a hot flash flare, igniting in a burst of unbridled burning. Unable to control the feeling any longer, I began to sob, muffling the sound of my weeping with my hands over my mouth. One after another, each tear came rolling down my cheek and plummeted to the floor like a steady dripping faucet. Overwhelmed with a deep misery, I stepped back and fell into a corner of the kitchen, butting my body in between the sink and the pots-and-pans cabinet. I tucked my knees to my chest, folded my arms, buried my head in the voided space between, and sobbed.

From inside the kitchen, I could still hear the echoing argument of the boys as they fought in the living room over who got to sit on which couch. Realizing that the fight was not going to stop and that being a mother right now outweighed my own despair, I raised my head, wiped the tears from my face, and used the countertop to stand up.

"Boys, stop fighting," I said, letting my shaky voice resonate off the ceiling. "Don't make me come in there . . ."

The fighting continued in the living room while I tried to wipe away my tears and snot with my hands, rubbing each swipe from my face onto my denim jeans. I tried to compose myself, but found that the only thing I could do was cry. A relentless stream of tears rolled down my cheeks and dripped onto my white embroidered blouse. I could hear screaming coming from the living room, but I was powerless as a mother to do anything but cry in the kitchen. I could hear Bowen, my oldest twin boy, screaming my name.

"Mommy! Mommy! Mommy!"

I could not move. My legs were like quick sand, and I felt as though if I took a step, the floor would swallow me whole. As Bowen's scream-ing got closer and closer to the kitchen, I panicked. He had run into the kitchen so fast that I had no time to wipe away the tears before he reached where I stood.

"Mommy, I'm hungry, and Zachary won't stop kicking me. He keeps . . . he keeps kicking me off the couch, Mommy."

I stood there, wrecked with sadness and dripping in tears. Bowen stood in front of me, begging me to be his mother, but I could not even function as me, let alone as his mother. I turned from him so that I could wipe the rest of the tears off my face and collect myself.

"Mommy . . . Mommy . . . Mommy, I'm hungry . . . Mommy, I want a snack!"

Bowen's shouting coupled with the flashback made the sadness turn into rage, a compound feeling of fullness in my chest. The sensation flooded every emotion out of my body like a tsunami wave, inflicting it upon the closest thing to me, my son. I spun around and quickly grabbed Bowen by his shoulders. Shaking him violently, I shoved my face three inches from his and in half-shouted scream said, "Get the fuck out of the kitchen!"

And then I crumpled to my knees, surrendering to my moment of emotional deterioration and broken failure as a mother. It was Bowen's first step into my world of suffering. Frightened for what I might see, I hesitated to look up at my child from my shattered expression of grief on the floor. When I did Bowen's face was glazed over with a mixed look of terror and surprise, as if he had truly seen my nightmares. His lips quivered as he started to cry. Tears welled up in the corner of his deep-blue eyes, spilling the salty tears over onto his cheeks. Remorse and regret swelled in my heart and supplanted my sadness and pain as he stood there crying in the middle of the kitchen.

In an attempt to soothe him, I outstretched my arm and moved forward to hold him. He stepped back from me and pulled his hands to his face, trying to shield himself from me like a wounded animal sheltering itself from a vicious predator. My own child cowered away from me, recoiling backward into the wall behind him. Paused in that moment, transfixed on his frightened face, I thought, "I'm a monster."

I wiped the tears from my eyes, knelt on the floor, outstretched my arms again, and pleaded, "Bowen . . . Please, baby . . . I'm sorry. Mommy didn't mean to yell at you like that . . . Come here, please."

Bowen hesitated for a couple of seconds and then slowly lowered his hands from his face and walked cautiously into my outstretched arms. As his tiny frame wrapped around mine, I held him in my arms warmly and gently, as though it was the first time he had ever been hurt. "I'm sorry, baby" was all I could say, over and over again into his ear as I held him to my chest. I pulled him back, and staring straight into his big blue eyes, I said, "I love you so much, honey. You know I love you, right?"

"You scared me, Mommy."

"I know, honey, and I'm sorry."

I wiped the tears off his cheeks, brushed his shaggy blond hair from off his forehead, and cupped his face with my hands. "Now, what did you come in here to ask me?"

"I'm hungry, Mommy."

"Dinner's in an hour, honey."

He gave me a look of disenchantment that drowned me in a downpour of mother's guilt. Out of shame for what I had done, I gave into him. "Okay, you can have a small snack." I pointed to the pantry and said, "Go ahead and find something."

As I stood there and watched him slide open the white pantry door and stare up at the tiered shelves full of food, I wiped my own tears from my face and gathered myself enough to walk over and help him grab the Goldfish crackers off the third shelf. I opened up the box, filled a bowl for him, and watched as he walked out of the kitchen as if nothing had ever happened.

It was hard to tell if Bowen had imprinted that moment into his memory as he walked off into the living room, but somehow I knew that he had.

The guilt of that day weighed heavily, even a month later as I sat there in bed wondering if I should double-check on the boys while James was in the bathroom, but the sound of the water turning on in the bathroom quickened my pulse and made me think back to the nightmare. I decided that the nightmare was still too fresh in my mind and that I was in no condition to check on the kids. I lay back on the pillows behind me and pushed back the tears that were starting to form. Trying to keep my composure, I told James the good news of the day, "I got a B-plus on my early-Brit-lit paper."

From inside the bathroom, trying to shout over the sound of running water, he said, "That's great, honey . . . Proud of you." He swung wide the bathroom door, sauntered out in his boxer briefs, stood in the middle of the doorway, and said, "You want to take a shower with me?"

"The last time you said that to me, we ended up with twins. Can we please just chill out on the baby-making factory for a while before you try to double-stuff me like an Oreo again?"

Once he was back in the shower, I took inventory of the papers scattered across the bed. I had fallen asleep while studying. Just as I was curling up in the indentation on my side of the bed and ready to let the haphazard memory of my deployment fade from my mind, I heard Zachary's voice.

"Mommy."

I peered at the cracked bedroom door. There stood Zachary with tears in his eyes.

"What's the matter, baby? Why are you crying?"

Sobbing and walking toward me, he said, "I had a bad dream."

I sat up and opened my arms. Zachary snuggled against me as tight as a newborn baby. I couldn't help but be moved by the visible pain on his face caused by his nightmare. I knew that pain. I rocked him slowly back and forth. "It was just a dream, baby. It never happened . . . You'll be okay . . . You'll be okay."

# 20

# To Kill, or Not to Kill

DARIO DIBATTISTA

From my turret in the gun truck, I was watching the ridge on the south side of the river when a Humvee exploded, most likely after running over a land mine. The noise of the explosion created a frenzy of activity. We had traveled out in full force. The whole 3rd Battalion of the Seventh Marine Regiment was on the prowl.

After the pacification of Husaybah in April 2004, our standard operating procedure was to send the entire battalion out to the different towns that made up Greater al-Qa'im in a show of force. The objectives were cut-and-dried: segregate a town and have patrols move through, trying to capture insurgents and their weapons caches.

My team, civil affairs (in a nutshell our mission was to fix things after the grunts blew them up), was on hand to deal with any collateral damage. This was our implied task on these operations—known as cordon and knock missions—but our direct task had us providing security for the battalion commander.

Our battalion commander believed very strongly in "leading from the front." This filtered down to commanders and leaders at every level. I don't think any of us ever felt our leaders would order us to do something they wouldn't do themselves. The price for this bold leadership, however, was high. The commanding officer of Lima Company and the company gunny from Kilo Company would both be killed in action during their deployment.

The battalion commander himself was even wounded in action. The secretary of the Navy flew in to present the Purple Heart. Al-Qa'im was so hot, the secretary needed to fly in with a massive air convoy for his protection. After quickly touching down, he was escorted to the ceremony and then right back to a helicopter that never even turned off its engines.

Back on patrol, in the moments after the land-mine explosion, we saw the villagers in the town scurry away as if, by some animal instinct to avoid larger animals, they sensed danger. We were the large animal, the undisputed top dog. And the insurgents wanted to at least challenge our place on the food chain.

Human beings, unchallenged at the top of the food chain, have lost this sense. That is, unless they are involved in a primal survival fight with other men. Service members in Iraq who engaged in direct combat with the enemy on a regular basis learned to rekindle those dormant instincts.

I was watching the ridge to our south just before the explosion. I watched the Humvee explode. I had just watched someone die.

Training and instinct kicked in, fortunately. Like a mindless automaton, I pulled back the charging handle of my machine gun, making it operable to kill, and searched for a target, all before the smoke from the explosion had a chance to dissipate in the sky.

Over the radio someone reported that the villagers who did not disperse and flee back to their homes were known to use grenades to fish, and that probably caused the explosion. "That's bullshit," I said calmly to Sergeant Hendricks, who was patrolling on foot alongside our Humvee. "There's the explosion right there." I pointed across the river. Somehow, I was the only one in our column who had seen it.

Ubaydi was a town located north of the Euphrates River. It was mostly unvisited by coalition troops. Only light-armored reconnaissance units, with their eight-wheeled armored vehicles, made presence patrols north of the river for the most part. No other units were mobile enough or well-armed enough for the task. Our whole infantry battalion would travel here for only a scant few hours.

Over the radio eventually came news that the Humvee did, indeed, run over a mine and that everyone was miraculously okay. But this meant that the insurgents were getting smarter; they were learning our tactics and predicting likely positions where we would stop during our operations.

An Iraqi civilian near our column worked himself up into overload and began screaming at us. About what, none of us could tell. He might have been complaining about a hangnail and looking for medical attention. The Iraqis were a dramatic people, very in touch with their emotions. But when he stepped too close for comfort, I drew my pistol and gestured for him to step aside. This was an advantage I had as a left-handed rifle shooter and a right-handed pistol shooter: I could threaten two people at once without taking my hand off either weapon.

Another Humvee across the river came to the rescue of the disabled and stranded Humvee and its crew, and it, too, struck a land mine. Again, miraculously, everyone was okay. The insurgents had used weak antipersonnel mines in both cases.

After the second explosion the crazy Iraqi man scurried off, and when we decided that the situation no longer warranted our attention, we also continued onward, along a road that paralleled the bank of the river. We drove into a small subsection of the village with the pace of a curling stone. I was surprised to see special-forces soldiers already there, seemingly just hanging around, mixing it up with the locals. Everyone wore smiles; the Iraqi children seemed happy to see us.

I spotted an older Iraqi man who was holding an infant in his lap. He smiled and played with the child in the same way I would play with my niece back home. He grasped the child's arms, and with a big endearing smile toward the child and then up at me, he waved his arm and the child's arm simultaneously. I surprised myself by waving back and smiling because I had hardened my heart in order to deal with the reality of this conflict. But seeing the older man and the baby—their smiles and waves—made me feel human for the first time in months. And the first time I felt good about this war. *Maybe all these people aren't really that bad.*

We increased speed for a few minutes and found ourselves in a wadi, a dry riverbed. The wadi became annoyingly bendy; at one point we had to travel sharply north and then sharply south, just to continue our northwest course. We paused. Still in the rear of the convoy, I was the only one facing southeast. That's when a small blue Iraqi car, about the size of a Toyota Tercel, suddenly came into view and was speeding around the turns of the wadi. At that point in the war, there had been very few vehicle-borne IEDs. Suicide bombers in Iraq were the modern-day Kamikaze. I hunched over and craned my neck inside the Humvee to report to the vehicle commander, Staff Sergeant Mallicoat. This was a situation I had never faced before, the prospect of having to decide whether a vehicle approaching was a suicide bomber. I tried to remove that responsibility by pawning it off to someone senior in rank.

"Uh, Staff Sergeant, there's a vehicle coming up on our rear pretty quickly," I said with no inflection.

"How far back is the vehicle, D-Boh?"

I wanted to convey to him that, even though technically the vehicle was quite a ways off because of all the turns, it really wasn't geographically far away at all.

"Uh, pretty close," I said. I couldn't think of a simple way to quickly tell him the whole situation.

"Well, let me know when it gets closer."

By then the vehicle was even closer, close enough that I could make out the driver and four passengers. Five people in a single car did not fit the profile of a suicide bomber because it just wouldn't make sense to kill five suicide bombers at once, instead of implementing them five separate times. Also, there couldn't exist much room to pack a significant amount of explosives inside a car that was so full of people. Vehicle-borne IEDs were usually driven by a sole occupant. So then I was wondering if the car held a small enemy fire team seeking to get close enough to engage us with small-arms fire.

"They're fucking coming really close, all right?" I shouted down to the staff sergeant.

With a new sense of urgency, galvanized by my observations, Mallicoat and the others in our Humvee bailed out and raised their weapons on the vehicle. The car closed to a distance of about 150 meters.

As the Humvee's machine gunner, my job was to disable the vehicle by destroying the engine while the others would take out the driver by hole-punching his brain with bullets from their M16s. But I didn't fire.

In a split second I decided that these Iraqis were not the enemy. Even a precautionary shot at their engine would have caused a magazine dump of rounds from all the other Marines.

And still the vehicle kept coming.

Over the radio Sergeant Golden, the driver for a vehicle ahead of us in the convoy, yelled frantically, "You've got a vehicle coming up your six! Shoot it, D-Boh! Shoot it!"

I fondled the trigger. That was a direct order to shoot. But I didn't want to kill civilians.

The vehicle slammed to a stop, now face-to-face with the business end of several weapons. The Marines with m16s swarmed the vehicle, forced out the occupants, and searched them. My job then was to act as the guardian angel for the situation, the overwatch, so I kept my finger on the trigger.

Turns out that three of the five occupants were Iraqi police cadets whom we saw frequently at the IP Academy. They were just driving home, not paying attention to the world around them. If we had killed them, we would have made a lot more Iraqi enemies, so I had made the right decision not to fire, or had I?

We moved on, and the patrol ended several hours later. When we arrived back on base that evening to break down our vehicles and weapons and to return the ammo, Stilling, a private first class on my team and technically one of my subordinates, and Sergeant Golden accosted me.

"What the fuck were you thinking, D-Boh?" Stilling said. "You should've shot those guys!"

Golden was in a rage. "You put your Marines' lives in jeopardy. What the fuck happened back there?"

Sergeant Hendricks, the driver of my gun truck, and Staff Sergeant Mallicoat came to my defense.

"Hey, relax," Mallicoat said. "D-Boh did everything he was supposed to do. He informed us immediately of the situation and followed through appropriately."

Hendricks chimed in an agreement: "He made a great decision. He weighed the situation and made an appropriate judgment call."

But Golden wasn't having any of it. "He was being a coward."

"That's the end of this conversation, Golden," Mallicoat said in a warning tone.

On the way back to our living quarters, a few minutes later, Stilling said, "You should've shot them, D-Boh. You put your Marines' lives in jeopardy."

"You would have made the wrong decision then," I said.

But technically, I knew they were right. I had jeopardized the lives of the Marines in my gun truck. I knew the dangers of a speeding car closing at an unusually fast rate on our position. Such an act warranted the use of deadly force.

Our rules of engagement defined hostile intent as something somebody is doing that can be perceived as a harmful act or the basis of a harmful act toward you, other Marines, or U.S. government property. Hostile intent could be someone pointing a gun at you or someone placing an IED in the ground or someone, like a suicide bomber, speeding up behind your convoy.

In Iraq, unfortunately, self-defense was not allowed unless you were getting shot at or someone was getting ready to shoot at you. Because the enemy wore no uniforms, we had to decide who they were by their actions. We never really had the advantage.

Young junior Marines, like me at twenty, have to make life-or-death decisions, and if their reasons aren't 100 percent solid and they do take action, their own military and country could imprison or punish them.

That day on patrol I failed in my duties. I truly believed that. I couldn't sleep because I couldn't rationalize my decision against the weight of what might have happened to all of us because I hadn't fired on a car full of civilians.

I had let them get too close under a suspicious pretext. Or worse yet, what if they had just been testing us? What if they were insurgents who had volunteered their lives to jostle up emotional support for the insurgency if we had shot? What if either way they had learned critical information about our tactics? No doubt, the enemy was watching. Maybe some Marines would die in the future because the leadership of the insurgency would decide that Marines in al-Qa'im were cowards and a suicide bomber could be successful there. All this because I hadn't taken the shot.

More than a year later, after my time in the never-ending war, back home in the Baltimore suburbs, I'd met a newly widowed Marine wife at a bar I frequented. She was there, with as many drinks as she could handle, to numb the steel-fisted sucker punch of the death of her Marine husband. The bartender, who knew I'd served overseas, sent me over to her.

Her husband, her high school sweetheart, I learned, had a day before sacrificed himself to save his men by stepping in front of a suicide bomber—in al-Qa'im, the same place where I did not shoot when ordered to.

And she's told me since how proud she is of him. And the Marines he saved—I met them at a memorial event for her husband—have told me the same thing. But they've also said that I made the right decision that day in al-Qa'im. And no one's angry at me. And they champion my empathy, my humanity.

But nothing can change the fact that I did not kill like a good Marine. And I don't really know the outcome of my decisions. I still can't really say whether what I did was right. And I still don't know whose life is more important.

But men are dead. And that very well may be because I chose not to fire when maybe the most courageous thing was to shoot to kill.

# 21

# How the Military Turned My Father a Genius

KIM WRIGHT

My father never made any bones about it: he saw the military as his way out of Sebring, Ohio, a small Steel Belt one-industry town that he unfailingly referred to as "the armpit of America." Dad was a high school dropout who was born in the dead center of a family with eleven children during the Depression, so God knows there weren't a lot of avenues open to him. By the age of sixteen, he had figured out he had three options. He could work the railway, like his dad. He could work in the pottery, like his mom. Or he could join the military.

My father's name was Harry Eugene Wright, and he was a great storyteller. He would sit back in his chair with a cigarette in one hand and a glass of cheap wine in the other, his cardigan sweaters frequently buttoned in the incorrect holes and his left middle finger and nose both bearing evidence of having been broken in childhood football games, but never set. He was a self-made man who had created a successful business and who had married, again in his words, "way above himself," but he never lost the common touch. He bought his clothes at Walmart and his breakfast at Burger King and his wine, which admittedly he liked a bit too much, by the jug. (In fact, his favorite joke was: *Q:* What two brothers gave man the gift of flight? *A:* Ernest and Julio Gallo.)

He attempted to make up for the Grand Canyon–size gaps in his education by reading the encyclopedia on the toilet and always carried a bit of a chip on his shoulder about his tenth grade education. This insecurity was heightened by the fact he had married into a family full of teachers who loved nothing better than to debate political and social issues around the dinner table. But when the high-blown theories and multisyllabic words began to fly, my dad had one ace up his sleeve.

My father, you see, was a genius. The U.S. Air Force had told him so.

What follows is the story he told me. I'm fairly sure this is not the true story, and perhaps it's not even close to the true story. I am a novelist by profession, and I learned everything I know about fiction from my father, who, though he never read a novel in his life, was genuinely gifted in the fine art of making stuff up. He loved speculation. He loved gossip. Whenever I would drop by the house, he would splash a little Gallo in a juice glass, settle down on the couch with a Salem, lean in confidentially, and say, "So, whatcha know?" He meant, of course, any spicy stories I'd collected since I'd seen him last. He would absorb them, mull them over, and retell them in whatever manner he chose. (And this was, of course, after I myself had already edited the original story to make it funnier or more dramatic. The apple doesn't fall far from the tree.)

So this story—told by him to me and then by me to you—is almost certainly inaccurate in the details, but I think the core of it is true.

Here's how it starts. Picture a half-man and half-boy, already several years into a length of service that would last from ages sixteen to twenty-two and eventually take him all over the world through three different branches of the military. Skinny, crook-nosed, with clothes so shredded that the wives of his friends sometimes mended them for him out of pity. Born—as were three of his sisters—creative and curious in a family that dealt only with grim reality. No one had ever told this boy he was smart. No one had ever suggested he might go to college or train for a profession. With nine surviving kids to feed on a railway man's salary, the subject of how Harry Wright might better his life had simply never come up.

But one cold December on a troop transport ship heading from America to northern Africa, everything changed. The men being transferred were largely National Guard and unseasoned in the ways of the military world. The ship had left the States, cruelly, on Christmas Eve. The waters were rolling. So much so that nearly everyone on board was sick, and your choice was either to be down below with the sounds and smells of hundreds of puking men or to be up on deck buffeted by a constant icy spray.

It was 1951, nearly 1952. A portion of the men on board were being delivered to a base that was experimenting with a new type of radar, a technology that would probably seem laughable to pilots and air-traffic controllers today but was cutting-edge for its time. To select the most promising men to learn and use this new science, the Air Force had given every man on the ship an IQ test.

I have no idea the state of mind Dad was in when he took that test, but the conditions were far from perfect. He was surrounded, remember, by National Guardsmen, many of whom I'd imagine were much like my uncle, also named Harry. He was blond and blue eyed and constantly smiling and had lived—at least in comparison to my father—a cushy life. These two men became friends during their time on the troop ship and later in northern Africa, which in turn is how I came to be. Once my uncle Harry was out of the service, my dad came to see him in North Carolina and, while there, went on a blind date with the woman who would someday become my mother. But I'm getting ahead of myself.

The point of this story is that under normal circumstances, my uncle and my father never would have met, but of course the military has a way of forging all sorts of unlikely friendships. And without the knowledge he was a genius, I'm not sure my father would have had the guts to marry into my mother's somewhat intimidating family. Because my dad was up on deck, hanging onto the railing for dear life as the storm blew, his CO approached and yelled out the sentence that would change his life.

"Son, did you know you're almost a genius?"

Note the word *almost.* The Air Force defined a genius as anyone with a 140 IQ, and my dad's tested at 138. But this was enough to get him into the radar program.

No one was more surprised by this news than my father himself. Nothing in his life up to this point had indicated there was anything unusual about his level of intelligence. But he suddenly found himself in a training program predominantly populated by, as he put it, "a bunch of those ROTC-type boys." During the next eighteen months they studied, they trained, they served as air-traffic controllers, they gambled, they drank, they had low-level heat strokes in the desert, and on their days of leave they ventured into Tangiers for the sort of adventures men don't discuss with their daughters. And my father got a new vision for his future. He began to see himself as someone who could hang with educated and advantaged people and keep up just fine.

A sweet little story, right? Pottery-town boy makes good, grabs a chance at a new life. But here comes the twist.

One day my dad is in the control room monitoring the position of several planes. There was a larger than usual number in the sky over the base, and he was a little anxious, so he made a mistake. He touched the screen with the metal fountain pen he was holding in his hand. He was also sitting on a metal chair, and immediately a bolt of electricity ran through him, knocking him unconscious and sending the chair flying across the room, where it crashed into a wall.

When he came to his first thought was that he was no longer smart. He had probably suspected all along, to be honest, that the first IQ test was some sort of fluke, perhaps incorrectly graded by a man too seasick to see straight. He was so worried that the bolt had zapped him back to ordinary that they gave him a second IQ test.

It went up two points. He was now officially a genius.

My dad was certainly smart enough to know that people score slightly differently on different tests and that IQ is not a fixed mark. But he loved the idea that a bolt of electricity turned him into a genius and repeated this story throughout his life. Because it had worked out so well for him, he set a great store by IQ tests, and when I was born he asked my schoolteacher mom to test me as soon as possible.

Either the results turned out well, or my mother lied to him for fear of what radio-in-the-bathtub type of experiments lay in my future if they didn't.

Sadly, my dad died suddenly of heart failure in his fifties, but he remains one of the greatest influences in my life. Right after he died I had a dream in which I was trying to ask him some question, and he said he would sit down and talk to me soon but that right then he was playing cards with some of his buddies from Buckner. I awoke mystified. It was an eerily clear dream and I was sure it had to mean something, but I'd never known my dad to be connected to a place named Buckner.

My mother had no idea what it meant either. Eventually, I called one of my aunts, who said that *The General Simon B. Buckner* was one of the ships he'd served on during his time in the Navy.

My dad never came close to active combat, but his time in the service most emphatically changed his life for the better. It pleases me to think of him back with the friends he made during those years, pulling up a metal chair with a scrape, cigarette dangling from his mouth and Gallo in the glass, saying, "Hey, guys, deal me in."

# 22

## War Stories

TRACY KIDDER

I am the author of *Ivory Fields*, a novel. I wrote it soon after I came home from Vietnam. Not many have read the book. After thirty-three publishers turned it down, I lit a fire in a trash barrel behind a rented house in Iowa and burned up all my copies of the manuscript. Years and years went by, and the book became a part of my distant memories of being a soldier, memories that would creep up on me when I was washing dishes or turning a key in a lock, memories that I wished away. Then one morning another copy of the novel arrived in the mail, from an old friend who was cleaning out his files, and I realized I was glad to have it back. From time to time I look at it, and I think.

The protagonist of *Ivory Fields* is a strange, doomed young Army officer named Larry Dempsey. He's a second lieutenant, just as I was when I arrived in Vietnam in June 1968. But Lieutenant Dempsey is sent to Vietnam to lead an infantry platoon in combat. Whereas I commanded, in a manner of speaking, a detachment of eight enlisted men who performed an indoor sort of job, a classified mission called communications intelligence, in support of the 198th Light Infantry Brigade of the Americal Division. We belonged to the Army Security Agency, but in Vietnam we worked under the false, though actually more descriptive, name "Radio Research."

I imagine this disguise was meant to confuse not only our enemies but also our friends who didn't have proper security clearances, but I don't know what difference it made. Our compounds were off-limits to most American soldiers, and we never saw the Vietcong or North Vietnamese. At higher headquarters in Chu Lai and in small airplanes, other Radio Research soldiers listened in on the enemy's encrypted Morse code communications, and what they learned—mainly locations—was passed to my detachment and passed on by me to the brigade commander. I remember an article in an overseas edition of *Time* that accurately described what units like ours were doing. I read the article in my hooch, in my detachment's compound, which was tucked inside the brigade's fortified base camp, Landing Zone Bayonet. The camp was situated at the edge of the coastal plain, at the base of the foothills of the central highlands, in the part of South Vietnam that the American authorities had labeled I Corps. I spent most of my year at LZ Bayonet, inside the perimeter.

I remember watching a small group of American soldiers head out one evening. The selections that memory makes often puzzle me, but I probably remember seeing the patrol because it was the closest I ever got to the infantry in Vietnam. I was standing on the hill near my detachment's antennae. I could see most of the base camp and, to the west, out beyond the bunkers and barbed wire, green hills with taller hills like a wall behind them, and on a rock face in white paint, "ALPHA 1/46 THE GUNFIGHTERS," the name of an infantry company that must have passed through in the course of the war and left that memento behind. The sun was setting on the hilltops, below great-chested clouds, and I was gazing out that way, glad to be apart from my men for a while, when I caught sight of the infantry patrol on one of the intervening hills, a group of olive-drab figures in procession, tiny at that distance, hump-backed beneath rucksacks. It would be dark soon. They were trudging away from the camp at an hour when I would have wanted to be heading in the opposite direction, toward hooches and beer and cots and mosquito nets and generators.

I had decided that this war was wrong. Not because of anything I had read recently or because of what I had seen so far. I opposed the war mainly because a lot of my friends were protesting back home. I watched the patrol with morbid fascination, with something like the feeling I used to get as a boy when I'd inch toward the edge of the roof of my grandmother's apartment building in New York, until the soldiers went over the hill in single file and disappeared among lighter shades of green.

I was glad I wasn't going with them. But what if I had to? What if I enraged some field-grade officer and for punishment got reassigned to the infantry? A fluttery sensation passed through my chest, and for a moment my hands felt weak. I imagined my civilian friends watching me.

I imagined my girlfriend, Mary Anne. She might approve of my being less than gung-ho, but not homesick and frightened. I had let some of those feelings slip into a few letters, and she had written me a sweet but keep-your-chin-up letter, in which she'd said, "Don't be so paranoid." I'd be more careful from now on. Soon my letters would suggest a stoical, even at times heroic, young fellow. And after all, here I was, standing on the edge of the dangerous highlands under an operatic Asian sky, in a situation she ought to find poignant, a reluctant commander drawing hazardous-duty pay.

I wandered down the hill, past our latrine, toward the enlisted men's hooches, and turned in at the one we had made into our lounge. Outside the screen door I heard beer cans hissing open. I went inside as usual. Five or six of my men were sitting around the TV set, awaiting that evening's episode of *Combat!* The title filled the screen: "What Are the Bugles Blowin' For?" Sergeant Saunders's platoon has volunteered for a dangerous mission, which takes them, through the pouring rain, into a bombed-out village in France. The one kid left in the village joins up with them. He wants to fight the Krauts, too, because they killed his sister. He wants to get the man who did it, so he keeps checking the faces of the Krauts that Sergeant Saunders's squad guns down. Sergeant Saunders is brave and wise and kind to children and women, especially nuns.

I had a good sergeant, a buck sergeant in his early twenties, three stripes on the sleeves. His name was Stoney Spikes, and he came from Alabama. He had a strong face, with a big square chin, and the other men obeyed him. He kept one of his two pairs of jungle boots polished more or less for the inspections we occasionally endured, which were for me almost a form of combat. The other pair he left unshined, at first perhaps because he saw no sense in shining them and later on, I think, because they made him feel more like the soldier he wished he was— because a real soldier, an infantryman, a grunt, would never wear shiny boots in the bush. Spikes had gone away on leave and had run into some buck sergeants his age who had combat infantryman's badges. "They got a name for people like us, Lieutenant," he told me when he came back. His jaw hardened. The term was REMF. It stood for "rear-echelon mother fucker." Spikes never seemed quite the same after he found out what real soldiers thought of soldiers like us. In my memory he sits forever in the lounge, at the end of another hot and dusty day. He opens a beer and tells the other men to hush, as *Combat!* fills the TV screen, and he is dressed for the show in those sad, scuffed jungle boots.

In a sense I put on scuffed boots, too, when I came home and began to write my novel about an infantry platoon and its lieutenant. Writing about experiences that I didn't have in Vietnam quieted real memories. A decade later I had become a magazine writer, and in 1978, in an article about Vietnam combat veterans, I wrote this about my homecoming: "Vietnam seemed so far away and everything seemed to be proceeding so normally at home that I thought the war must have ended." But that wasn't all I felt. Ten years after the Vietnam War had ended for me, I was still curious about those experiences that I had merely imagined. So I traveled around the country, interviewing Vietnam combat veterans, to gather material for my article. And what a lot of strange and violent experience had been transported back into the United States, into jails and treatment centers, and at least as often into houses on quiet, tree-lined streets. I met a former infantryman who remembered getting a black eye when a piece of his best friend's skull hit him in the face, a former combat medic who had finally weaned himself from morphine but still had lurid dreams about the men whose lives he hadn't saved, a government official who had lost an arm and both legs to a hand gre-nade, and dozens of others with terrible stories, all certifiable.

Also, in Lexington, Kentucky, I met a man whom I'll call Bill, who told me a different kind of story, a tale about a tale.

In a bar one night, after listening to a bunch of other Vietnam vet-erans tell war stories, Bill had said, "*We* were ridin' on an APC outside Pleiku, when *we* got hit." Bill had told the barroom that he could still see those tracer rounds, like little red-tailed comets coming at them from the tree line, and the way his buddy who was sitting beside him on the armored personnel carrier slumped over and, as if in slow motion, fell by the side of the trail. Bill was scared, he told the bar. Fuckin' A, who wouldn't be? But that was his buddy, that was a GI lying wounded and dying back there on the trail. The captain, though, was yelling at the driver to *di di mao*. And Bill was yelling at the captain that they had to go back, and the coward told him to shut up and shouted at the driver again to *move out*. So afterward, back in base camp, the captain, to cover his ass, busted Bill to spec. 4, and Bill brooded and brooded and finally made up his mind to get payback. He had to kill the officer. He had to frag the lifer.

Bill was sitting on a sofa in his parents' living room when he described himself telling that story. He said that he really did experience some moments of near combat in Vietnam and that there really was a captain he wanted to kill, who busted him in rank. And in fact, Bill did come home wounded. But his actual offense was repeated drunkenness, and he received his wound when he fell in a hole in a base camp and a friend, also stumbling drunk, fell in on top of him and broke his jaw. Bill had come home feeling miserable and had moved between the city's drunk tank and its barrooms, where he told his story again and again. "It just came out one time, and it felt really good. Then each time I'd say it, I'd make it a little more glorified," Bill told me. "When I came home the other veterans always had big, wild stories, and I didn't have anything like theirs to tell. And theirs were probably as fictitious as mine." He looked down at his hands and seemed to smile at them. "It takes the place of things you didn't do. After a while, if you tell 'em enough, the ones people like to hear, you almost start to believe them."

When one considers the suffering of actual combatants and the much more numerous sufferings of Vietnamese civilians, it seems like sheer perversity for a rear-echelon soldier to come home wishing his experiences more dreadful than they were. But I'm sure that Bill was not alone. Most of the American soldiers who went to Vietnam were boys, whether they were twenty-two or just eighteen. They had watched a lot of movies and TV. Many set out for Vietnam feeling confused or unhappy, as adolescents tend to do, and deep down many probably thought they would return with improved reasons for feeling that way. But of the roughly three million Americans who went to the war dressed as soldiers, only a tiny minority returned with combat infantryman's badges, certain proof of a terrible experience. Imagine all the bullshit stories Vietnam inspired.

My own wasn't exactly a story, just a freighted suggestion. I made it twice, the last time on a night in the mid-1970s. I got drunk at a Christmas party. Afterward, imagining that I'd been insulted by the various people I'd insulted there, I started crying angrily in the backseat of my car. A friend was driving. He asked me what was wrong, and I felt the need for a better explanation than the real one, whatever the real one was. My friend knew I'd been in Vietnam. "Did you ever kill anyone, buddy?" I said.

"No," he said. "Did you?"

"I don't want to talk about it."

*Ivory Fields* was a more elaborate war story. In late 1968, just back from Vietnam, I sat down at a table in my parents' house, and I began:

*When we were there, things were on the increase, not the wane. The coonskin cap was still nailed on the walls of Cam Ranh Bay, so speak.*

*About this time is when the sad story begins. It is the saddest story you ever hope to hear.*

There was a man the others called Pancho, and he stared at me openly, with his head cocked to one side, as if I were a curious variation of the species lieutenant. He was short and smooth-skinned and slightly round in the middle, not fat at all but round in the belly like a baby. He had jet-black hair, always longer than anyone else's. I noticed that right away, but something had kept me from mentioning haircuts to him during those first days of my command. I couldn't see his eyes because he wore sunglasses, day and night, it seemed. He'd look me over and then amble away, dragging his heels, a compact, graceful, package, brushing his sleek hair off his forehead. Sometimes I'd hear him laughing softly to himself.

On a day during that first week after Pease had left, I woke up feeling tired and ornery, and then, on the way back from briefing the colonel, I noticed that the jeep was almost out of gas. The men seemed to use the thing whenever they wanted, heading off to a place they called "the Ville," and it seemed to me they ought to be grateful that I let them use it, or at least considerate enough to fill up the tank. The time had come to draw some lines. When I got back to the detachment, some of them still hadn't gotten up, and a couple were wandering back from the shitter in their underwear and Ho Chi Minh sandals.

"I want some men to come with me and fuel up this jeep, goddamit," I said through the screen door of one of their hooches. Eventually, a couple of them came out and climbed aboard. They seemed sullen to me, though they may have just been sleepy. I hadn't been to the fuel depot before, but when we got there, I assumed command. The brigade's fuel was stored in huge black plastic bladders, as big around as backyard swimming pools. I saw a hose connected to one, and I grabbed it and stuck the nozzle in the jeep's fuel tank, turning back to glare at the men.

They both looked startled.

I thought, *That's good. I've made my point.*

"Lieutenant," one of them said, "I think you got the wrong hose. That's diesel fuel."

He got out and found the proper hose. I stood aside. "God, I hope I didn't wreck it."

The jeep sputtered a little on the way back to the detachment. A week in command, and already I had wrecked the jeep. "What do you guys think? Think it'll be all right?"

"Yeah, no biggie, Lieutenant."

"Jesus," I said, when we'd dismounted. "You really think it'll be all right?"

"Don't worry about it, Lieutenant," one of them said. As he turned away I saw the flash of his teeth, a piece of a grin he hadn't meant me to see. When I passed by their hooch that night, I heard what seemed like more laughter than usual from inside.

In *Ivory Fields* Lieutenant Dempsey gets off to a bad start, too. Soon after he arrives at LZ Old Smokey, he meets his platoon. The next day his company commander says to him, "Did you give your men a speech? Don't do it again, Ace. They don't need to be told what they're fighting for, Dempsey." The commander goes on, expressing sentiments I'd heard from a veteran infantry officer at Fort Benning: "Joe Bazatz came off the streets. With the lowest fucking IQ in the world. And he'll shit all over you. You know what he'll do, Dempsey? He'll shoot you in the back. You know who I'm talking about? Your men, Ace." Then the captain says that he's sending Dempsey and his platoon of Joe Bazatzes out on a combat patrol the next day.

The platoon hikes away from the base camp into the boonies. Dempsey gets lost, through the connivance of his platoon sergeant, the short and stocky Sergeant Fisher. Finally, the platoon bivouacs on a ridge, and the sergeant takes Dempsey aside and gives him some remarkably bad advice: "Lieutenant, I seen disciplined men go all to hell and damnation without the necessary leadership. Are you gonna kick some ass, sir?" He puts his face close to Dempsey's. "Care about this platoon until she hurts. Then you're doing a job." The sergeant salutes him and says, "You're gonna be a fine one, sir."

The men are lounging on the ridge. The sergeant walks among them, making congenial remarks. Then Dempsey visits them, too. But Dempsey, "because he was ashamed of his map work," issues unnecessary orders. "Soldier? Get off your back. This is a perimeter. Soldier, start cleaning that rifle now." Then Dempsey moves away. While he sits alone eating his lunch of C-rations, the men mock him behind his back. "And so when Dempsey looked behind, he found no eyes on him, but he did not see them working on their rifles either. And while he sat, the sun strode over the top of the sky and took the morning away." Dempsey thinks to himself, "Everyone gets lost once, but this platoon would never get lost again. And the personnel, the men, they would come to see him the way the Sergeant had. He was just getting his feet upon the ground. When the time came, the men would come to him and thank him for making them clean their weapons. 'Saved our lives,' they'd say. He conjured up his homecoming. Walking down Anstice Street in his uniform, he could see it now. Though that was many days away, it seemed quite close, and he would not wear the medal, but . . ."

Of course, my sergeant, Sergeant Spikes, wasn't disingenuous, although he didn't always tell me everything. And among second lieutenants, getting lost in the field was a much more serious and probably more common error than putting diesel fuel in a jeep. But while our jeep ran fine the following day, that incident brought an end to the first period of my command. The men were done with waiting and watching to see what their new lieutenant was like. They'd seen enough. I found this out a couple of nights later, from Rosenthal.

We were finishing up my briefing, he and I alone, in the front room of the operations hooch. He cleared his throat. "I don't believe in talking about a fellow behind his back," he said. "There was a meeting about you last night, Lieutenant."

"About me?" I said. I shrugged. "So what did they say?"

"Pancho did most of the talking. He doesn't like the fact that I'm not on some of the duty rosters. Pancho does a lot of talking, Lieutenant. It's just big talk."

"Oh, well, let 'em talk."

I went down to my hooch, got into my cot, and tried to read. I saw myself telling Spikes to leave Rosenthal off those rosters. I sat right up, to drive that image away. I lay back with my book. An old mosquito net hung from a rafter, surrounding my cot. I stared up into its folds. Things had gone so badly already, there was no point in trying to fix them now. I thought of Lieutenant Pease bitterly. He hadn't had these problems, because he hadn't even tried to do this job. A faint, dry smell, like fine dust in the nose, came from the netting. The nightly artillery barrage had begun, American mortars firing nearby at regular intervals. It sounded as if the shells flew right over the roof of my hooch. In *The Heart of Darkness*, which I'd recently reread, a European ship sits off an African coast and fires its cannons randomly into the jungle. I, too, was surrounded by violent absurdity, and I was part of it. Those mortars might well be firing at targets I'd supplied to the colonel today. I didn't want to be associated with that noise, with this place, with these men who talked behind their commander's back, with this dusty hooch, the rats skittering around beneath the floor.

A mortar round went overhead. In the silence that followed, I heard a banging at my screen door. I looked up and saw Pancho saunter in. I was in my underwear. He was fully dressed, still wearing his sunglasses. "Hi," I said, brushing away the mosquito net. I swung my legs over the side of the cot. "Can I help you?"

He sat down on my footlocker and said, very calmly, "Lieutenant, you know what a lifer is? You know what a lifing, begging puke is, Lieutenant?"

"What?"

He went right on. "It's a flatdick who lifes and begs and pukes all over EM scum, Lieutenant. Ain't like a man, Lieutenant."

The Army had films and pamphlets to instruct a soldier in all the activities of daily living, and I had gone to training camps for more than a year and learned to avoid venereal disease and march and make my bed and fire weapons, but I had never received a single instruction in how to handle troops. I remembered how, during her first year of teaching high school, my mother would come home almost every day in tears. The Army should have sent me to an inner-city high school for six months and let me try to keep order in the cafeteria. As it was, I had an idea that, being an officer, I would be obeyed. I didn't know exactly what this short kid in dark glasses was talking about, but I could tell it was impertinent and I shouldn't put up with it. I said, "Now wait a minute, Specialist."

Pancho said, "We don't like some of the things you're doing around here, Lieutenant."

"Well, that's too bad," I said.

"We can shoot you anytime we want, Lieutenant," he said.

"Oh, yeah?"

"Yeah, Lieutenant. We can."

"I'll shoot you first, asshole," I said to him, but under my breath and after he'd gone and I was sitting on my cot under a bare lightbulb, staring out toward the dark. The light reached only a few yards beyond my rusty screen walls. I couldn't see out, but anyone could stand in the patch of tall grass near my hooch and see my lighted silhouette.

# 23

# Hulls in the Water

JEFFERY HESS

Sunrise lit Egypt from behind as the USS *San Jacinto* steamed out of Alexandria, two days early, on August 1, 1989. *Steamed* is a term we used in reference to ships of an all-but-forgotten era. Our propulsion involved gas turbines that ran on jet fuel. We were brand-new and had cutting-edge Aegis radar systems, Tomahawk missiles, Harpoon missiles, and a pair of antiaircraft Gatlin guns that looked like R2-D2. Aboard ship, we were prepared for World War III.

My sea and anchor station was on the bridge. They needed an interior communication's electrician standing by in case any equipment that communicated voice, heading, speed, or one of our multiple alarm systems on the bridge or down the passageway in Command Information Central malfunctioned. This was the fourth month of a seven-month deployment in the Mediterranean, and this rarely happened on such a new ship. I carried a soldering iron and the most common replacement bulbs in my tool bag, just in case.

As Egypt grew smaller behind us, I stood in my usual spot outside the bridge, near the Signal Shack, talking shit with the chief signalman. We bitched about the smell of the place we had just left and also about not wanting to head back out to sea so soon. We'd been delayed pulling into Alexandria because we'd been ordered to follow a Soviet submarine. We had been in similar cat-and-mouse situations before, but nothing ever materialized from them—much to my disappointment. I was twenty-three years old with a mere 137 days left to serve on my 6-year enlistment. If I was going to get any action, it couldn't happen soon enough.

In a quiet moment out on the bridge wing, I stared at the water between me and the horizon, watching whitecaps crest and fall into the ink-dark chop of deep ocean. It was the same view almost every time I had occasion to go up on deck. At sea it wasn't unusual for days to pass without being outside, but on this day I leaned on the life rail, weight on my forearms, hands clasped as if in prayer. I didn't pray then, because if I did, it might have been for something to put my training to the test.

The captain secured us from sea-and-anchor detail when we got well into open sea, but before we had time to get a soda or hit the head, he spoke over the 1MC (the ship's public address system). I don't remember the captain's exact words, but something was going down in Lebanon, and we were headed to meet up with our battle group off the coast of Beirut. There was a civil war raging, and we might have to get involved. He ordered High Threat Condition 3 Watch Stations. We ran to our battle stations amid the echoing gongs of the General Quarters alarm.

The anticipation of action immediately filled the passageways and decks. There were a thousand guesses and scenarios in those early minutes, but I'll never forget the collective mood that made us feel like all the training and practice of the past year and a half since the ship had been commissioned would finally be called into action.

A ton of nervous energy came with the waiting. Instead of weighing me down, it fueled me like the JP-5 that ran our jet engines. I thought, *Holy shit. I may finally get to see some action!* I also remember thinking, *Ah, shit. I came all this way and I didn't get to see the fucking pyramids?*

I didn't dwell on the contradiction, but now that I'm twice as old as I was then, this two-headedness is something I realize that I brought with me when I enlisted.

I enlisted in the Navy in July 1983, two months after I graduated high school. My father drove me to the recruiter's office. I was seventeen, and he had to sign for me. On the way he asked, a half-dozen times, "Are you sure you want to do this?"

I was and I wasn't. I don't know what I said in response. I couldn't have had the ability to articulate my two-headedness then. On one side, I'd wanted to find my future, but on the other, I didn't want to leave my past or present. I knew, even at that age, that I couldn't have both. My parents had already told me they'd support me in whatever decision I made. That made it easier, but also more difficult.

I must have answered yes, because we went inside the recruiting office that day, and we both signed our names.

Even then I didn't know my father had planned on going into the Navy before my parents got married. That was something I learned years later looking at his yearbook when one of his old friends visited. Or maybe I did see it, but no one ever discussed it. Maybe that was something that influenced my decision.

Maybe it was because we had a boat when I was a kid growing up in Florida. It was a sixteen-foot, open-bow ski boat. We'd motor down the Caloosahatchee River and into the Gulf of Mexico. I was pretty nervous the first time on the boat. The floor beneath my feet was unsteady, and I felt like I'd fall, even while seated. After a while my body adjusted to the rocking and rolling, and I enjoyed the ride. Rushing over water that I could reach out and touch, the wind in my face, this all became the sensation of being superhuman somehow. Maybe it was because of land shrinking and then disappearing behind us. Maybe it was the freedom from roads or stop signs and the practical recklessness of leaving terra firma and trusting our souls to a boat and a motor. Maybe it was the unknown that could happen out there. Maybe that was compounded by the notion that if something did happen, odds were there'd be no one around to see it or to help, and we were all reliant on ourselves and each other. Maybe it was just the love of speed and the wind in my face and the promise of getting to some tropical spot along the coast and turning around and skipping like a stone all the way back again. All the while being mindful, even as a six-year-old kid, that shit could go seriously wrong. I don't know what it was, but I loved it.

Maybe it was the day I saw the movie *Midway* with my father. My breath caught in my chest as the theater darkened in that moment before the movie started. I was ten and knew the movie was going to be about war and ships, but as I sat in the theater next to my father, excitement made me vibrate in that thick foam seat. The action of shooting down planes and firing torpedoes looked like the coolest thing ever.

That movie piggy-backed off memories I had of third grade when Miss Dickerson's brother visited our class in dress blues—looking like the guy on the Cracker Jack box. He gave me the $CO_2$ canister he'd used to fill his flotation device. It was brass, if I recall correctly. Flotation devices changed by the time I got aboard ship.

It had been hot as balls in Egypt. A bunch of us had played golf at a local course the day before we had to ship out. Bubba and Hearns kept quoting the *Biloxi Blues* line, "It's Africa hot!" I'd played the best round of my life that day, largely due to a caddy who cost all of six dollars. Afterward, despite the smell in the air, we ate KFC. If not for the pyramids, I would have been happy to get the hell out of there. Instead of going to Cairo, though, I spent twelve hours a day in Repair Locker 3.

Repair lockers are rooms that house damage-control equipment like fire hoses, axes, flooding pumps and more hoses, oxygen breathing apparatuses and canisters, rubber boots, and, for those of us on the fire team, helmets and flame-retarding Nomex coveralls. I volunteered for this duty because I'd learned years earlier, on my first ship, the USS *Proteus* (AS-19), that the best way to ensure your survival at sea in the face of emergencies was to take matters into your own hands.

I'd left my first ship in the spring of '87, while the Soviets were doing nuclear tests in eastern Kazakhstan. I transferred from a submarine tender to a guided missile cruiser. This was the U.S. Navy's equivalent of getting out of a semitruck and stepping into a souped-up Mustang. I felt like a Minor Leaguer being called up to the Show. I flew ten thousand miles on four planes from Guam to Pascagoula, Mississippi, where my brand-new warship was being built. The excitement had made falling asleep difficult for weeks before and after the move.

Now, in the repair locker, it was my job to man the nozzle and direct our fire team in snuffing out any fires that broke out in our portion of the ship. With the nozzle on, I could direct the spray pattern wide to begin cooling the room or switch to a steady stream for power and distance. I was well under six feet tall and weighed only 150 pounds, but I was strong enough for the job. The fire hose wasn't just heavy, but hard when charged with pressurized water. Picture holding a giant boa constrictor that maneuvers like a bucking bronco, but sideways.

We did a lot of drills, pretending to fight engine-room fires, flight-deck fires, and mass conflagration. Everything we did involved sweating. Those Nomex coveralls were thick and heavy enough to keep out flames as well as air.

I remember the next day's dread of having to put on the still-soaked coveralls that smelled of mildew no matter how much talcum powder you wafted inside. After countless drills and exercises during shakedown cruises and battle-efficiency trials in the Caribbean, the Nomex suit was like a second skin. And I'd have a lot of time now, floating off the coast of Lebanon, to wear it during endless drills.

I didn't know much about the Middle East at that age. We were more focused on the Soviet Union. We'd had some tense times such as when we followed that Russian sub and again while sailing into the Black Sea on our way to dock in Constanța, Romania, as we passed Soviet ships.

If you knew your ships, you'd recognize each distinctive silhouette—like knowing all the different types of cars on the road. Distinguishing a particular ship was dependent upon how many hull numbers you had memorized. Hull numbers are the bright-white numbers near the bow in the typeface you recognize from old-school digital clocks. The U.S. Navy began assigning these Naval Registry Identification Numbers way back in the 1890s. My ship, the USS *San Jacinto*, is hull number 56.

The other half of this official identification system uses letters to differentiate the various classes of ship. For example, BB means battleship, FFG is guided missile frigate, CVN for nuclear-powered aircraft carrier, and CG for guided missile cruiser, like my ship. The letters and numbers are separated by a dash when used to identify ships in Navy reports or newspaper articles.

The Soviet ships also had hull numbers on their bows, but these numbers were in a totally different typeface. The ships cut all the right angles, and their weaponry appeared not just lethal, but threatening. I don't know if everyone held their breath in that instant of seeing them, but the tension slithered down my back and made it hard to swallow. The sky matched the haze gray of the ships, which was a shade darker than our own. I knew a little about the classes of Soviet ships from what I'd seen in *Jane's Fighting Ships* and what I read in Clancy novels, but I had to guess that the ships were destroyers in their twilights.

World War III always felt imminent to me. I sort of wanted it, back then. If it didn't kill me, I'd likely get some medals out of the ordeal. If it did kill me, so what? I'd never considered myself suicidal. Instead, my fatalistic mind was convinced that I wouldn't live to see thirty. I felt that in order to enjoy my remaining time, I'd need to have done something heroic. This hero delusion may have been exacerbated by the books I was reading at the time.

I read a lot of books in the Navy. I was big into Hemingway, and I read all the books I probably should have read in high school. My girlfriend at the time gave me a box filled with books from her prep-school days.

I don't remember who gave me Tom Clancy's book *The Hunt for Red October*, but I read it obsessively. The book fascinated me because he wrote about classified information so convincingly and because I wanted that level of mission—something big, important, and death defying.

In the downtime during this High Threat Condition 3 Watch Stations, while we sat or stood in the passageway outside the repair locker, amid the chatter of other sailors, what we called "tell-a-lie time," amid the smells of mildew, talcum, and Skoal spit, I thought of the uss *Stark* (FFG-31). It was the one thing I knew about the Middle East.

The *Stark* was on patrol in the Persian Gulf when it was struck in the port side by two Iraqi Exocet missiles. The first missile didn't detonate; the second did. It was May 17, 1987, and thirty-seven men were killed. The hull was ripped open; the ship took on water, listed, and eventually limped into Bahrain for repairs. The *Stark* never fired a single weapon in defense or retaliation.

When I'd heard of the attack, I sort of jealously imagined the noise of the missiles piercing the ship's steel hull, the explosion's percussion. The sound of the fire bell and the ear-splitting gongs of the General Quarters alarm sending boots pounding down passageways to battle stations. I hoped someone cut off power quickly so the guy doing my job on that ship would be able to lug his hose and put down as much water as his brass nozzle would allow.

The loss of so many fellow sailors angered the hell out of me when I heard the report, but I sort of envied them, too. Whether they were killed instantly or while trying to put out fires or stop flooding, their deaths were honorable. I figured if it were me, the honor associated with such a death would ease my parents' grief, at least a little. I'd still be dead, but dying "in action" had to be easier on them than a car wreck or alcohol poisoning. At least that's what I thought back then.

I didn't think of the sadness those sailors' parents and wives and girlfriends would experience upon learning their sailor was one of the thirty-seven killed that day. Those who survived would be decorated not only for having endured the attack, but also for their efforts to restore the natural order in the face of such challenges.

To this day I don't know what kept the *Stark*'s captain from defending the ship, but I was convinced that we'd return fire immediately and destroy the enemy bastards.

The Iraqis later apologized for the attack, by the way, but that doesn't bring back any of those sailors.

I didn't know any of the guys injured or killed on the *Stark*, but they couldn't have been much different from the other sailors I'd known over the years. They'd each come from some town where they'd had families and at least some semblance of happiness, or comfort, or maybe just a sense of familiarity they were all anxious to get back to. They wore the same uniform, took the same oath, and boarded their ships just like everybody else. Just like me. They might have done their best on their fateful day. They might have let fear overtake them. I hoped, if the time ever came, that I'd step up. What's the use of studying if there's never going to be a test?

While steaming off the coast of Lebanon, spending twelve hours a day in the repair locker, I kind of had a feeling that something would happen. I didn't know if it would happen when I was already dressed out in the firefighting gear or if it would happen in the middle of the night when I was asleep. The worst case would be getting caught with my pants down on the shitter, but that was possible, too.

The one night I really thought I was going to die came during a typhoon evasion aboard the *Proteus* in '86. The *Proteus* was a submarine tender homeported in Apra Harbor, Guam. Yes, Guam. As in, head out into the Pacific, find Hawaii, pass it, and keep going another four thousand miles into the great blue deep.

This ship was a welded-together husk we called the *Old Pro*, which happened to be the oldest ship in the fleet. She was a weathered hulk built during the early days of the Roosevelt administration and had been present at the Japanese surrender with six enemy submarines moored on each side.

Her sole purpose was to serve as lactating sow for all her submarine pups. The ship didn't have enough firepower to burst a balloon in a clown's mouth at the state fair. At the time I resented that fact. I felt trapped on the little island when we were in port and vulnerable to the enemy while at sea. Years later in civilian life, I realized that our weapons weren't the guns aboard our ship, but rather the submarines that we tended. Each sub that stopped by for refueling, restocking, or repairing was like a giant torpedo filled with missiles and more torpedoes. Collectively, we were a powerful and important factor in the Pacific during the Cold War.

But that night during this typhoon evasion, I was awakened in my rack when my head hit one end and my feet, the next moment, hit the other end. Back and forth as the ship pitched and rolled. We were caught in the outer bands of the very typhoon we left port to evade. The ship groaned and creaked as if it might snap apart. I almost wished it would happen.

It wasn't battle, but would still entail a valiant effort as I sprang to action on the flooding team. I didn't want weather to be our ultimate enemy, but this was the most violent movement I'd ever felt. There was no predictable pitch or roll. It was rather like being Yahtzee dice in a half-century-old can, but in slow motion.

The noises I remember are the crashes and tumbling roll of unsecured items knocking about. Shipmates doing the same and cursing afterward. The creaks and moans coming from the ship's steel. The ship had been cut in half during a refit to accommodate Polaris missiles as cargo. My life was in the hands of the welders who rejoined the ship's hull. I was sure one of the seams would separate and we'd take on water. Capsize. Sink.

For the better part of three days, the rough seas kept the weather decks secured, meaning no one could go outside. The seas were so rough the cooks had to close the mess decks for anything other than crackers and the industrial Kool-Aid they made from little brown envelopes of neon-colored powder. There were no smells of chow, but rather of blown chow. It smelled in all the passageways and in the berthing areas, and just when you got away from the smell, someone else would spew and you'd have to smell it all over again. Fresh and hot. I was lucky to avoid the sickness, but the price of feeling good was having to pull the load for those who were incapacitated in their racks or stinking up the toilets and sinks and garbage cans.

Certain noises made me jump to my feet if I was sitting. Others made me brace for impact if I was standing. I was prepared at every minute, like living on heightened adrenaline, to hear the alarm for General Quarters, where I'd rush to the repair locker and take my position on the flooding team.

I wanted to hear the alarm. I wished for it. I wanted to save the ship from sinking or die trying. Instead, we survived the storm, and all I got from the experience was the benefit of having to work extra while my shipmates were laid out, seasick beyond the pale. The prospect of action was why I'd enlisted, but action wasn't necessarily dependent upon enemies or the weather.

We'd been out at sea participating in battle-group exercises in the Caribbean on April 19, 1989, when word spread aboard ship that the uss *Iowa* (bb-61) had an explosion in its sixteen-inch gun turret 2 and needed assistance. We were only a couple miles away. There was no way to know at that moment, but the explosion and the fires that followed killed forty-seven sailors. It was the single worst loss-of-life event for the surface Navy during the Cold War.

I imagined the carnage and chaos based on the training films we'd seen. I don't know if I would have been fighting one of those fires had I been aboard the *Iowa*. I don't know if I would have been killed.

There's no way to know exactly how I felt the day the *Iowa* exploded, but I know I was excited that we were dispatched to assist. There was talk aboard the ship that a repair locker might be sent over to help with damage control. I wanted to be one of those guys. I was heroic in every scenario I played out in my head.

Another part of me withered a little from the fear that something like that could happen to our ship. While in my heroic fantasies I was instrumental in minimizing damage and saving lives, I also cringed at the thought of burning metal curling in thick black smoke from flames that melted steel and suffocated countless men as they ran toward or away from the destruction—running through passageways, hurtling through the opened water-tight hatches.

In the end another ship was closer and called in. I was disappointed. Later that night I might have spun the combination on my locker slowly or I might have leaned on my rack for a while, but I remember this surprising sense of "better them than me" for the first time. And this led immediately to guilt.

We patrolled off the coast of Lebanon for weeks. I kept hoping we'd launch missiles. I also kept worrying about being blown up like the *Stark*, or the *Iowa*.

On October 1, 1989, I was just "seventy-five days and a wakeup" away from becoming a civilian. After evening chow the bridge sounded the alarm for General Quarters. Drills were rarely conducted at that time of day, so we all hustled into action. There was a fuel oil leak in Auxiliary Machinery Room 1. A busted pipe pissing fuel into a space with moving metal parts could explode in an instant. I suited up in my Nomex coveralls and harnessed into my breathing apparatus and casually braced for the shock such an explosion might make. In the tense minutes that followed, I heard Hanson spitting Skoal juice into a Pepsi can. I heard the master chief holler, "Damn it, Hanson! Spit out that dip and straighten up!" Many of us laughed. It was funny, because it was typical. To have something typical in such a tense moment was a welcomed distraction.

The dangerous leak was isolated before it ignited, and a cleanup team had been dispatched to remove the flooded fuel. It seemed my remaining ten weeks in the Navy would go uneventfully.

But then, immediately after securing from that, the captain spoke over the 1MC to inform us we were going back to High Threat Level 3 because we were sailing close to Lebanon again. This time with the *Iowa* and to be her antiair firepower. The rumor was the *Iowa* would fly a drone over Lebanon to take pictures. Drones were new then, and this was a first for us to witness or be a part of. We would sit back and make sure no planes or missiles launched against her.

And just like the last trip to Lebanon, our missiles were armed. I figured that we would surely see some action. After twenty-four hours the missiles were taken off-line, and we headed west again.

On October 11 we pulled into Naples, Italy, our first port in thirty days at sea. Somehow, the Navy routes mail so we had a good mail call. I got a care package from my parents filled with Doritos, Charmin, Skoal, and magazines and letters. I also got a book from my sister and letters from my girlfriend. And then liberty call.

There's not enough time here to describe all the ways we amused ourselves in foreign ports. Everything you've heard about sailors on shore leave is true. And none of it is true. Some of the stories involve alcohol. Some are sweet stories like when a newly married guy spends his entire day in Istanbul searching for a music box for his wife as a souvenir. A lot of times alcohol is involved. Once in a while the best intentions can take a turn for the worse. Sometimes there's a girl involved or an irate store owner. But usually alcohol is involved. Then there are fights and tattoos and brokenhearted phone calls home. Alcohol makes everything better.

I played golf in places like Cuba, Egypt, and St. Thomas.

I bought diamonds in Israel, china in China, and an inexpensive painting in France.

I drank rum in Puerto Rico, plum wine in Romania, and beer in more countries than most people ever get to visit—more countries than I've visited U.S. states.

I toured the Vatican, the Colosseum, and the ruins of Pompeii. I danced in the streets of New Orleans, broke the speed limit in Hollywood, and stumbled back to the ship in the Philippines.

I entertained lady friends in dozens of beds, a couple of swimming pools, and once on a toilet.

I rode the Korean bicycle I bought while stationed on Guam on the French streets of St. Tropez, where I got drunk on red wine and met the host of the old *Gong Show*. But more important than the admirals, politicians, and celebrities I met, I made friends from places such as Kentucky, Texas, Maryland, Georgia, and Jamaica.

We complained about everything, the way sailors always do. The chow was never good enough, we never slept enough, we were hot, bored, tired of suiting up for drills, anxious to get to the next port, to see some action, and to return home.

We were out at sea, again and still, on November 9, when we got word via Teletype feed in the Comm Shack that the Berlin Wall had been torn down. The news spread fast around the ship, as it always did. There were high-fives and *Hell, yeahs!* and the definite joy of victory in the air. I don't remember chants of "U-S-A," but I wouldn't be surprised if they were there. I was proud, too, for our country, but I didn't know if the wall coming down was a victory or a gateway into a greater confrontation. We didn't have the benefit of live footage or talking-head analysis. There was no way to know at that time.

What I did know was that we returned home to Norfolk eleven days later.

Hundreds of people waited for us on the pier. Big crowd. Wives, girlfriends, kids, parents everywhere. Cheering. Banners. Balloons. Signs waving. Flags.

Just over a month later I signed my honorable-discharge papers, signifying the end of my enlistment. While half of me was excited to get out and go to college, the other half was pretty sure he wanted to stay around, give him some more years to find some sort of action. I was well set up for advancement and I was due for shore duty, and unless you've got pictures of a naked congressman, there's no better leverage to getting the orders you want than when reenlisting. If I stayed, I probably would have negotiated staying right where I was. Instead, I signed my name and left with my honorable discharge.

In those early years of civilian life, the stories I told sounded rehearsed and some would say juvenile. The less I talked about it, the less my contribution seemed.

Over time I came to realize I wasn't just *in* the Navy, I was *part of* the Navy that was partly responsible for closing out a win in a forty-four-year conflict with the Soviets. Just as submarines were my first ship's weapons, I, myself, was one of the Navy's weapons. Always at the ready.

I never established myself as any kind of hero by doing any heroic things. But in the coming years as I settle into a rocking chair, I'll tell stories of how we took down the Berlin Wall and, with it, the Soviet Empire itself. I've come to believe that though I never experienced one giant challenge on one particular day, so many ships in the course of history, the *threat* was what appeared to have mattered most to the Soviets, and to me.

# 24

# Proud to Claim the Title

THOMAS VINCENT NOWACZYK

Joining the Marines was to be the first honest thing I ever did for myself. I had dreamed the dreams my parents wished for me, the ones forever etched into the deepest recesses of my memory, their innocence forever intact. Memories that included my father building model airplanes with me—the p-51 Mustang, p-47 Thunderbolt, p-38 Lightning, and half the series of bombers, including the b-25 and the b-29. My hands were half the size of his, and he carefully explained what each part was and how it made the plane fly. He had grown up with the newness of airplanes and thought it was pretty nifty to be able to soar through the air like a bird. In 1943 the draft board cut him short, his eyesight being what it was. They told him to eat a lot of carrots. The closest he got to any of those World War II airplanes was walking across Europe a few hundred feet behind Patton. In his mind, I think, he wasn't raising merely a son. He was raising a pilot.

Mom was the ambitious one. "Remember this," she said, holding up a Chicago newspaper in front of my high chair, pointing to the picture of John Glenn in his space capsule, Friendship Seven. "This is important!"

The only variable in my parents' plan was the strength of their marriage. After the divorce we moved, and moved again. My mom was a skilled waitress; the jobs just didn't pay much. At any rate their plans for me were an early casualty.

In high school, in the early 1970s, I grew my hair long and dreamed of going to Berkeley, and all this drove my parents nuts. I enjoyed knowing they would not talk to each other about it. And that is why, with a logic possessed by only a teenager, I dropped out of high school in my senior year to join the Marines.

I had grown up with the Viet Nam War, which is how it was spelled before people who pay journalists by the word wised up. I had fully expected to come of age and go to war. But by the time I was old enough to join, the war was over. Life felt safe again. Still, the Marine Corps felt like the last great challenge, even if there was no war to fight. And if I needed an ace in the hole as far as my parents were concerned, I had only this: John Glenn was a Marine and a pilot, and my parents had started it.

But after three weeks at Parris Island, for a number of us in my boot camp platoon, life would never feel safe—anywhere, ever again. We discovered how bad things can get when a good plan goes sideways, as demonstrated by our three drill instructors who, after using and abusing everyone in Platoon 222, ended their careers with a matching set of courts-martial.

My favorite bumper sticker to come out of post–Viet Nam veteran America proclaimed: *If it wasn't for flashbacks, I'd have no memories at all.* As they say in places like Berkeley, California, I can relate. I can relate because for nearly thirty-five years, I have tried to forget what happened. I have tried to forget what it was like to desperately need to use the head (toilet) and know it was useless to ask, because the answer would be worse than *No.*

I have tried to forget how it felt to watch Private Fuckwad (the drill instructor's pet name for one of our recruits) finally piss his own pants, and the look of humiliation on his face when he did, and the way he tried to hold back the tears as piss ran down his shiny black boot into a puddle on the deck. I have tried to forget the shock of Sergeant Smith screaming about the piss. I cannot forget the revulsion, disgust, and utter self-loathing I felt when Sergeant Smith made Private Fuckwad roll around in his own piss to mop it up.

I can't forget the full length of Sergeant Smith's fist and forearm through my gut and damn near out my back. Or of tripping backward over my footlocker when he slammed my head against the steel post of my rack, and slammed me again, head first, onto the cement deck.

I would like to forget standing at attention in the barracks with a stream of blood running from the shaving cut beside my lip down my neck that collected in a bright growing circle of crimson on my clean white T-shirt. I could feel it, warm, spreading. Others could see it, but no one could say anything. No one, that is, except the recruit standing at attention on line next to me. "Dude, your face is bleeding," he whispered out of the corner of his mouth.

"I know," I whispered, surprised that anyone other than a drill instructor had spoken to me.

"Put your finger on it."

"No."

And then, "What the hell kind of tea party we got going on over here?" yelled Sergeant Smith as he ambled toward me with Sergeant Giles on his heels. They both walked slowly, deliberately. "Well, what do we got here?"

"Looks like a bloody face to me," Sergeant Giles said.

"Private Motherfuckin' Alphabet," said Sergeant Smith, referring to me, "did you cut yourself shaving?"

"Sir, yes sir!" I said.

"Does it hurt?" he said.

"No, sir!"

"You're just a tough guy, ain't you?" he said.

"Sir . . . ," I said.

"Shut up," he said, and stuck his finger against my face and swiped away a fingertip full of blood. He stuck his finger in his mouth, grinned, and smacked his lips like a barbecue judge. He turned to Giles. "B positive."

"Is that right?" Giles said as he, too, swiped my face and stuck his finger in his mouth, smacking his lips lightly, almost demurely, as if he were sampling a new bottle of fine wine.

"Nah . . . A negative," Giles said.

"What's your blood type, dumb shit?" Smith said.

I shouted, "B positive, sir!"

Smith laughed and walked away.

Giles shook his head and walked toward the front of the squad bay. Smith addressed the platoon. "You people can't even shave without cutting yourselves. A lot of good you're gonna be in a combat situation . . ."

"You with the bloody face, come here," said a different voice. I could barely make out the words and wondered if I had hallucinated them. "You with the bloody face, come here." The voice was coming from the quarterdeck area, which is a small indoor patio at the front of the squad bay with a shiny cement floor on which we were never allowed to step. I leaned for a peek. Giles was holding aloft what appeared to be a cotton ball pinched between the thick fingers of his left hand. "You with the bloody face, bring your dumb ass over here," he said.

I ran to the quarter deck and stood at attention in front of Giles. The cotton ball appeared wet. Giles poked it into the cut on my face. It stung, and the scent of astringent made my eyes water.

"Put your finger where mine is." I did so, and he immediately removed his. "Get back on line." I ran back to the empty spot in the row of human clones and stood at attention. I was the sole exception to the row of perfection with my right elbow bent sharply, my finger shoving the cotton ball into the cut.

It has occurred to me that those of us in Platoon 222 that February and March 1976 must have looked as much like prisoners as we were being treated: heads shaved, white T-shirts and skivvies, barefoot, afraid. I remember only fear, in its purest primal form. I had been thrown to the dogs, and they had tasted my blood. In retrospect, I should have been grateful; it could have been much worse. I didn't realize this until I witnessed what they did to poor Private Horwitz.

Private Horwitz, granted, had a funky rebuilt ankle and probably should not have been let in the Marine Corps, but after the series of Houdini-like stunts my own recruiter pulled, I know how desperate those salesmen were in those days. Vietnam had been officially over for only eight months; there was no line at the recruiting office door.

One day, Horwitz twisted his ankle while we were running. He was limping around—in formation and in line at the mess hall. Several of us insisted he go to sick bay. Horwitz was too afraid to ask. When he could no longer bear the pain, he finally asked for permission. Sergeant Smith asked why, and Horowitz said his ankle was hurt.

"Your ankle hurts?" Without warning, Smith kicked Horwitz in that very ankle. "How about now?"

Horowitz cried out.

Smith kicked him again and, joined by Sergeant Giles, again and again. Horowitz lay on the floor in the fetal position, crying, "Ow! Ow! Ow!" as Smith and Giles kicked the crap out of him and his stupid ankle. I stood by helpless, and in shock. I had insisted Horwitz take care of himself, and here was the result.

Maybe this is where I should confess to playing fill-in-the-blank a bit. The blank comprises a good chunk of the space between my ears where there used to be conscious thought and pretty memories of things at Parris Island such as sunshine glittering off the choppy waters of the Atlantic or the sound of taps late at night when everything on "the Island" finally crawls into the rack, exhausted. These are just two gems I unearthed when I finally started probing my memory for answers to what happened so long ago and why the experiences in boot camp affected every personal decision afterward. Every decision, it seems, can have ramifications somewhere down the road. Heavier decisions, greater ramifications. Truth be told, for every horrible and intrusive memory from that boot camp era that has thrust itself to the forefront of my awareness for the past thirty-five years, to which I reacted poorly—costing me jobs and ruining relationships, and unable to defeat the memories with drug or bottle—I have fifty memories that are no longer there. Or there, but buried too deep for my own consciousness to reach. I was eighteen in boot camp, and my eighteen-year-old mind is still trying to protect me today from the horror.

I hope this goes a long way toward explaining why I have lived my life the way I have and how I found myself living in my car in the Chicago version of Winter Wonderland before finally checking into the Stress Disorder Treatment Unit run by the Veterans Administration in North Chicago. And why sometime later, I mustered the courage to request the official paperwork from the courts-martial of our drill instructors.

The paperwork . . . I am reminded of the cartoon of the guy sitting on the toilet with a seemingly oversize roll of toilet paper hanging on the wall beside him to emphasize the point in the caption: *No job is finished until the paperwork is done.* From paperwork came paper trail, and from paper trail, I, Hansel (Gretel left me years ago), found my way back to the cottage of memory.

The paperwork is a collection of manila folders, stapled stacks of printer paper, scrawled notes on loose-leaf pages, PDF files on my computer, Word documents, and copies of e-mails. But it's the PDF files—my God, the PDF files. Damn the PDF files. They showed up in the mail one day, a computer disc in a plastic case with a curt, perfunctory note from Navy JAG in response to my Freedom of Information Act request.

I insert a disc, and the CD-ROM spins. The hard drive starts scratching itself like a puppy with a skin allergy. My eighteen-year-old mind starts screaming, *What the fuck are you doing!?* I put my hands to my face, covering my mouth and nose, breathing shallowly, quietly, desperately . . . and then a window opens on the computer screen. PDF symbols appear. There are words below them. I hold my breath and read.

*Giles, Michael (Vol 1) redacted*

*Giles, Michael (Vol 2) redacted*

*Smith, William (Vol 1) redacted*

*Smith, William (Vol 2) redacted*

I am eighteen again and a Marine recruit. I am standing at attention, on line, in a squad bay on the third deck of the recruit training barracks for Fox Company, 2nd Recruit Training Battalion. I stand perfectly still, a line drawing of a Marine recruit at attention, unmoving, unbending, unyielding. My clothes, faintly damp, stick to my skin, but in standing so absolutely, perfectly still, I can feel the slightest, most deliciously cool breeze wafting so gently that something as airy as a breath would cause me to miss it. My reverie is interrupted by the sound of a door opening—the door to the drill instructor hut (office). I hear footsteps at the front of the squad bay, and I know my drill instructors are surely coming for me because I have their court-martial records. "Private Motherfucking Alphabet!"

I jerk myself upright out of the chair. I am back in the present, shaking. It takes two cigarettes, coffee, and a walk along the railroad tracks contemplating a call to my counselor before I get myself sorted out. I make my way back to the computer and look at the names again. *Giles. Smith.* Two out of three is not normally bad, but why there is no court-martial record for the senior drill instructor, Staff Sergeant Bellene, seems a rather curious detail. The cursor floats across the screen and settles over *Smith, William (Vol 1) redacted*. Double-click.

Boom. The first piece of good news is that Sergeant Smith appealed his court-martial as far up the chain as he could, and they all told him to go fuck himself. At least that's the way I read it, and I like the way I am reading it. The cold, hard fear that drove me from the room has been replaced by a warm sensation that starts in my gut and grows hotter as it spreads. Just as intimately as I know my fear and how to deal with it, so have I learned to deal with my hate, but there are times such as this when it's best to just let that puppy roll and experience it, and I do, for hours, through record after record after record. In unearthing the facts, I start unearthing my memory, long since crushed into little jagged pieces of glass that now begin to reflect hints of things I used to know, and things I did not know, and things I could not even imagine.

All three of my drill instructors went to battalion office hours (a formal hearing in front of the battalion commander), and all three were referred to General Courts-Martial (in front of a general). Giles went to trial and was busted to private, paid a big fine, and spent a year in Leavenworth before receiving a bad-conduct discharge.

Smith went to trial on fourteen counts, including his assault on me. He got the same sentence as Giles, except three months in the brig instead of a year in Leavenworth. In my mind, it should have been the other way around, since Smith was far more brutal and Giles was the only one to ever show any compassion. But Smith's lawyer worked his ass off, and I came away with a picture of Smith's poor parents trolling around Annapolis, begging friends to write letters for their poor, misguided son, the school bully whom everyone thought they were finally rid of when the Marines (thank God!) took him. But that's my picture.

And then there is Staff Sergeant Bellene, which may be the strangest part of this twisted tale, because it would be entirely proper to say "and then there is *no* Staff Sergeant Bellene." The only reference in any of the records to Bellene is a statement, apparently in his own writing since it is signed by him, refuting a molestation charge. Somewhere along the line, one recruit in 222 was forced to fondle another recruit from another platoon. Smith's and Bellene's names are all over the accusation. After that, Bellene seems to have vanished.

I dig deeper through Smith's records, through appeal after appeal after appeal, until finally I hit the mother lode. Three-quarters of the way through *(Vol 2) redacted*, I find the transcript from Smith's court-martial at Parris Island. There is the charge sheet. There is my name. History is voices mumbling in a courtroom, the sound of a fan whirring, the clearing of a throat, a gavel against a bench, a proceeding coming to order. On the historical time line, I know I should be halfway across Parris Island, in the Reassignment Platoon barracks, waiting for the set of orders that will send me over to Casual Company, where I will stand around in civvies all day with everyone else, smoking cigarettes, and waiting for the set of orders that will send me back home and far from the violent confrontation of Parris Island. Yet a question nags and pulls me back to the trial. My name is all over the place and Smith's lawyer refers to me by name in his closing argument, but my little assault charge is one of Smith's lesser offenses and I don't get it.

Some people take a stroll down memory lane. Others pack a lunch and take a long, strange, trip. My friends the Aussies (anyone who rappels out of helicopters head first is my friend) have a term they nabbed, I believe, from the Aboriginals: *walkabout*. The purpose of a walkabout is to go off for a nice, long hike until you run into yourself. I dig through that trial record, looking to run into myself along the way, and there I am . . . a photo of me staring back—large hazel eyes, blinking in disbelief, me at 165 pounds, still wet behind the ears and scared to death, but very much standing tall and pointing a finger during the trial at the accused, and it is not my index finger.

You see, one day the JAG had come through the barracks and taken statements from all of us in response to what we had witnessed or experienced at the hands of our drill instructors. Every statement is in the record. As I read each statement and each name, I begin to remember, smell, hear, and feel. Every other statement varies from a couple of sentences to a paragraph. Some are longer. Mine is a page and a half. Though the sharp, pointy letters of my high school cursive contrast with the rounded letters of my later years, there is no mistaking whose handwriting this is, and there is no mistaking the intention of my writing; I all but damn the man to hell.

The lawyer, also a JAG officer, had a statement he wanted all of us to sign. The statement read:

> We, the recruits of Platoon 222 wish to state our feelings toward Sergeant William E. SMITH as our Drill instructor. We have been informed that he has plead [sic] guilty to various orders violations and various specifications of hazing and assault and we firmly believe that Sergeant SMITH always had the best interest of the platoon in mind and that he never seriously harmed any member of this platoon. We humbly ask the Court to take our statement into consideration when arriving at a sentence. We all feel that our learning experience and knowledge gained from Ser-

*geant* SMITH *will make us better Marines. Our remembrance will be one of an excellent Marine in which we had the pleasure to serve.*

Now, Smith, Giles, and Bellene all in fact had seriously harmed people, but that did not stop the lawyer or the signatures. Epperly signed first, and the platoon lined up. The names are all there, as the defense lawyer will also note in his closing statement: Felmer (who had been choked), Hemric (who had been choked and slapped), Flagler (who had been punched in the stomach), Avery (who had caught a rifle butt in the gut), Boehlert (who nearly got his eye poked out by Smith), Issa (who had been choked), Mizzoni (who was denied sick call) . . . Nowaczyk . . . and so forth and so on.

I was standing by my rack while everyone signed the lawyer's statement. Out of forty recruits, not everyone had signed it. The lawyer looked around the room and then at me.

"You haven't signed yet."

"No, sir," I replied.

The others, who had signed, looked at me. So did those who had not.

"You're not going to sign this?" said the JAG.

I did not answer.

"What's your name?"

"Private Nowaczyk, sir."

"You're Nowaczyk?"

I cringe as I write this now, at the incredulous nature of the lawyer because I would not sign *his*—our—statement, at the disbelief that after everything we had been through, that *anyone* would sign it. But we did, and I did, too. I was a member of Platoon 222. I cringe at the peer pressure and the way I caved. When I signed, so did Lonnie Burchette (who had been hospitalized by these criminals).

I cringe again as I read the lawyer's closing argument, and the way he uses this piece of paper against us, specifically against me and Burchette: "Gentlemen, if you look at the names in relation to the charge sheet—Burchette, Nowaczyk, Roman—just look down the list, gentlemen, and you'll see the names . . ."

Trial lawyers are smart cookies, and when they bring their A game, watch out. But trial juries are pretty smart, too, and this one was not bad. Sure, they saw my signature on that page. They also saw the charge of Smith assaulting me and probably noted that he pleaded not guilty, though he pleaded guilty to more serious allegations such as choking people, denying sick calls, refusing head calls, and assault after assault after assault with fists, feet, and rifle butts, all ostensibly for our own good if you read the man's testimony. He "wasn't getting no backup." He was working for a slack senior. And although Smith had never been to war (he labored in the bookkeeping trade for the Corps), he did have a solid Vietnam combat vet in Giles at his side. To hear Smith tell it, Giles was just as ineffective as Bellene.

But the jury saw through that. When Smith says he put a finger up to a recruit's eye and said, "Eye, this is your eye," and if he touched it at all it was on the closed eyelid, and I say he jammed his thumb into the recruit's eye until he screamed, whereupon Smith said, "You ain't hurt," well, one of us is obviously lying.

In the end I was left all those years since to deal with a fear and mistrust of anyone in a position of authority. A fear so great that when our new drill instructor team raised his hand in the four-fingered manner of a drill instructor illustrating a point to a recruit, my mind inferred an attack, and I grabbed his wrist. I knew in that moment I would be thrown out of the Corps, and I did not care.

Soon after, I was standing in front of some captain who was yelling at me. He threw a roll of toilet paper, I think, at my head that crashed against the wall locker behind me, and I lost complete control. I stood there and cried like a little girl.

Next, I'm ordered to spend the night with a third-phase platoon. I am led there by someone, possibly the lieutenant. The third-phase platoon is gathered around the feet of their senior, who is sitting on a footlocker. They are spit-shining their boots, and when I am "introduced" to them and they are told I will be their guest for the evening, they all turn and grimace at me and growl. I believe that I have been brought to stay with them so they can beat me in my sleep. I start crying again. They laugh at me. I lie awake all night, certain of a blanket party, but it never happens.

A few days later I'm sent to Reassignment Platoon and to a psychologist. I'm to be discharged for "the good of the service," as if I have done something horrible to the Marines. I suppose, in a way, I have, for I said no to a drill instructor and put my grimy little recruit hands on him, and no amount of my thinking I was about to be beaten could change the facts. But what does it matter? I'm not exactly fighting to stay in.

So I settle into my role as a bench sitter in Reassignment Platoon. Horwitz, the guy with the messed-up ankle, is there, as are a couple of others from Platoon 222. More will join us in the following weeks. Horwitz and I become friends. He's a laid-back, thoughtful, easygoing guy with a sad smile and a sense of humor. We talk about everything: growing up, school, politics, and religion. I go with him to temple. He goes with me to mass. We drink Cokes and talk about life. We meet other Marines who are nothing like our drill instructors. Horwitz eventually collects his discharge and returns to Texas.

I wait my turn, sitting it out on a bench in Reassignment Platoon. I think about home and how my homecoming might be, having dropped out of high school to join the Marines and then not succeeding at this either. The letters from home confirm everyone loves me and can't wait to see me. There are phone calls of support, too. There's even an apprentice electrician job waiting for me if I want it.

And then one day a gunnery sergeant who runs the show walks into Reassignment Platoon, where all of us soon-to-be-ex-recruits sit on benches. He calls a private's name and throws a rifle card down on the table in front of him. "Get up here. There's nothing wrong with you. Sign this rifle card. You're going back into training."

The kid starts crying. The gunnery sergeant picks up the rifle card and shoves it in a pocket. "Ah, shut the hell up. I'm just kidding, ya big crybaby." And he walks out.

Something about this cruelty irks me and stirs up the old childhood memories. I am here to become a Marine, to be able to say I have accomplished something of significance. Parris Island was to have been my proving ground. Others in Platoon 222 have dutifully marched onward. Why can't I? And that's when I learn that if you truly want something, you'll never really stop wanting it.

Without requesting permission, I stand up and walk toward the desk where the duty sergeant is reading a book. "Yes, Nowis*check*?" he says, without looking up, and purposely mispronouncing my name. And this pisses me off, too.

"I want to talk to the gunny," I say. "I want to go back into training."

The sergeant, startled, drops his book and looks up. He's speechless.

Finally, he stands and walks toward the gunnery sergeant's office. I can feel every eye behind me burning holes in my back.

I have come to Parris Island to become a Marine. And no one is going to deny me, even if no one but me really gives a shit if I earn the title.

So I stand at attention, and wait.

# 25

# Passages

CAROL EVERETT ADAMS

I sat one morning in a crowded waiting room at the Olin E. Teague Veterans' Medical Center. This was the clinic vestibule, from which color-coded medical teams pulled patients through sets of double white doors. *Wait! Have you checked in at your team's window?* Cheerful men and women in scrubs of many colors came out from behind doors at random to call one name at a time, while everyone in the waiting room froze his chosen pastime for a fraction of a moment—his reading, his staring, his chat with a neighbor—hoping the name fitted. Only one lucky winner at a time, though. And then that fellow, whole or broken, would lunge forward off a wall or shuffle gracelessly to his feet with the aid of crutch or wife, and move toward the possibility of rebirth at the hands of the expectantly smiling nurse.

The rest of us watched each soldier—his lurch through the narrow rows, the chairs nailed down like pews and just as unforgiving. We couldn't help looking—some outright, some discreetly—at the number and size of each veteran's holes, passages left by bullets and bombs.

Each combat veteran in that room was the usual shape of a man (the older ones are more often men), his face intact, features arranged in a recognizable expression, his limbs present (mostly). But an actual gaping emptiness, a quietly dreadful disk of air, occupied each torso.

These types of holes usually begin as a slight depression rather than a true opening, and they start with a small circumference. Some of these little pits enter the crater stage rather quickly, the flesh underneath caving in but not giving way altogether for years. Most older soldiers have an enormous hole that goes all the way through—window without pane—so that you can see what's on the other side of the man, even put your whole arm through if you're so inclined. These are real spaces, cavities that begin at the moment the man is launched into warfare—

the shielding from death or the taking of life, either one a devastation. Either action begins the excavation.

Each soldier's hole is a fascinating study, as individual as a snowflake and just as blameless. Most veterans are abundantly perforated, and the biggest aggregate of holes you'll ever see in one place is at a busy veterans' hospital. I always recommend one that serves a sizable Army post if you like to look at extra-large holes with your morning coffee and your *USA Today*. Some holes are so small you'd need to stand right next to the guy to see one—a child could stick her pinky in it, as if she'd gotten to the page with Mummy's ring in *Pat the Bunny*. Others, especially lately, are so huge you really wonder how anyone could still be capable of walking around with such gigantic missing pieces.

On that particular day, however, in that particular hospital, with so many men freshly home from the desert (where they'd learned an essential spelling lesson—everyone wants two de*ss*erts, but no one wants to fight in the de*s*ert a second time), all the folks in the waiting room were so riddled with holes, I could see clear through to the other wall in spite of the crowd. Veterans' spouses almost always have chasms as extensive as the ones their partners carry, the children not so much—depends on age. All the holes belonging to families have ragged edges, but the holes of combat veterans are often smooth and clean around the circumference, because they are issued a multipack of circular cookie cutters at basic training—their instructors think it best that everyone be prepared for the inevitable.

Today, the younger wheeled and walking wounded were there to try to fill their holes—*silly Sisypheans*—but I knew the most they could hope for was a temporary plug. They could shove in medication, time in the chapel, a nurse's concern. These Army nurses understood, surely. Most of them had clean white bandages over their own holes.

My father sat beside me in a wheelchair, waiting for a paper to sign. His newest holes were the medical kind—small, internal, and growing rapidly. The kind that show up in doctors' pictures. But the aperture he'd had for more than forty years was so large we'd stopped seeing the rest of him long ago. He'd folded himself origami style into his own gaping absence, become one with it. There, or not there—it didn't matter anymore. Blank, white paper, changing in the light depending on how you held it in your hands at a given moment. Look at him, look through him, there in the rolling chair. I could see all the men behind him clearly enough, lined up for their turn to sign a paper, too.

My uncles tell me that my father had some slight fissures even before the Vietnam "military engagement." These small cracks were formed by lack of food and poverty of attention. He tried to pour into them some football fame, first on a smaller field, then a larger one, until his knee permanently tackled him. He tried to fill his holes with stolen, siphoned gas, so he could race Mustangs with his friends. He used to leave us kids wide-eyed with tales of the taste of gasoline surprising his mouth at the end of a hose.

He tried to fill himself up with mayonnaise sandwiches on Wonder Bread, but that was not feast enough, so he and his best buddy hi-hoed off to the jungle. Patriotism! Adventure! Exotic locale! Like a really fucked-up boat ride where the jokes fall flat and the robotic animals eat you.

His friend caught an audio-animatronic bullet on their very first day, and, to their eternal surprise, actual blood appeared. His friend's wound hole came so quickly that his real vacancy never had time to form, and that made him a kind of fortunate son.

My father only ever told me one story about his time in Asia—the rest of it was small bits I had to piece together from my mother, my uncles, his doctors, or, near the end, his own almost incoherent memory mutterings. But that one story . . . oh, that was the truest of them all. That story included the one great shining moment, the balance upon which the entire seesaw shifted to one side with a hard thump. Yes, that story was a pleasure for him to tell, and retell, the words so well rehearsed I learned to notice any accidental slip from script.

Here's how it goes: He was walking along one day, so slowly, so quietly, first in line, like he'd won a place in the teacher's heart. He was worried about punji pits, which are shallow holes camouflaged and lined with stakes. Suddenly, he heard a man's voice from above, saying, "Stop now! There's a land mine in front of you!" He stopped, of course, even though he didn't know who'd said it. The whole line had to stop, too. He looked carefully, and, sure enough, a Bouncing Betty was buried right there in front of his feet. But no person was ahead, around, or above him. He realized that God had sent an angel to tell him to stop on that path, so that he would live instead of die, and so he accepted Jesus Christ into his heart to be his personal Lord and Savior.

The interesting thing about Jesus Christ the personal Lord and Savior is that he does do an amazing job of temporarily filling up a Vietnam veteran's largest abyss—the hole that chews him out after the sun goes down every night, that reprimands with, "Why did you live, when others died?" and "What did you do to your enemies so that you would survive?" The hole with so loud a rebuke that if a land mine didn't get him, his own trigger finger would have to sooner or later.

My father spent the rest of his able-bodied days telling us all about Jesus's doctoring skills. I listened closely when I was young. I covered my ears as I grew older, but I could have told the youngest soldiers in the waiting room that day that if they limped on down to the chaplain's office instead of seeing the Green Team doctors, their minds and bodies would probably last much longer than the medics could predict.

But nothing in heaven or on earth can ever permanently fill the holes that a year in Vietnam digs and scrapes out of a person one forkful at a time. Jesus kept his thumb in the hole in my father's wall for more than twenty years before that homemade dam began to weaken where the rotten air pressed against it and light started spewing from the cracks. The Savior stopped saving, and who can fairly blame him? He's had an awful lot of holes to fill these past few decades.

Before the rest of my father's mind began leaking out of the ever-widening gaps, he did try to repair some of the damage himself. Since his youth had raced away with the last car at the antique auto show, he gave up those memories of stealing gasoline and, instead, tried to patch his hole with the Bible, with other Jesus-plugged people, with handwritten and highlighted scripture verses on index cards, and with NavPress printed pamphlets such as *How to Get Results through Prayer* and *How to Know the Will of God* and *Claiming the Promise*. And, knowing for himself the power of the cross to stop the carnage, he tried frantically to push Jesus into the holes he encountered in fellow veterans, shoveling prayer into other men as fast as he could keep up.

But the waiting room refilled daily and had such capacity, such long halls, and always room for more. The soldiers rolled down like justice, like waters, like the righteousness of an everlasting stream, flowing like the blood of the Savior in his last moments, and every day more high tides and fewer low ones, as if the end times would soon be upon us, everyone with holes washed clean by the rapids of the va system, bones broken and rebroken on every jutting rock of doctors, new wounds ripped into being with each call over the intercom.

*Next, please.*

It's our turn.

This last hole of my father's, this new one, was not repairable, not even by Jesus, I was told. And so I explained, as best I could, to a man who now remembered only fast cars and the dark tunnels they could race through. And so we all signed the papers.

Once at home he did not want to leave his last bed for some reason, though Jesus was waiting. The nighttime hospice nurse, a large, friendly man with the most clean, tidy, and squared-away hole I'd ever looked through, centered neatly over his left pocket, told us that our father maybe had one more problem to resolve, one more question to ask, or one more person to see, and possibly that was why he wouldn't drive away just yet. The nurse also told us to lift the bedroom window a crack, because the spirit needed an opening through which to leave.

So, on that last night, I sat beside him—to listen, to answer, if I could. And I waited while he trudged the narrow and highly traveled routes, where opposing forces had concentrated their mud-ball mines, their tin-can grenades, their punji pits.

Finally, he asked the central question of his life—the fulcrum, the thesis statement, the turn of the sonnet, the edge of the deepest and widest chasm:

"Did he just die in combat?"

Yes, Dad, he did. You did. They all did.

We all did.

And the little that was left of his spirit, rent and torn, left through the last passage.

# 26

# Letter to a Drowning Sailor

RONALD JACKSON

Father, you died in 1980 at fifty-nine, pancreatic cancer. That was the year the Phillies won their first World Series, a team you tried out for, thick-muscled slugger that you were. I now have you by seven years, become more your elder each year, hope I am good and whole enough at some point to fully embrace you as my child-father.

*Dementia praecox*, it says, the diagnosis on the U.S. Navy medical records released by the Veterans Administration to your five children. Schizophrenia. Later the doctors called it bipolar. PTSD has to be in the mix, given your long hours of shelling by the Japanese in World War II, as you dripped sheets of sweat in the steamy bowels of your ship. As the bombs shook the ship and rattled your bones. You kept the turbines pulsing in that hellhole and then broke down yourself when it was all over. The vessel stayed afloat, and you were sent home. But that Pacific drowning field never did release you.

You came home to your wife long enough to make five kids, and then you hightailed it before the youngest was of school age. What was your life like those years you retreated to the Wild West, prospecting, drifting, retreating from your war, your fanatical religious upbringing, and other specters unknown to me? While we, left behind, watched, smelled, felt our mother's cancer take her slowly and listened to her call out "Take me, Jesus!" in the night? While we were shuffled off to aunts and uncles?

Your letter in the VA records—the one where you describe your sortie as a fighter pilot over Germany—that read loonier than PTSD. I recall you had taken private flying lessons at some point, but I don't need to be a diagnostician to flinch at the leap of fantasy in that letter, offered so casually as the truth.

Over the years I've wondered, what *was* the source of your problems? Your upbringing? Great-Grandma Lucy Willhoit and Grandmother Jasmine marched arm-in-arm with Carrie Nation and saw visions in the clouds as they knelt in the dirt streets of Dodge City and other Kansas towns, awaiting God's commands. "Murphy's Saloon," came one message in the sky, the history books tell me, and that army of battle-axes marched into poor Mr. Murphy's establishment and hatcheted the hooch right off his shelves. Growing up in that family, you had to know many times how Mr. Murphy felt.

Another constant speculation: you were a midwesterner who never really cared for anything east of the Mississippi and had great difficulties living in the deeply ethnic, closed-in neighborhoods of Philadelphia. Your wife was kind and loving. But so many in her extended family were mysteries to you. Some were kind, but many were dark-thinking eastern Europeans, often showing little tolerance for your condition or behavior. I have no trouble understanding that part.

I imagine it was exotic at first, like docking in a foreign port. You were a sailor out of the Philadelphia Navy Yard, hungry for civilian food when you weren't out on maneuvers, getting ready to take on the Third Reich and the Imperial Navy. You first met our mother at the famous Fisher's Seafood Restaurant in 1939. She had to be the prettiest waitress there. I am certain you two had a storybook time flitting about town, you in your Dixie-cup hat and Cracker Jack uniform and Mom dressed to the nines.

After the war? Seems you never did blend in with the Old World ways of our family and felt isolated almost daily. You left often just to breathe the clean air out West, open your eyes to the light, clear your head, and get back to someplace that made sense.

Good riddance was the common sentiment in the family. But no boy wants to lose a father, no matter how ill-suited to the task, no matter how abusive. I remember mainly the beatings—few tender, happy, or simply idle father-son moments. You applied the belt like John Henry hefting his sledge, raining down on a spike. One! Two! Three! When you got tired of numbers, you used words rich with rage to pace the pelting. Remember that? One cry for each lash: *You! Sunuva! Bitch!* I can still see the sharp leather of your belt whip high across your dark crew cut and flash past your blue eyes. And I swear I can smell the belt, acrid as snake venom, pouring down from the needle fangs of your fury.

While you were about your business, I must have felt this in some deep recess of my soul: *This is what bad is like, and surely I am bad. Else why the beating?* Usually, at some late moment, I sang, "I'm sorry!" An incantation to stop the rain. But I didn't mean it. What I meant is: *Fuck you, Daddy-o. I won't cry; you will not see the hurt.*

Afterward, when the squall subsided, you were off somewhere, and I lay in my sagging heart of darkness, licked my hot wounds, sloshed through the gloom that pooled at our place like runoff, biding my time, waiting for the next storm to strike.

So in so many ways, it was good to see you go.

Then out of the blue, 1966. There you were, in a hospital coffee shop at Keesler Air Base, Mississippi, on the sunny Gulf Coast. I was sent on a peculiar errand by my supervising sergeant from the hospital kitchen where I worked and waited for my training to begin. "Airman, I need you to go to the canteen for cigarettes," he said. As I entered you stood, handsome as ever, that thin-lipped smile, leaning heavily against the post counter, a Styrofoam coffee steaming at your elbow. Not as if you were holding up the room so I could make it in and out safely. Fat chance. You stood as if to say, *Here I am. Isn't it great? It's up to you, son. . .* Or maybe, *Hey, let's let bygones be bygones.* A man stood behind you with a stack of stripes and rockers on his sleeve. You two eyed me up and down in tandem.

How do you show up like God's gift, after eight years of *gone for good, who needs you anyway, what happened, where were you?* I hadn't thought of you. I'd swept you under the rug. So I passed you by, numbed and stiffened by the poison dart of recognition, didn't know how to interpret that scene. I walked to the sundries counter, asked for the Marlboros, and high-tailed it out of that place and back to kitchen duty. The man with the stripes, the guy standing next to you in the canteen, came to me as I was cleaning an oven, asked my name, what I did, how long I'd been there. Was he your chaperone onto the base? And how did you find out I was there?

Father, I got my war too, a quarter century after yours, supporting the fighting in Vietnam from the Philippines and Thailand, with stops at Da Nang Air Base. I never got as close to the action as you did. But I did my job. Brought home a Filipina woman and, like you, could not make it work. She died of cancer before her time, too. But two fine children came out of that marriage—children I love and have supported.

I want to go back those forty-six years to that canteen and march up to you, grab you by the collar, be damned if I care how big you always were to me, grab you and shake you, till something jiggles loose in your brain and you become the man I needed, wanted, all the years you were there-not-there, a boogeyman, the years you were gone for good, all the days when I needed just a word, the simplest phrase, like *Nice!* or *Let's go!* or *Hey, look at this!* All the days since, when I had to do my job and yours too, both of us failing far too often. Over the years I looked for the few good men around in my life, men who were willing to stand tall, walk away from the post counter, come right up to me, show me a son's photo, a letter from home, a new key chain, anything, and say, hey, look at this.

Could I grab you by the collar and shake you? You spun the illusion that you were larger than life. My hands do not wrap around a baseball bat powerfully enough to smack a ball far over a distant fence. My hands are not the work tools you used to split a log, dig a trench, build a chicken coop in that half-finished house we lived in. My hands are not your threatening paddles raised in air as if expecting a transgression at any moment.

So what am I left with?

My own hands, to start with. I have come to make friends with them. The proportions are just right, and I would not have it different. My nails have a healthy shine. My knuckles, gentle undulations—not the crusty knobs of your tree-trunk fingers. The veins on the backs of my hands pulse out well enough. My palms are cleanly lined and able to dribble a basketball with a sure grip, feel the energy of the ball rebounding from the ground, delicate in my palm, as if I have the world in my hand and I can carry it where I like. My fingers are deft from years of dancing over guitar strings with some delicacy and feeling.

The ring from your hand lies in a silk purse in my nightstand drawer. Every once in a while I try it on, slide it on my finger, twirl it about, marvel at its girth and looseness—I could slip some folding money into the space between finger and ring. Then I put my own ring on and smile. You could not wear it.

Again, what am I left with, old man?

For one thing, your absence had another side to it. With you gone I inherited some of my mother's gentler nature, and that has saved me so many times in moments of frustration and rage. For another, I have not abandoned my own children, though I have not always been the father I have meant to be.

What am I really left with today, Father?

Your son from your second marriage—my half brother—recently contacted me and told me something I do not remember ever hearing from you. He said you spoke of us. He said you loved us. He said you were a troubled man, an image that has visited me more frequently in recent years, slowly taking its place alongside the schizophrenia, the hurt, and the damage. What if the medications you got later in life had been available in your years with us? What if you had received full disability from the government in 1945, instead of 1962, after a long and hard fight (which tells me you had something in you—you weren't a total quitter)? It's almost painful to imagine a loving father of sorts, but from time to time I do it anyway, part of my healing, I am sure.

So yes, troubled. We have that in common. We battled our way through two wars and the aftermaths: you in your dark world below the surface of that ocean, me swimming stronger every year.

# 27

# The Intimate

DONALD MORRILL

On my right hand I wear my father's class ring, Omaha Central High, 1943. He received his draft notice two weeks before graduation, so the planned celebratory trip to exotic California was never to be taken, and like many of his generation, he found himself sent on another journey altogether. The ring came into my possession after his death in 1995, a consoling surprise since I hadn't known of it. I admired its modest elegance. On its thin, almost feminine band, four Art Deco platforms mount to a black, leafy shield bearing the letter *C*, the whole structure flanked on each side by the year now more than a little worn away. Here perhaps was the grandeur once associated with a high school diploma, a flourish allowed after a Depression-era childhood. I wear it to remind me of a young man I could never know, that recruit in basic training whom the Pepsi-Cola company allowed to record a message home on a wax 78 now lost to heat and cracks and final misplacement. "Hi, Mom! Hi, Dad!" he began. I know this for sure because we, his children, made fun of that reedy, callow voice when we played the disc now and then, callow adolescents ourselves. He had nothing to say, really, like all the other kids making those records, and there is no loss in its vanishing— except that voice. On the flip side he played the piano and sang a ballad, probably a recent hit. No one remembers which one.

He was Navy Air Corps, a radioman on a submarine killer, stationed first in Panama and then Brazil. They flew up and down the coast, searching for Nazi vessels out to harass merchant shipping in the region or coming to oil in Argentina. It was long hours in the air, with multiple crews trading off, napping in hammocks on board . . . and occasional machine-gunning of sharks out of boredom. He almost never reminisced about those years. So only a few highlights: his gunnery instructor had been the actor Robert Stack; he lost his virginity with a whore at the Mayflower Hotel in Panama City; he nearly crashed once, thanks to a drunken pilot.

He never traveled like that again. In a memoir called *A Stranger's Neighborhood*, I've written of him and his time there—partly out of what I learned after his death. While in the service, he had a friend, a Brazilian pilot, Renato:

> We also discovered six photographs of Renato the matchmaking Brazilian, as well as two brief aerograms and a postcard from him. Why Dad had separated these items from the other mementos in his Navy chest immured in the attic no one knows. Dated from November 1944 to December 1946, they testify to a relationship of greater duration than Dad's brief remembrances had suggested to me. The photographs bear dates different from each other and from the aerograms, perhaps accompanied by other letters now lost.
>
> In the aerograms, Renato's English—easily broken—displays an unremarkable propriety, bounteous with good wishes for Dad's mother and sisters, or calls for quicker replies and longer letters. Yet several of the typed inscriptions on the backs of the photos give pause. "Ren" stands barechested and square-shouldered on the roof of a house: *At Yacht Club. I am not so fat as this photo is showing.* He sits in the cockpit of his single engine wing-over: *Would you like to fly with me?* He smiles suavely, a Latin Gene Kelly in Navy whites: *I like coffee / I like milk / I like you / Do you like me?*
>
> These communications invite me to peer more deeply into other, formerly ordinary passages, such as: *I should like very much to shake your hand, as you are the greatest friend of mine. I am very sorry I was unable to say goodby as I wanted very much to do, but I suppose that's the way things must be at present. It seems we never did get to go swimming or do anything that I would like to have done. . . .*
>
> Why—at the end of World War II—does Ren begin one letter with warm wishes in faulty German? In this same communication—the last in this group—he writes: *I was glad to hear that you are free to make your own choice about a good girl to get married with, if I were you I would choose a beautiful blonde with green or blue eyes, what's your type?* Yet he concludes, as always, with eager wishes to see Dad again and: *Why don't you come down to Brazil now that you are a civilian, and you'll see that everything is quite different.*

This ring also reminds me that thirty years after my father's conscription, I graduated from high school and America was still fighting wars. In 1973 the conflict in Vietnam was winding down at last and impressment suspended. But the draft lottery was still held. My birth date, July 24, was the thirteenth drawn. Perhaps this "near miss" had seemed even less momentous since I'd applied for conscientious objector status and was granted a partial (or so it seems to me now, as I have no record of it). My letter justifying my application displayed bad faith, mostly. I professed a rectitude beyond my understanding, a religious conviction long abandoned. Not that there wasn't good reason—given the lies of the Pentagon and Nixon's machinations—to believe loyal opposition was the more patriotic stance. Quite simply, I was afraid of dying in a rice paddy—wasn't everyone?—and it was no longer a society in which a rich son (even if I had been such a thing) could personally hire another, less fortunate, to serve in his stead. My surmise was as conventional and of its moment as the assumption behind the contemporary variation of *dolce et decorum est pro patria mori*: "America: Love or leave it."

I never told my parents about the CO application, though my mother knew I feared, and perhaps she feared, as well. I recall crying to her in my bedroom at thirteen or fourteen (the last real little-boy breakdown) after seeing particularly visceral news footage of burned bodies. There was also the mental nausea as I sat over the map of Vietnam yet again appearing in the *Des Moines Sunday Register*—the North that hideous shade of pink, the South that green. These instances, these introductions, were perhaps analogous to my father's tenth grade teacher telling her class that Hitler must be stopped, so all the boys present would one day be fighting in Europe. You can imagine the peering around the room then, around that speech, all straining their wonder like those of us later wearing an MIA bracelet, the fashion item of 1970, nonplussed ultimately by the unstoried name embossed on it, alone somehow with that.

Selfish, untested, ambitious, vague, I'd also learned from the zeitgeist to give my father's apparent dreams and their results a fine fuck you; who couldn't do better than that life, right? In any case, long before my draft number came up, my patriotic parents had turned dove, unable finally to understand the enemy and "our goals over there" with the clarity allowed them decades earlier.

At one point I began this essay with the conviction *There's hardly a thing more alien to me than the military.* But alien is only partially the case—alien but intimate, familiar but unrecognized. My deep prejudice against the powers that control the military, perhaps more than any marking my generation, is borne of a pity and rage at what soldiering can exact from those given to its bond; it seethes at the manipulators of honor and loyalty, who elide the distinction between those who serve and those who compel service, in order to evade judgment; it remains ever wary of the motives, too frequently cynical, for which armed forces have always been a convenient instrument—political ends and, yes, economic interests all too inevitably, wretchedly, shrewdly entwined with those of every citizen . . . myself included.

As children we played war, of course, and killed and died in the backyard. But just a few doors down, Jack Huxford's pink-striped prosthetic leg—courtesy of the Korean conflict—stood propped with its leather straps in the corner of his bedroom, a still-life in late-afternoon sunlight as I passed with his son Lenny, hurrying as though it might catch me glancing at it. Later, another childhood friend, Jim, the son of a Marine drill instructor, purveyed seductive military lore to our late preteen circle. He and two others—one of them sickly and eager to belong—thus alluded daily to the feats of Chesty Puller, super-jarhead. They called each other "gyrenes" and took dares from one another and sung out to the day they would go for basic at Camp Pendleton (where on TV Gomer Pyle seemed forever stationed without concern about deployment to Southeast Asia). We spent summer days leafing through Marine yearbooks, the photographs there of Jim's father inspecting rifle barrels amid rigid shoulders. He'd served sixteen years. (Why not twenty, I wonder now, a full career? Busted out?) We revered his smoking Camel straights and imitated that in our clubhouse. He poured concrete for a living, a man with fading bluebirds tattooed on his chest, compact but powerfully restrained and somehow ancient, though he couldn't have been more than thirty-six or -seven. When he spoke his son jumped, and you were glad you were not his son. Before I lost track of them completely, Jim and the stronger of the other boys did indeed enlist in the Marines, both becoming platoon honor men, the latter also part of Nixon's guard at Camp David.

These days I think of another high school friend, one of the clique of smart kids whom I sought out and hung around with each morning in the library, under the flag, before first period. Who would have guessed she'd grow up to be a mother of Ithaca, giving a child to war in Troy. This time the far-off land was Afghanistan. There she is, with her notable tresses in 1973, and her thick glasses, her dry wit, her debate notes on index cards. Her unimagined son will become a West Point graduate, a captain, one day killed with a younger man under his command by a roadside bomb.

I haven't seen her in years, though mutual friends keep in touch. I have no children and don't presume to imagine her grief. But the young captain's image, there on the commemorative website—he has her cheeks, her smile. That girl.

"The last full measure of devotion," Lincoln called it at Gettysburg.

There is a keening through the ages that is mostly silence. Hear it in the photograph of the one in uniform, never to be put away, that one in living rooms around the world?

At the university where I work, a colleague—a scientist liked for his dark, engaging humor—brings that silence, that intimate, closer to me as he thanks nursing graduates for the crucial work they will do. Briefly, almost reluctantly, he tells them of his dire condition forty years ago, a POW just released from the "Hanoi Hilton"—acute pneumonia, broken orbital bone, anemia . . . and two-thirds his normal weight.

"Doctors get you well, but nurses keep you alive."

We shake hands afterward, as usual, but this time I feel my father's ring in the midst of it. My ring now, too, and not.

At the Buddhist temple here in Tampa, on Palm River Road, a handful of baby-boomer vets serve Sunday lunch, some speaking Thai, some Vietnamese learned from their wives. Beside the Hyde Park vfw Post, a few blocks from the porch where I write these sentences, a bbo smoker billows; the windows of the recently refurbished bar there are extra-small as if obliging a privacy . . . And this past month it was revealed the Army only last year, in 2012, began testing body armor designed for women, nine years after the first combat death of a female U.S. service member in Iraq.

My father's single ongoing contact with his Navy days appears to have been an annual Christmas card and letter to one Archie Mackinnon, in Wisconsin.

About Renato: "Your dad didn't say much about him," Mom replied, when I asked about the relationship. "Only that he helped Renato's sisters with their English, and they were a very prominent family. And after your dad came home from the service, Renato sent him a kind of love letter, and your dad didn't answer it. He didn't want no part of that."

Though that scandalous letter is missing, my brothers Greg and Mike are convinced that something substantial, most likely amorous, occurred between these two men, and it may very well have. They believe that even if Dad and Renato never touched, Dad encountered powerful desires that he suppressed at great cost over a lifetime.

"The night the war started," my father said (meaning America's entry into the conflict), the radio news bulletin from Pearl Harbor interrupted, "I Don't Want to Set the World on Fire," by the Ink Spots, at the Reeds Ice Cream shop where he worked part-time. *I don't want to set the world on fire. I just want to start a flame in your heart.* He was alone. So he locked up and walked home along the cold streets, among the suddenly bright and anxious houses, to see what next. Sixteen years old—he who would one day order for his epitaph the inscription *World War II.*

# Dependent

REBECCA MCCLANAHAN

In one of my earliest memories my mother is standing on an unpacked crate beneath the ceiling of a Quonset hut. Barefoot, she balances like a circus performer, testing her weight gingerly as she leans toward the curved wall, trying to hang a picture of waves. This is the only image in my head that hints at any desperation my mother might have felt in her long career as a military wife. If hers was a war against rootlessness and loneliness, she fought it privately, in small physical skirmishes. She made a home from whatever was given. If the kitchen in our new quarters had a window, she'd size it up as we walked through the empty rooms. The next morning I'd wake to find she'd stitched and hung yellow curtains, creating an illusion of sunlight that tinted the linoleum and bounced off the toaster she'd polished with her sleeve.

My father was like her in this way; he did what he could to shield us from the difficulties of military life. Because he was a Marine we could not accompany him on overseas assignments, some of which lasted fifteen months. And because he was an officer we were able to stay in one place longer than the families of enlisted men. Except for a few months in temporary quarters—the Quonset hut, an apartment building, the officers' guest suite—we lived in sturdy houses within driving distance of the base. As we approached the gate the uniformed guard would glance at the sticker on the windshield of our station wagon, click his heels together, and salute.

We children would salute back. If our father was present, he'd reprimand us, reminding us that a military salute was not to be taken lightly. Once out of our father's sight, we took it lightly, as we took lightly everything related to the military. Cushioned from hardships, we saw the base as one privilege after another—free swimming, dime movies, twenty-five-cent bowling and miniature golf, discount toys at the PX, cheap groceries (unlike our neighbors with their civilian pints of ice cream, we never had less than a gallon in our freezer.) The only privilege we did not welcome was free medical care, which seemed to encourage our mother to splurge on tetanus shots and throat cultures.

I was vaguely aware that our sense of privilege stemmed from the fact that our father was an officer, and occasionally I caught glimpses of what my life would have been like had my father been, say, a corporal instead of a major—and later, a lieutenant colonel. On our way to the base swimming pool I counted the stucco duplexes surrounded by dirt yards where khakis and diapers flapped on makeshift lines. Children's faces were plugged to the front window, hostages along with their carless mothers, while we whipped by in our blue station wagon, creating dust swirls that must have settled minutes later on their wet laundry. Turn another page in the story, take the next bend in the road, and it was time to leave again—the luggage carrier packed to the gills, the U-Haul trailing. Yet no matter how many times we moved, how many friends and towns we left behind, there was always a passel of warm bodies to fill the station wagon and the empty new house. We were our own portable town; my siblings were my constant allies. Of course, we fought (the veins in my brother's forehead pulsing as he lunged toward me), but when the dust settled and the blood cooled, peace was always restored. The more heated the battle, the more dramatic the truce that followed. We knew better than to turn on each other permanently, for soon we'd be moving to a new town where strangers waited at the bottom of the U-Haul ramp. In the long run we were all we had. Because we had each other, we never felt alone.

And never homeless, for in the distance was our grandparents' farm where we returned every summer. To the same feather beds, the haymow with the rotting floorboards, the attic crammed with outgrown clothing, the worn path to the creek. We were hybrids—half Marine, half farmer—and whenever we grew tired of packing and unpacking, we knew the farm would be there. Old as dirt, the saying goes. The land would be waiting for us. I was born a Marine brat and spent my childhood in service, but until my twenty-first year my life had been lined with escape hatches. Except for one brief remembrance—Mother hanging a picture of waves—nothing prepared me for my stint as a military wife.

I'd been married less than a year, and everything that could have gone wrong had. Pete's parents had divorced, and his father had been hospitalized with severe bleeding ulcers. When Pete quit two consecutive jobs because he refused to take orders from supervisors, I doubled up on my hours at the printing shop and continued full-time studies at the university. A brilliant linguist, Pete had been studying for a degree in German, but at the height of the Vietnam War, his student deferment was canceled. A few weeks later he received his draft lottery number. It was a low number, which almost guaranteed that he would be drafted. And almost all draftees were sent to the front lines. If he joined the Army, rather than wait to be drafted, he might avoid an infantry assignment. Then again, he might not. I tried to comfort him, but with each step I took toward him, he took two steps away. Being a wife, I'd come to believe, was not something I was good at. Pete's fingernails were chewed to the quick, and the tic on the side of his face had intensified, the spasms more frequent than ever. The draft was breathing outside our door, and we were holed up behind it. I felt helpless, under siege from without and within.

Then, just as the draft was about to break down the door, Pete uncovered a window. Following a tip from a fellow German student, he took a qualifying exam and won a coveted slot at the Army's language institute, four hundred miles up the California coast. The timing, it seemed, could not have been better. It would take Pete two months to finish basic training and three more months to complete the introductory language course. Then he'd send for me. In the meantime, if I moved in with my parents, I could quit my job at the print shop and finish my literature degree. I told myself that this turn of events would also be good for Pete: he could escape Vietnam while being paid to study languages. My father had never been fond of Pete, but as soon as Pete joined the Army, my father's feelings seemed to soften, and for one brief moment I imagined my husband and father joining forces, their arms linked, rocking me between them as in a child's game. The day Pete left for boot camp, I stored our belongings and moved back to my parents' home—my father had recently retired from the Marines. Jennifer and Tom had left for marriage and college long before, and Claudia and Rick, having claimed the empty bedrooms for their own, were not about to relinquish their privacy. I moved in with my youngest sister, Lana, who had recently turned nine.

Several times over the first few weeks I looked up from the book I was studying to see a little girl standing beside Lana in the doorway, staring at me silently. Each time it was a different little girl. Later I learned that Lana was charging her friends a quarter to see the bride who was now her roommate. She'd told them that my husband had been killed in the war, and did they want to see the veil?

Every night as I climbed into our shared double bed, I felt a great relief. Surrounded by Lana's stuffed animals and the nursery rhyme comforter, I was rocked backward into another time. I slept longer and deeper than I'd slept since I'd left my parents' home. And waking to the clatter and bang of breakfast, my mother working in the kitchen, was a pleasure so exquisite I couldn't imagine why I'd ever left. These feelings worried me. I had a husband. Shouldn't I be missing him?

I wondered if my mother had ever felt this way. When my father was overseas she stayed busy every daylight hour; I never saw her cry. But on nights when insomnia claimed her, I'd wake to the sounds of table legs scraping across the wooden floor, casters squeaking as the sofa was rolled to one spot and then another, the electric mixer whirring, the rat-a-tat-tat of the Singer accelerating to unsafe speeds. Then the pause. The quiet. The click of the presser foot being lifted and, in the space between seams, fragments of a top-ten song from the radio. I'd lie in the dark, wondering if they were playing American songs where my father was—in Japan or Korea or Hawaii or Vietnam. For years I counted the distances between my parents in time zones I traced in the Rand McNally atlas.

Their lives, it seemed, ran smoothly on separate, parallel tracks. The moment my father returned, the tracks converged, the double seam healed, and only the white strip on his arm, the place where his Japanese watch had lain, recorded the lost time.

Reunited, their bodies made a spoon curve on the sofa—my mother in a pink housedress with covered snaps, my father behind her with his hand cupped over her waist. I thought all married people acted that way. It did not occur to me until many years later that their union was not typical, that it lacked the quality of dailiness that dulls the shine on marriages where partners eat and work together and sleep beside each other every night. The Marine Corps built a wall of time and distance, a wall my parents were forced to scale again and again to reach each other.

Perhaps that's why their marriage wore so well and why they had so many children. My aunt tells of the day, forty-five years ago, when my mother announced she was pregnant again. The child would be her fifth. The fourth, Claudia, was nursing at my mother's breast. My aunt's reaction to the news was, "How could you let it happen again?" My mother simply shrugged her shoulders and laughed: "I'm just always so happy to see him."

Weeks grew to months. I began to miss the sputter of Pete's motorcycle in the driveway, the damp fossil his feet left on the bathroom rug. I missed his blue eyes, his rough freckled hands, and his smell, an odd mixture of motorcycle oil, cigarettes, and English Leather. Surprised by the force of my longing, I wondered if Pete was missing me, too. Maybe the Army was what we'd needed all along. The day Pete called to say our apartment was ready, I rented a U-Haul van. My father and Rick loaded the furniture; in the cab I piled clothes, boxes of books, my grandmother's wedding-ring quilt, my framed diploma in English literature, and my mother's portable Singer. Early the next morning I was on my way, driving the first leg of the four-hundred-mile journey up the California coastline. How many times through how many years had my mother made a journey like this while my father waited for her in their new quarters hundreds of miles away? On the radio Roberta Flack was singing "The First Time Ever I Saw Your Face." Sun glinted off the waves. With each tick of the odometer, the difficulties of the past year receded like the images in my rearview mirror. Suspended on the road between my parents and my husband, with the ocean to my left and the sun overhead, I felt hopeful. A fresh start in a new place. Things were going to be better.

But the man who met me at the base welcome station was not the man I had married. His eyes were gray, not blue. He was thinner. He had poked an extra hole in his belt to cinch the trousers around his waist, and the fabric puckered above his buttocks and thighs. When I ran to hug him, my legs weak from the ten-hour drive, his kiss was hurried and dry. He smelled of beer and an unfamiliar brand of cigarettes. The tic was alive on his cheek. When we got to our quarters, we made love on a pallet spread on the living-room floor, but the lovemaking was as hurried as his kiss had been, and as dry.

Military dependents is what they were called, the wives and children living beside us, below us, and on top of us, in apartments identical to our own. Theirs was another world, one I'd never seen from the inside, the underground world of the enlisted. The officers' wives I'd known throughout childhood had been anything but dependent. With their husbands gone for months, sometimes years at a time, these women not only shopped, cooked, cleaned, and sewed, but balanced checkbooks, mowed lawns, made house and car repairs, and negotiated all necessary public business. If their responsibilities were doubled, so were their freedoms. They came and went as they pleased, subservient only to their own needs and the needs of their children. When my father was overseas, our household ran on a different clock. We stayed up later, slept later, played more games, ate more child-friendly foods—beanie weenies, macaroni and cheese, fish sticks, Frito loaf, and my favorite, a dish I named Train Wreck, a Sunday-night treat in which the week's leftovers collided in one large iron skillet, topped with Tabasco sauce and sopped up with white Wonder Bread.

And over it all my mother presided. I never doubted her authority or her ability to keep us safe and happy. She moved easily through the days and nights with a grace I associated with her mother. Poor farmers are another breed of independent women. Partnered by necessity, they work as equals beside their husbands in field, garden, and pasture. Both my grandmothers, trained in self-sufficiency, not only managed the indoor chores expected of farm wives (stoking kitchen fires, frying chickens, making sausage) but also chopped the wood that made those fires possible, wielded saw and hammer to build chicken coops, repaired the fences that encircled the hogs waiting to be slaughtered. This was my heritage, a legacy of independence passed from grandmother to mother to daughter.

But there were no pastures on this Army base, no squads of officers' wives gathering at the pool or golf course. The young military wives who surrounded me were trapped without cars, without jobs, with two or three preschool children crammed into a two-bedroom apartment, their only escape Wednesday-night bingo or a rerun at the base theater. Or morning classes in the damp, windowless basement they called the Craft House, where they painted ceramic Santas, Virgin Marys, pumpkins, and elves while their children scuffled on a rug at the child care center, overseen by women with bad teeth who stared at the television bolted high to the wall.

Despite what my ID card proclaimed, my laminated face and name stamped with the word *dependent*, I was determined never to become one of those quietly nervous women I saw in the Laundromat of the apartment complex. I renewed my prescription for birth control pills, hung my diploma over the kitchen sink, and set about camouflaging the apartment. I covered the khaki walls with daisy contact paper, painted a Seven Sisters constellation on the bathroom ceiling, and strung a mobile of kites and balloons over the dinette table. I draped my grandmother's quilt over the couch, and at the windows I hung colored beads that rattled when an occasional civilian breeze found its way through the maze of concrete hallways that led to our third-floor unit.

The language-institute position might have been a plum, an assignment draftees would have killed for, but it was still the Army. Privates like my husband still stood inspection, still pulled 7:00 KP. And all-night guard duty, a task made all the more demeaning by the fact that they were issued shovels instead of rifles. It was a pretend war, the enlistees were constantly reminded, but to Pete it might as well have been Vietnam. Each order given, each exam, was an enemy rustling in the bushes. In sleep he thrashed at the covers, and when I reached to calm him, his chest was beaded with sweat.

Late one night I woke in an empty bed. I called Pete's name and searched the apartment, and when I looked out the window I saw him slouched inside a phone booth across the street, his boots pressed against the glass. He had left the door open to darken the booth, but the streetlight silhouetted his lean body.

One hand held the phone against his cheek; the other hand caressed the cord, his fingers running up and down its uncoiled length. Suddenly, what had encased him, the exoskeleton of phone booth and bone, of boots and jacket, fell away, and what had been invisible to me came into microscopic focus. It wriggled on the slide—blood and tissue, muscle, the soft inner membranes—a secret life pulsing on its own. I knew that he was talking to a woman.

I ran a bath and soaked until my fingertips were shriveled. Only four more months, I told myself. Then the Chinese course will be over and we'll leave for the next base, but this time I'll be with him from the first day on. And I'll be pregnant—that way, he can't leave. Until then I'll wait it out. You can survive anything for four months. I climbed out of the tub, powdered and creamed my body, combed the tangles from my hair, and sat by the space heater until my hair was silky, spilling over my folded knees like the hair of the Oriental woman in the painting my father brought back from overseas the summer I turned twelve.

An hour later, perhaps two, Pete climbed into bed. When I asked where he'd been, he turned his face to the window. I never asked again, not when he began disappearing for hours at a time, not when he stayed out all night. I put the unpacking on hold and attended to him. I would cook more of his favorite foods, steam his khakis with a cleaner pleat. This thing I was living was my life.

Even when I missed the second period, the possibility of pregnancy still didn't occur to me. I'd been sleeping fitfully, troubled by a low-grade nausea that weakened my appetite, and as a result I'd lost several pounds. Yet my body felt strangely heavier. My breasts had begun to swell, and there was a strange metallic taste in my mouth. One night I woke with a tightness in my belly, a wrenching, as if something were twisting me from the inside, a vise clamping down.

Pete stirred but did not wake as I left the bed. At the bathroom door I flicked on the light. The fluorescent tube above the sink flickered, went black, buzzed, and flickered again, coloring the room in a bluish wash. The toilet seat was cold. The vise gripped me again. I concentrated on the veins in my thighs, tracing the intricate network, and when the vise came again, I closed my eyes and pushed the pain out my mouth in rapid, nearly silent animal pants.

When I finally stood and looked down, what I saw was the size of a man's outspread hand. I watched it floating, a viscous crimson island, watched the edges peel away into strands that thinned and separated, marbling the water with pink streams, leaving only a thick dark center. Then I lifted off. My bloodied nightgown billowed, and I rose toward the ceiling where my mother and grandmother were waiting.

*What took you so long?* read the cartoon bubbles over their heads. Long fingers reached out to me, caressing the sleeves of my gown. We hung there suspended, looking down at the scene below, where a woman's hand was reaching for the chrome handle. I heard the flush and saw the water swirling in ribbons of red and pink and black, a child's pinwheel spinning dizzy circles.

A few weeks before the scheduled move, my mother arrived to help out. Boxes were stacked in the living room. The walls were bare once again. "Looks like you've got everything under control," she said brightly, but I could tell she had sensed trouble. As the hours passed she kept checking the clock; she never asked where Pete was. "You look thin" was all she said. "Are you eating enough?" She spent the evening at the Singer, altering my dresses and mending Pete's civilian clothes. I lay on the bed, comforted by the whir of the machine, the drumming regularity of the stitches. It was a rhythm as old as my first memory of her, lulling me into a safe place. I sat up on the bed.

"He's having an affair. I know who she is. He's there right now."

My mother's lips, pressed together to secure a family of straight pins, opened, and the pins scattered to the floor. I told her everything—about the dark-haired neighbor, about walking in on her and Pete in the Laundromat. I told her that the woman's husband was overseas, that I suspected it had been going on even before I'd arrived, and that now every evening when I went outside Pete was on the playground with her sons, pushing them on the swings or throwing baseballs he'd bought at the px. I said I couldn't wait another minute, that I was going to the woman's apartment to confront him, to ask him to come home.

My mother raised her hand as if hailing an invisible cab. Her index finger was cocked. Then slowly her hand drifted down. Her eyes brimmed for an instant, cleared. "Do what you need to do" is all she said. I knew the words she was holding back.

She would not have gone. Years before I'd overheard her comforting a neighbor. Women often came to my mother for help pinning up a hem or doctoring a fevered child, and one neighbor came by often, her face tight and red, the seams in her stockings a little skewed. On this particular night she was crying fitfully and loudly, the way I thought only children cried, those sobs that lift your shoulders and deepen your voice.

"What. Would. You. Do?" the woman cried, each syllable punctuated by a jerky intake of breath.

My mother's voice was even and calm. "I've never had cause to doubt him. I would swear by it."

"But. What. If. He. Did?" It's the kind of question you ask when you're desperate. What you want is for the other person to tell you it's okay, to pat your hand and say everything will be all right. My mother gave the truth, and I could tell by her tone that she meant it. I could also tell that she had considered the question more than once and the decision had been reached long before this moment. Her words flowed like water: "I'd walk out the door and never look back. The more I loved him, the faster I'd walk."

"But. What. About money? Where would you go?"

"I'd live in a shack before I'd take a penny of his money."

"But. The children."

"We'd manage."

I sat on the bed and looked across the room at my mother. Her dark eyes, lit with anger and pain, held no answers. In desperation I reached back in memory, past my mother's eyes, past her fierce pride, searching for another way to finish this, a way that would better suit me.

What I saw was Grandma Sylvie cutting off the dying dog's leg to save him. Whatever it takes, you do. Then I saw her decades before I was born, standing at the back door of the farmhouse, with two children at her side and a baby, my mother, asleep in her arms. Suitcases are stacked beside her, and she is facing my grandfather. Her words are like bullets. "Look at that woman again, and we're gone."

I don't know how long she stood there before he gave his answer. Knowing my grandmother, not long. My grandfather must have played his part well, for she never took that first step through the door, into the garage and the waiting car. The scene freezes in that moment—the suitcases, my grandmother's silent stare, my mother waking in her arms as if from a bad dream, releasing a strong, hoarse cry.

The marriage ended at the runway of a California airport where I boarded a plane to Columbia, South Carolina, my brother's city. After I'd confronted Pete with my knowledge of the other woman, we'd attempted a halfhearted reconciliation, but it soon became clear that he was not going to end the affair. "And even if I did," he said one night during dinner, "I can't promise that it won't happen again." I looked across the table at him, and the years stretched out before me. I knew I couldn't live that way. I packed my bags that night.

Once in South Carolina I underwent the initiation rites common to newly separated women. I wept, lost weight, cut my hair, found a minimum-wage job, bought a used car, rented a studio apartment. Fort Jackson was a few miles away, and over the next few months I often found myself cruising its perimeter. My half of our furniture was delivered to me courtesy of the U.S. Army. Officially, I was still a dependent and would be for another year, the grace period the Army had extended to me. Desperately close to the poverty line—I now qualified for food stamps—I told myself I could use the services. I needed groceries, I was past due for a medical exam, and my first troublesome wisdom tooth was starting to push through.

When the long-distance divorce decree arrived in the mail, I contested nothing. With one signature I swept away the previous three years, agreeing to no fault on either side. Only one remnant of the marriage remained: my military ID card, which I found, to my surprise, I did not wish to relinquish. It had taken months to mourn the marriage, the man, and the almost-child.

But my tour of duty was not over. Something yet remained, a loss that ambushed me one winter afternoon as I was driving past the base. This time my car turned, headed toward the front gate, and stopped. I pulled the ID card from my wallet and held it out to the guard. With a snappy salute he motioned me forward. It might have been any of a dozen bases I'd known. Fort Ord, Fort Belvoir, Fort Meade, Quantico, El Toro, Corpus Christi. Bases named for generals, chiefs, bulls, the bodies of lesser and greater gods. Bases so familiar I could have driven their streets in my dreams—and I had, many times since I'd left California. I'd also been dreaming my future, in dreams that took place outside the gates of the military and prefigured the circumstances of my new life—a new husband and a home on a civilian street, a marriage secure though childless, the death of my grandmother and of the farm.

Once inside the gates of Fort Jackson, it felt as natural as breathing, this tour past the barracks, the commissary, the PX, past the swimming pool and tennis courts with their tall fences, the officers' quarters and the Quonset huts. My gums were aching. The tip of the wisdom tooth had pushed through the surface, and my swollen jaw was pulsing with pain. I passed the clinic once, twice, and then circled back to the parking lot. I stopped my car and sat for a few minutes, staring at the entrance and watching the parade of soldiers and dependents. A woman emerged holding the hand of a little girl who was rubbing her upper arm (a vaccination, I suspected) and sporting an imitation medal on her shirt, some Army doctor's award for courage in battle. I'd earned the right, I told myself. Even the Army thought so—that's why they called it a grace period. I got out of the car and walked toward the clinic, tonguing the swollen gum. No question about it, the tooth would have to go.

# 29

## Pictures Don't Lie

CHERYL LAPP

The letter I hold in my hand is faded and wrinkled. I laugh at how we numbered the envelopes during the Persian Gulf War so we could read the news in chronological order. A photo slips from the envelope and falls to the floor. I pick up the grainy, color photo and smile at the naive girl I once was as I posed for Mike. *Oh, what a sad time,* I think. In the photo I'm posing on a bedspread of flowers surrounded by dusty pinks and creamy whites. I had looked into the camera lens with tear-filled eyes, with an almost dreamlike gaze. *War can do so much,* I sigh. The memory and the night when this photo image was captured open their arms to me now, and I am whisked back to October 1990. Mike had already been deployed for two months. On that night, outside Lynn's house, a light October rain had fallen, while a cold storm raged inside my heart.

I had pulled Mike's dirt-brown, two-door 1985 Oldsmobile in front of the familiar yellow rectangular ranch-style house. It was one of many houses nestled neatly in its row along the carbon-copy streets in staff quarters, military base housing in Havelock, North Carolina. The October night, barely settling down on the damp streets, failed to swallow me up as I had anticipated. I was a mess. A frightened cat, frozen with guilt, hackles up, guttural sounds echoing somewhere in my mind, yet there I sat with the engine running, seeking—something like solace or possibly a distraction from the stressful day.

I had been overwhelmed with the emotions of the past few days, and a "party" was the last thing on my mind. I wasn't sure why I had driven over to Lynn's house in the first place. Lynn had planned this "girls-only party" three weeks earlier. *Plenty of time to back out,* I had thought back then at the office. Lynn had joked that it was our own private therapeutic party. Her choice of words was intended to be humorous, because we worked in the office of a local psychologist.

We vented almost daily since her husband, Ben, and my fiancé, Mike, had deployed with the Cherry Point Marines in August for the Persian Gulf as part of Operation Desert Shield. Lynn suggested holding the party as a way for a few military wives to get together and do something special for their men. Her idea of something special was a lingerie photo shoot. Maybe I was tired of being alone, tired of waiting and wondering, or tired of making decisions. I can only guess it was a combination of dealing with Mike's business as well as my own since he'd been deployed. Mike's business included taking care of his twelve-year-old son, Joe, and cat, Boo Bas. My business included working full-time and raising three children of my own.

After days of stewing I found myself in Mike's car facing another decision. Ill-fated or not, I sat at Lynn's front curb and needed to decide what to do next. Was I gong to drive on or join the other lonely military wives gathering inside? I couldn't use my old *sitter excuse*; the sitter had arrived on time. As I toyed with the idea of driving home, the rain stopped.

I turned off the wipers and killed the engine, and as if on cue, Lynn's smiling face appeared at the front door. She was talking to someone, another wife maybe—no, certainly. I was the only single one she invited. Single. Committed. Dedicated. *Semper Fidelis* or *Always Faithful* as the Marine Corps saying goes. Who was I fooling? I was failing miserably at being good for anyone at the moment.

Home was a ten-minute drive north, but loneliness or guilt threatened to accompany me on this night of nights. *Which emotion would win me over this evening?* As I waged the debate in my head, I reached into the backseat for my bag of lingerie. The garish contents in the damp brown paper sack in the backseat reeked of guilt. I remembered Mike's last letter. He wrote that he was lonely, too, and was dreaming of holding me again. I shouldn't have felt guilty about taking a few sexy pictures to send him then. Holding the bag of lingerie, I thought of Mike and his cat. I had promised to care for Boo, and then he was gone— found him dead in my bathroom. I had to cancel the late-afternoon vet appointment. Surely a victim of some illness, Boo's health had deteriorated rapidly. *How had I had missed the signs?* As I quietly resigned to the fact that guilt would be my companion, I punched my nerves into drive and stepped out of the car.

I paused before I reached Lynn's front door. She had stepped inside, enveloped in conversation. The mood—the sounds were lighter inside, and music mixed like a tonic, pulling me closer. But I wasn't ready to laugh. *How does one prepare for this, for a lingerie party in the midst of a military conflict thousands of miles away?*

I entered the house to find Lynn's living room, though small and charming, with soft, low lights, lending a sense of coziness, which was a blanket for my edgy nerves. The ladies smiled and chattered like birds, and someone offered wine, beer, or coffee. I took a glass of red sweet wine, hoping I could survive the night, praying I would survive Mike's deployment. Aside from distressing over the cat, I worried more and more about Mike's son, Joe. He's been acting like a jerk lately—lying and sneaking out of the house at night and generally pissing me off. But this afternoon, Joe had been nothing short of amazing. He'd been surprisingly calm after discovering his dead cat lying still in my bathtub, bundling him in a green Hefty trash bag, digging the shallow grave with my one short shovel in the side yard near the maple tree, and crying with me as we covered Boo for the last time. Knowing Mike could not share this moment with us, Joe had been amazingly open to my friendship and compassion as he awkwardly let one arm pause on my shoulder.

When I arrested my thoughts I noticed other nervous smiles on unfamiliar faces, and eventually their voices danced to my ears. I sighed, forcing the breath caught in my ribs to release me. No one knew me here, except Lynn. Amid a tightly connected band of military wives, a fiancée could feel like an outcast. A fiancée of only two months, without an engagement ring, can easily be rated number one on the gossip list.

"Hey, any news from Mike?" Lynn asked, catching me along the wall between the living room and kitchen.

"Not much, really. Just that he is running the troops, doing laps on the *Iwo Jima*'s upper deck," I said. "He did say they are scheduled for two liberty calls through December. They'll be somewhere in or near Oman. You?"

"Oh, Ben's last letter was all about missing me and sex. You know how they are." She laughed, slid her glasses down with a neatly manicured nail to roll her blue eyes with maximum effect, turned, and moved gracefully down the hallway. Her strawberry-red curls bounced along her slender shoulders, and all five foot two of her almost skipped into the last room on the right.

One of the wives waiting on the couch pulled out pictures and passed around beach shots of her family summer vacation last June, and I'm transported back to then. A week after Mike and I met, we took all four kids to Fort Macon, where we climbed, played, and later picked up shells along the Atlantic Beach. My three children and I along with Mike and his son had made some good memories in the short two months we shared before he deployed. When Mike was gone I moved Joe into my house off base. I expected the kids to have a period of adjustment. My eight-year-old daughter, Michell, thought it was exciting to have an older brother figure around. The boys, John and Matt, ages six and three, respectively, seemed fine. Before Lynn's party we had a quiet dinner after talking about burying the cat. Jack, my ex-husband, called to talk with Michell, John, and Matt. Joe begged to go out with friends to ride bikes, but I had to say no. I needed him to stay close to home in case his grandpa phoned in. Joe had been trying to reach him to tell him about the cat. Besides I had a sitter coming, and I knew Joe would settle down for her, because she was older by two years.

I had rearranged two bedrooms to accommodate Joe's needs. I bunked Joe and John in one room and Michell and Matt in the second room. There had been some problems in their bedtime differences, so Joe went to bed about an hour or two after John. Of course, there had been the expected grumbling and complaining from both boys about sharing closet space, dresser drawers, when the light should be on and off, and the volume of music at night. Thank God for headphones. While we were working through these issues, I hadn't thought much about the cat.

I could understand Mike's cat, Boo, being slightly depressed over the new housing arrangements. I realized cats don't like change, and Boo had made some grand-scale adjustments with the move. I got it, but I didn't neglect him either. I fed him, vacuumed up his silky long gray hair, cleaned his litter box, stroked him when he let me, and trusted him enough to cry myself to sleep in his presence at least several times a week. This had been a privilege reserved for Boo only. I couldn't let the children see me cry. They were dealing with the recent changes in their resilient, childlike ways: arguing, crying, telling tall tales, and bouncing back. They simply survived in the way of children. On the other hand—in the world of adulthood, it seemed I had long forgotten how to play.

"Okay, ladies," Lynn blurted out as she returned to the living room smiling. "It's all set up in my bedroom. Let's see what y'all brought!"

A stone tossed into a gathering of peacocks—sudden colors ablaze in a show of alarm or even passion. In slow motion the room transformed into a pallet of color as bags of all shapes and sizes were flipped open, turned over, dumped, or tossed across the room. Giggles crescendoed, and I could smell the charge like the toxic scent of sweet liquor, as raw energy emanated from the small group of women anticipating what was to come. Sexual tensions erupted as the lonely ladies embraced the purpose of this mission, to do something special for their husbands.

Colors spun across my vision, and I didn't recognize my own laughter escaping the deep prison of my chest. I settled back on the end of the couch and anxiously unfolded the wrinkled edges of my own brown bag, dumping its contents into my lap. There it was, a neatly folded dusty-rose not-quite-sheer gown, trimmed with matching lace along the sleeves and hemline. The panties were tucked neatly within. I tilted my head forward, letting my deep red hair fall like a veil over the blush of embarrassment that burned down my neck, warmed my shoulders, and rested on my chest. But no one really noticed; no one judged; no one scolded or cheapened the moment, as I had feared.

The room had become a living, breathing garden moving in tune with the Righteous Brothers' version of "Unchained Melody," the background music for this dance of colors. Black-licorice silks flowed long like liquid coal across eager hands. Fire-red satins trapped the light and heat of the room, mingling with smoke-deep black laces mixing in the awakening excitement. Rose hot pinks, cool lavender purples, innocent azalea whites materialized in gowns, and stockings, and garters. Dove-like feathers, silver heals, and satin slippers of black and gold sparkled on the floor where they laid in expectation for the feet that would dance them down the hall and into the bedroom. And as I pulled one dark feather boa through my hands, I pictured holding Boo's tail once again. How he loved to flaunt his gray feather-like tail, inviting me to bury my fingers in its softness.

The thought of Boo's tail made me smile as I recalled the first time I met Mr. Boo. Mike had taken me to his assigned quarters, his home in base housing. It was an early warm summer evening in June. The children were out playing with their friends. Mike's shift at the MP station had ended, so he was starting his three days off, and he had one thing on his mind—sleep, with or without me. Having devoured dinner, we curled up on his ancient brown hide-a-bed and put some lame show on the television. I curled into his arms just as Mr. Boo, a blue-point Himalayan, made his regal appearance.

Flipping his tail to announce his arrival, he sprawled on the cool, bare linoleum floor in front of the TV and set his saucer-like green marble eyes on us for interrogation. He was master; we were merely party to his show.

Mike laughed in his easy way, calling out to Boo, "Hey, Boo. Come on up here and see Cheryl. She won't bite!"

I laughed and called, "Kitty, kitty." Boo peeled his eyes off mine and turned his head. Swishing his thick gray tail, he ignored me.

"Watch this," Mike said. He tossed a rolled tissue onto the floor, and I was amazed. Boo transformed immediately, leaping from regal demeanor to playful kitten, but Mike's playful kitten. The two of them had been together for years. Mike knew how to make a game of almost any inconspicuous household item, from tape, dust globs, tissues, gum wrappers, bits of dried food, or virtually any paper item. When Mike was home, the game was on.

But Mike wasn't home. I cleared the lump in my throat, chasing it with the last swig of wine in my goblet. "Cheryl," Lynn called me back to the lingerie party, "it's my turn now. Come on!" With one swoop she had me by the wrist, dragging me down the hall to the last room on the right.

"Okay, I'm going into the bathroom here to change. Just wait and check out my camera," she said. "Oh, and I am doing two outfits!" she chirped from her adjoining bath.

"I'll be right back," I called over my shoulder as I turned to head out the door. "I want some more wine."

I returned to find her there on her bed, posed among the pink magnolias blooming across her bedspread. Her black silky long gown draped like a flag around her legs startled me. Against her pale skin, it looked like death. She was curled up, holding a pillow on her lap and a teddy bear near her heart. Light-pink lip gloss freshly applied added a cherry glow to her smile, and I tried to blink away thoughts of death. She removed her glasses, and her naked blue eyes betrayed her facade of bravery. Her eyes held the sadness her smile couldn't defuse. Surrounded by the pink and white flowers on the spread, she smiled for Ben, a blossom among flowers. She held a picture of him for the next shot, blowing kisses to the framed photo of her husband, not in military uniform, but in jeans with a Calvin Klein smile. Click. The shot was done, but my hands trembled. Lynn hopped down and went into the bathroom, closing the door to change for the second set of photos, and I heard tears in her voice when she called out for a refill of wine.

"Oh, shit. Where's my bag? Where's my stuff?" I mumbled to myself as I returned to the living room. My small pile was still nestled on the floor, under the far end table where I'd left it hidden from prying, poking hands and waiting patiently for my return.

My turn. I dressed and applied my own lip gloss, ran my fingers through my shoulder-length dark-red hair, and silently wished I was as tan as some of the others waiting down the hallway. I took two small steps back from the brightly lit bathroom mirror, trying to glean a look at my reflection. For a moment I didn't recognize the person staring back at me. I was thinner, resulting from a diet of anxiety and stress. My hair—messy—would have to make do. Soft freckles dusted my face and shoulders, and my blue eyes teared against the bright lights, as red veins swelled around dark pupils. Closing in the front with a few strategically placed ties and small pink bows, the dusty-rose negligee hung loosely around my hips. It fell from my waist to the floor, sides tapering around to the back of my ankles. I was barefoot; the cold tiles kissed my feet with a longing for warmth and comfort I knew I wouldn't have this night or many nights to come.

I realized I had no props, no teddy bears, photos, or pillows of my own. So I sat on the edge of the bed and took hold of one of the four tall posters as if it were my life raft, and I held it tight. From somewhere they came—waves of tears welled up and rushed over me. I was drowning. I needed Mike home and wanted Boo alive again. Needing to reach out and touch them both, my hands gripped tighter to the wood post, turning my knuckles white. Trying to disguise my fear, I wondered, *How often did Mike do the same thing? Did the men crowded in the berthing areas on the ship talk of fears? Did they share stories or retain silence as a shield of strength?*

"Well, smile!" Lynn commanded from where she stood, pressed back against the bathroom door, pointing the lens toward me. "You can't cry! Pictures don't lie!"

Click.

It was over. I could have released the bed poster, but instead I held on, thinking of Mike. After the photo shoot I found my way back to the front room and started to pack my things. "Are you okay?" Lynn asked as she walked with me to the door. "It wasn't that bad, was it? I mean, this isn't a high-fashion lingerie magazine shoot, so relax. Mike will be so surprised," she insisted. "Call me tomorrow or we'll talk Monday at work."

My mind had drifted to a different topic. The cat. "What?" Lynn asked. "You said the cat . . . ?" she repeated. I started to laugh, softly at first, holding back what my eyes threatened to spill.

"How do I tell Mike about Boo?" I mumbled. "I don't even know what happened to him or how it happened to him." I forced the words out as a choking sensation pressed my throat, and tears licked the back of my eyes.

"Just go home and get some sleep," Lynn said.

As I turned north for the ten-minute drive home, I thought about when and if I needed to tell Mike about Boo. Maybe he didn't need to know right now.

Thinking of Mike, I wondered why he had trusted me to hold everything together. I had him, yet I didn't. We were in a relationship, yet we weren't able to talk or touch. He had trusted me to manage his files, talk to his son's teachers, drive his son to school, face the doctors, answer the questions, deal with the grandparents, answer more questions, pay the bills, and play with the cat. Now, above all else, I wondered why Mike had never mentioned Boo had a history of feline leukemia. For once I was grateful that I could not call him. I would write a letter. If I chose my words carefully, I could probably hide my anger in a controlled tone as I explained to him that his beautiful cat was dead.

# 30

# Tenuous Tethers

DAVID ABRAMS

In the summer of 2005 I was trapped in a cyclic eleven-hour workday in Baghdad, serving as a noncommissioned officer in Army Public Affairs. Day after day I cranked out press releases from my task force's headquarters building that lay within spitting distance of Saddam Hussein's former palace.

Outside and miles from where I sat, my fellow soldiers baked inside their helmets and ballistic vests, patrolling the streets, knocking on doors and politely, diplomatically, asking shriveled old ladies if they knew the last known whereabouts of their grandson, and then later kicking down doors and tossing flash-bang grenades when they confirmed the address of the "suspected insurgent."

These soldiers were as remote and unknowable to me as movie actors projected on the screens of a shopping mall cineplex. Me, I was cocooned inside the humdrum of war, just another mouse in the maze of a military headquarters. I had it good, as far as wars go: three hot meals a day, a dry place to sleep, and a comfortable desk chair. Apart from the occasional mortar landing outside in the parking lot, my environment was not all that different from the movie *Office Space*.

With the luxury of air-conditioning cooling me in my cubicle, I spent hours writing officially sanctioned dispatches about roadside-bomb attacks, discoveries of terrorist weapon caches, and laudable efforts by the U.S. Army to rebuild Iraq's crumbled infrastructure of utilities. I agonized over sentence structure and struggled to come up with new ways to say "liberated by democracy" before getting the releases approved by the military chain of command and distributed to the nearly two hundred news organizations in my e-mail address book.

The majority of editors and reporters back home in America deleted my work without even reading it. I was certain of this without having proof.

I knew my "news" was stale and lagged far behind the media's need for instant information. I was hobbled by delays in waiting for confirmation of facts to trickle in from division units and then trying to convince reluctant commanders that releasing the information would not mean a breach in security. My reports of soldiers' death and dismemberment often reached newspapers and television stations hours, even days, after the fact.

I was okay with this.

I was working my ass off in a combat zone to a useless end—yelling into a void—but I didn't take it personally. It was just a job, and I was a mere cog in a large machine whose wheels were turned by a tiny crank on someone's desk back in the Pentagon.

I toiled in the here and now and saw only as far ahead as the next coordinated attack on terrorist hideouts. This is what happens when you're isolated in the bubble of war. You get tunnel vision, the demanding taskmaster of the military collapsing the boundaries of your world until you're on a hamster wheel of work, sleep, work, sleep, work.

I often thought about taping a sign in my cubicle: "Another Day, Another Death, Another Press Release." This is also an unfortunate by-product of life inside the bubble. You get laser-focused in your cynicism, unable to see beyond the regularity of death, the daily schedule of terrorist attacks, and the molehill duties that the Army has convinced you are mountainous.

In Baghdad we were disconnected from our comfortable universe of friends, family, and fast food. News from America reached us, but it was through the wrong end of a telescope. Iowa felt as distant as Antarctica, and most days it seemed we were connected to a place called Home only by the tenuous threads of our Internet connection. We were tethered with a cord no thicker than a copper filament.

There were days when I thought the Internet was more of a curse than a blessing. Sure, we had the ability to instantly touch our families through the long reach of e-mail, but it could also distract us from the military operations at hand. Past wars never had to contend with this magnitude of attention deficit. I've often wondered if the Greatest Generation was more focused at Normandy because they weren't tweeting about the weather.

That spring and summer distractions abounded. Natalee Holloway disappeared, Terri Schiavo's feeding tube became the symbol for a movement, smoke curled up from the Vatican as another pope died, Katrina roared into New Orleans, and Michael Jackson shuffled to court in pajamas, walking as if his legs were made of glass.

None of these events had anything to do with our reality. It was a circus out there, but we were engaged in the most serious of struggles inside our bubble: trying to raise Iraq like a phoenix from the ashes.

On the same evening the pope died, sixty terrorists assaulted Abu Ghraib prison (also within pissing distance of my base), simultaneously ramming suicide car bombs at the front and rear gates, and firing grenades and AK-47s at the U.S. soldiers and Marines guarding the place. I was sitting in the forward operating base's Internet café at the time, having just gotten off shift (and gearing up for the moment, seven hours later, when I'd have to return for more of the same). I clicked and surfed, clicked and surfed, filled with longing for that foreign land, America. Tenuous threads.

I was reading a story about the sloppy breakup of Brad Pitt and Jennifer Aniston when the ground started rumbling from the attack. I barely flinched. This was just another explosion Out There, the alien landscape beyond the base's concertina wire. The next morning the pope was still dead, and the terrorists had limped home, repelled by our soldiers guarding the prison.

Because of my duties in division headquarters, I rarely left the forward operating base and was, therefore, scorned as a "Fobbit," a soldier with a marshmallow center who fiercely clung to his desk. Like the small, trembling characters in J. R. R. Tolkien's *The Hobbit*, I rarely ventured outside the safety of my shire. If the FOB was a mother's skirts, then I was pressed hard against the pleats. As a Fobbit, the attack on Abu Ghraib seemed as remote to me as the pajama-clad King of Pop. Not only was I cut off from America, but I was isolated from the very war I was supposed to be fighting.

Most days the only things keeping me in touch with other "real" soldiers were the photographs that arrived at my desk from our journalists and Combat Camera teams. I sat in my air-cooled cubicle in the palace and scrolled through what looked like stills from a horror movie. The bloodbath was happening less than five miles from where I sat, but it might as well have been Mars. My only link to reality was the photos. More tenuous threads.

*Click.*

Here's a picture of an infantry scout platoon out on patrol. The lead soldier is heading up a hill toward the cameraman, his buddies behind him scanning left and right with their M240s. The point man is covered with blood from the neck down. It looks like he's been shot in the shoulder, but still he's humping up the hill. I stare at the wet, dark magenta of the sergeant's shoulder wound, and I marvel at the apparently casual look on his face. If it were me, I know I'd be writhing on the ground screaming for my Mommy in five different languages. But this guy just has a fierce, determined look on his face as he continues to climb the hill.

*Click.*

These photos show the aftermath of a car bomb at a bus station, in which dozens of Iraqis were killed in the flash-bang of an instant. There are the usual pictures of men in long white robes and red-and-white-checked *shumagh* standing around the metal chunks of what used to be cars. Then there is a photo that stops me short: a pile of about thirty sandals, which no longer have owners, next to a puddle of purple-black blood.

*Click.*

Another day, another bomb. This one detonated at a restaurant in Sal-hiya. The public affairs officer at the scene who sent the photos said the blast killed twenty Iraqis, one of them a child. Witnesses said the suicide bomber wore a belt rigged with explosives and timed the attack for the height of the lunch hour. The first photos show the restaurant gutted by a swift, lethal fire. Part of the ceiling is gone, and hot sunshine floods the charred interior. Viscera smeared across the floor. Tables and chairs, inextricably married in a tangle of chrome legs and plastic cushions, rest against a back wall where they have been flung by the explosion. Bright packages of crackers, tins of tea, and cellophane-wrapped candy are still neatly arranged on a shelf next to a cash register, waiting for someone to come along to make a purchase. A shell-shocked man, presumably the owner, stands in a still-smoking doorway—the door is gone, thrown halfway down the block.

Fingers shaking on my computer mouse, I open the next batch of photos, labeled "The Remains of the Suicide Bomber," knowing these are not images I can ever release to the media, but needing to see them for myself. My stomach clenches as the first one pops onto my screen.

A head. Two legs that appear to sprout from his neck. A hand, fingers twisted and broken, located in the place where you'd normally find the right hip bone.

That was it. Nothing more. Everything else—skin, bone, muscle, organ—had been vaporized, a brickred mist splashed through the dust and rubble of the restaurant. The bomb rigged to his belt had subtracted more than half of the body.

In the blackened head the eyes were squeezed shut, as if in final reflex before he pulled the det cord. His feet on the ends of those neatly severed legs were turned in opposite directions—one up, one down. If you didn't know better, you might mistake his legs for arms, his feet for hands. He was a crude, meaty reassembling of parts—with those feet-hands, he looked like a child's drawing of a traffic cop, one hand saying *Stop!* and the other beckoning *Go!*

My head seemed to fill with air, swell like a balloon. I drifted a few feet above my desk, rose to bob against the ceiling. I felt even more amputated from the world around me, as neatly sliced away as one of the terrorist's limbs. To paraphrase a New Testament verse, I was in the war, but I was not of the war. In another six months, I knew I could board a plane and be home filling my mouth with fast food while I watched *Survivor* on my big-screen TV. But at that moment sitting in my office cubicle, I was untethered from both the reality of war and the surrealism of life in America. I was a real nowhere man, sitting in a real nowhere land.

# 31

# Sea Mommy

ELIZABETH "LIBBY" OBERG

I was a rebellious youth. Smart, bored, and ready to make my mark on the world, I sported a peacock-blue streak through my duck-down short hair and wore clothes more appropriate for clubbing than school—when I went. I dropped out despite my high SAT scores.

Unable to find purpose and direction, I sought out a Navy recruiter who tried hard not to laugh at me when I showed up in his office. He asked all the standard questions. No, I answered, I had never been arrested, ticketed, used drugs, or abused alcohol. (I know he didn't believe me, but honest, it was the truth.)

Then he found his excuse for keeping me out. In the late 1970s women were not permitted aboard ship in the Navy, so recruiters were limited in the number of women recruits they could sign. My recruiter, and the Navy, could afford to be choosy. You see, a man could join with a GED (general equivalency diploma); a woman needed a high school diploma.

So I got one. I simply enrolled in night school, challenged the tests for the two courses I required, and two weeks later returned to the recruiter's office with my diploma. I swear that his jaw unhinged when he saw it. I was going into the Navy, and I had not one clue as to what life would be like.

If you had told me back then that I would spend a twenty-seven-year career with the Navy, meet my husband (another sailor), and raise two children while serving, I would not have believed you. If you had told me that I would eventually reach significant rank and respect in the intelligence field, I would have laughed. I would have howled with laughter had you told me I would someday find myself standing in the sands of the Middle East. Yet this is exactly what did happen, and there, standing in the middle of the Middle East during an evening call to prayer that drifted across the sands, I would long for the family I'd left behind.

Ours had become a military family, through and through. My husband and I met in the Navy and continued our careers through to retirement together while raising our two children. I guess it should have come as no surprise, then, when both my son and my daughter chose the military lifestyle. I may have even encouraged it, God help me.

The separations were never easy. In the early years my husband deployed frequently. I remember standing on the cold pier, the wind biting and threatening to freeze the tears on the children's cheeks as we waved good-bye to Daddy on the ship until that enormous hunk of steel glided away from the pier and into the horizon. Funny, it was a cold day years later when my daughter retreated into silence and waved good-bye to me as I boarded the plane that would take me away from her for several months.

There were those times. Somalia. Grenada. Desert Storm. The bombing of the uss *Cole* and, of course, 9/11. Our kids knew the unique tension that only a military family can feel when the body counts begin. The news became *personal*. Anxiously, I'd look to the television for a glimpse of my husband or any news that might reassure me that he was safe. Before e-mail and video were commonplace communications, we could go for weeks without any communications before the mailbox would be stuffed with a packet of letters dated a month earlier. Years later my husband and I would sit huddled in front of the TV, holding our breath when breaking news announced a horrific helicopter crash involving our son's squadron, and this made me fully realize what he and his sister must have gone through during scary moments such as these—silently praying that no one was hurt, *but please, please, not my husband/wife/ mother/father.* Paybacks are hell. Now, it was our turn to suffer.

Both my husband and I were senior enlisted leaders and responsible for managing and leading a number of sailors. Dinner-table discussion was often about leadership strategy or the latest mission rumors spattered with typical griping about our seniors. The kids soaked up the military jargon and lifestyle. In our house a floor was a deck. The bathroom, the head. A mop was a swab. *Sailor* was always capitalized. A ship carried boats, but a boat couldn't carry a ship.

While Navy women weren't so numerous in those early days, I always felt at home and comfortable in uniform. That is, until I showed up at the school play or the PTA meeting in uniform after work and tried to mix with the other moms. I seemed to be a magnet for the judgment that women doled out on each other but never admitted to. Many simply kept their distance. Others were curious. I heard the whispers when my back was turned.

"I'd never put myself at risk like that—what about the kids?"

"Wonder who raises her kids when she deploys?"

And "How selfish of her."

A few felt the need to tell me directly what a terrible mother I was. Most just asked pointed questions that were meant to let me know that I was wrong to be in the military as a mom. I was wrong to leave my children. They simply couldn't imagine what would possess a woman to choose long absences from her own offspring.

And frankly, I wrestled with the same idea. As much as it tries, the military still is not exactly family friendly. By nature of its work, it never will be. My commanders often told me that the Navy did not issue my children with my seabag. When I was pregnant with my son, I became incredibly ill, for which I suffered humiliation and retaliation because I couldn't stand my normal watch hours. My "shipmates had to carry my load," and I was made to feel that my pregnancy was some kind of excuse to get out of work. Mission is always the priority, even when you promised to be in the front row at your daughter's ballet recital and she refused to go on, standing backstage and crying until you bribed her with a promise of something easier to deliver than time.

In a man's military women are still struggling to balance duty to country with duty to family. After trying to come to terms with that tug-of-war, I have decided that I don't believe there is such a thing as true balance for military mothers, just the juggling of competing emotions that threaten to crush you if you let one feeling sit too long.

When is it appropriate to put your country before your child? Always, or never? When do duty and honor outweigh the importance of parenting? On one level, I hoped that both of my children would learn that a life lived with honor, courage, and commitment was one well lived despite the challenges. I wanted them to see that helping others meant sacrifice greater than writing a check or donating the cheap canned vegetables to the food pantry. On another level, I hoped that they would be proud of me for serving rather than resenting my choices. Book me one ticket on that guilt trip.

When my daughter turned sixteen, I wasn't there for a sweet-sixteen party. I was in the Middle East, acting as the senior enlisted adviser for a forward joint services intelligence command. I missed her birthday. I missed Christmas. I missed her junior prom. Eight years later I can't shake the feeling that maybe if I had been home during those precarious teen days, I wouldn't be paralyzed with fear and guilt when breaking news and her unit name appear simultaneously on the cable news crawl.

There is a term that Navy sailors use: *sea daddy*. A sea daddy is the senior guy who takes you under his wing and teaches you the ropes. I was responsible for a hundred or so young sailors, soldiers, airmen, guardsmen, and Marines who were in desperate need of leadership, discipline, comfort, empathy, and protection. I became their "sea mommy," even though I would chew them out if I ever heard them call me that aloud. In my heart, though, I smiled when I heard it. Being a sea mommy meant that I had earned their trust. It meant that I was needed.

Someone else's son or daughter was in my charge. I not only had a duty as a military leader to protect them and send them home in one piece, but as a mother felt an obligation to do for their parents what I could not do for my own children. After all, these rough, tough boys and girls had once been smiling toddlers wobbling into their mothers' outstretched arms on first steps. They were loved unconditionally by someone out there. And I'd take a bullet for any one of them without a second thought. I'd step in and deny my own children their mother for any one of my troops. And they would do the same for me. I would cry with them when they got bad news. I'd rejoice with them when they got good news. I'd sit in a tent with a flashlight looking at the pictures of the three-month-old baby left at home by the young sergeant-mother. I'd drink a beer and cuss with the best of them. This was my military family for whom I was mom.

When my son announced that he was joining the Navy, I knew that the military would change him forever. I was also acutely aware of how difficult the Navy lifestyle was and not sure that I wanted my son to have to put up with what his father and I had put up with as we climbed the ranks. His joining meant that I would forever relinquish my right to rush to his side if he was hurt or in need. I would have to acknowledge that as a mother, I was no longer needed. Empty-nest syndrome takes on a whole new meaning when your firstborn may come into harm's way because you drove him to the recruiting station.

When it came time for my daughter to go to college, however, I had actively encouraged her to seek a military academy appointment or a Reserve Officers' Training Corps scholarship to pay for her degree. She had always expressed an interest in the military and flourished in her high school ROTC program. Smart and determined, she got an Army scholarship and thrived.

When she graduated and commissioned as a second lieutenant in the Army, I couldn't have been prouder. Or more apprehensive. I knew personally how difficult the military can be for a young, bright girl (been there, done that, got the T-shirt). My knees nearly buckled when I waved good-bye to her as she pulled out of the driveway on the way to her first duty station. My nest was now truly empty and still. Just like in the field during military operations, it's the quiet makes me nervous. Every square inch of me begged to follow her, to protect her, to advise her. I harked back to the days when I would meet the anxious parents of my troops and reassure them that I would take good care of their sons and daughters.

So here we are, my husband and I. We have surrendered our two most precious possessions to the military twice now. As children they endured absentee parents, anxiety, and constant change. As adults they have chosen to serve their country. Now there is a new generation of sea daddies and sea mommies ready to dole out advice, discipline, and, hopefully, love to my children.

And I'm grateful.

But I'm also a little jealous.

# 32

## Growing a Soldier

TONIA STACEY-GÜTTING

A ghillie suit. Funny. You teach them their ABCs, and then they find a new combination and teach it back to you.

"G-H-I-L-L-I-E," my son spells for me. "It's a Gaelic word from Scottish hunters. The frayed material and yarn make it blend in with the surroundings. I need it for sniper training. Will you help me with it? Please?"

I see my baby and the young man he is becoming at once, inseparably. His hazel eyes mirror-twin mine. Mine hold deep concern; his, growing deep conviction.

The same deep conviction in his father's eyes in 2001. I married a pastor. He had already earned his stories of being a Marine embassy guard before I met him. And though he occasionally spoke of going active duty, I said it was all fun and games until there was a war. My family stories were mostly of farmers who stayed behind to feed the nation's soldiers. But the confused, grainy images of planes and towers in a distant land on a friend's TV in bush Alaska spurred my man in a way I hadn't seen before. Please help me understand, I asked him then, when we're in a safe, quiet corner of the world with baby boys to raise, why step back up to the front line now?

*Because someone needs to be with those soldiers as they face hell,* he had said, *and because no one comes in my backyard, gives me a black eye, and gets away with it.*

And so with a prayer and my husband's signature, I became an Army wife, my boys a soldier's sons. Within months he said yes to a phone call to join the first Stryker brigade from Fort Lewis, Washington, deploying to Iraq.

"The American military is a warrior culture embedded within a civilian society," Steven Pressfield puts forth in *Warrior Ethos*. Less than 2 percent of us know much about it.

But I learned quickly. I learned that George Orwell wrote, "People sleep peaceably in their beds at night only because rough men stand ready to do violence on their behalf." While my gut churned with *Why mine?* my eyebrows lifted with *Yes, mine does your dirty work.* I heard the battle cry of a thousand warriors and learned how it sears your soul. I learned that pride of knowing we are the biggest, baddest boys on the block. I learned, and survived, that dead horror of driving your lover in the middle of the night to his deployment pickup, wondering if you were taking him to his execution. I learned the spouses' strength, too, as we built playgrounds, bought and sold houses, figured out repairs, turned off the news, turned to our children with a smile. I learned to be strong for my soldier in the insane charade when he's being strong for me. I learned the order of service in a military funeral. And our children learned it, too.

But it's one thing to send your husband to war. You can't control him. You have confidence in his ability. You are not responsible for protecting him. It's another to offer up your son.

As my boy marches off after his daddy, I backtrack. Maybe while strapping on his mite hockey gear, I should have cooed like another mother, "Here you go, sweet pea." Instead, I roared from the stands, "Be aggressive! Fight for it!" Maybe I should have taken away their toy guns, made them play golf, drugged them up to calm them down, downplayed their father's courage and capability and honor. Maybe I should have interfered instead of telling them to defend themselves. Maybe we should have read more fairy tales and less history.

Maybe I shouldn't be cutting out this ghillie suit for his role-play.

But no. Not only am I the one kissing my husband good-bye for months at a time, but I am the one raising my child to take that full thirty-six-inch step forward to volunteer for the nation's service.

So I sit with needle and threads of cotton to defend my little boy by hiding him in the reeds. I join the thousands of generations of mothers of soldiers sewing coverings, shining metal, slipping notes of love and baked food into the pockets.

And desperately searching for another way. Could we send out our best ten men and they theirs, living with whatever the matchup decided? Anyone for a game of chess? Yeah, right. Can we discuss and compromise and let live? We've been trying that for centuries.

The more enlightened we get, the more enlightened ways we find to kill each other. Those with no conviction die to those who live with conviction.

"War is an ugly thing, but not the ugliest of things," said British philosopher John Stewart Mill. "The decayed and degraded state of moral and patriotic feeling which thinks that nothing is worth war is much worse. The person who has nothing for which he is willing to fight, nothing which is more important than his own personal safety, is a miserable creature and has no chance of being free unless made and kept so by the exertions of better men than himself."

My thoughts and vision blur as I wrestle with frayed loops of yarn on the back of the ghillie suit. Couldn't I please go for my son? I prick my finger on the pointed needle pushed through the camo. What kind of a man would let his mother fight for him? Neither of us would respect that character. So am I really closer to the samurai mother who smiled when she heard her son died with dignity?

Garrison Keillor said no war was without controversy. I guess the cause seems just until it's your child marching out the door.

What absurd gluttony to even be thinking these thoughts. Most women of the world's history had no choice. Their men went to war, or they all died. Their choice, my choice, was denial, refusal, or simple gratitude and pride.

I tie the final knot on the ghillie suit.

My thoughts are cornered. They coil and strike: in creating the kind of man I want my son to be, I am signing his future enlistment papers. Please God, not his death certificate.

The infamous Spartan 300 weren't chosen for their strength. They were chosen for their mothers. So goes the theory Pressfield tells. If the mothers caved at the inevitable death of their sons, all would be lost in the war for the whole society.

"The warrior ethos . . . rests on the will and resolve of mothers and wives and daughters—and in no few instances, of female warriors as well—to defend their children, their home soil and the values of their culture," said Pressfield.

*Faith.*
*Family.*

*Freedom.*

*Some things are worth fighting for. Most never will.*

So reads the tattooed forearm of a young soldier who was eating dinner at my table one evening.

I step up to my boy and strap on the ghillie suit, checking it for any weakness. I meet his eyes and say with the spirit of the Spartan woman, "Come back with your shield, or on it."

# Contributors

**David Abrams** is the author of *Fobbit*, a comedy about the Iraq War that *Publishers Weekly* has described as "an instant classic" and named a Top 10 Pick for Literary Fiction in the fall of 2012. *Fobbit* was also a *New York Times* Notable Book of 2012, an Indie Next Pick, a Barnes & Noble Discover Great New Writers Selection, a Montana Honor Book, and a finalist for the *LA Times*'s Art Seidenbaum Award for First Fiction. One of his stories also appears in *Fire and Forget* (2013), an anthology of short fiction about the wars in Iraq and Afghanistan. His short stories have appeared in *Esquire, Narrative, Salon, Salamander*, the *Connecticut Review*, the *Greensboro Review, Consequence*, and many other publications. He earned a BA in English from the University of Oregon and an MFA in creative writing from the University of Alaska–Fairbanks. He now lives in Butte, Montana, with his wife. Abrams retired in 2008 after a twenty-year career in the active-duty Army as a journalist. He was named the Department of Defense's Military Journalist of the Year in 1994 and received several other military commendations throughout his career. His tours of duty took him to Thailand, Japan, Africa, Alaska, Texas, Georgia, and the Pentagon. In 2005 he joined the 3rd Infantry Division and deployed to Baghdad in support of Operation Iraqi Freedom.

**Carol Everett Adams**'s essays have been published in the *Journal of Ethics and Information Technology* and the *Journal of the Society for Philosophy in the Contemporary World*. Her poems have appeared in *CAIRN: The St. Andrews Review*, the *Carquinez Poetry Review*, the *MacGuffin*, the *New York Quarterly*, the *Owen Wister Review, Soundings East*, the *Quercus Review*, and others. Adams works as a technical writer at a software company in the Kansas City area. She is earning an MFA in writing from the University of Nebraska and raising two young children and a spoiled dog.

**Linda Adams** is a former enlisted soldier who, she insists, was least likely to have joined the Army. Adams served during the first Persian Gulf War, when it was still strange and new for women to be at war. She has published short stories in *Enchanted Spark* and *Fabula Argentea* and is working on a contemporary fantasy/action-adventure novel. You can visit her blog, *Soldier, Storyteller,* at http://garridon.wordpress.com/.

**Caleb S. Cage** was appointed executive director of the Nevada Office of Veterans Services by Governor Brian Sandoval. Cage is a veteran of the U.S. Army, serving from 2002 until 2007. Born and raised in Reno, Nevada, he attended the U.S. Military Academy, West Point, where he studied American history. Upon graduation in 2002, he was commissioned as a field artillery officer and was assigned to the 1st Infantry Division in Bamberg, Germany, for a three-year tour. During this period he served as a company executive officer and later as a motorized rifle platoon leader in the city of Baqubah, Iraq. Less than a year after returning to Germany, he received orders to return to Iraq. His second deployment was to Baghdad in support of Operation Iraqi Freedom IV, where he served as an information operations officer for Multinational Corps–Iraq. Before this appointment to Veterans Services, Cage served as senior policy adviser for rural and veterans issues for the Nevada lieutenant governor.

**Tracy Crow** is a former Marine Corps officer and an award-winning military journalist. Her essays and short stories have appeared in a number of literary journals and been nominated for three Pushcart Prizes. She is the author of *Eyes Right: Confessions from a Woman Marine* (University of Nebraska Press, 2012). Under the pen name Carver Greene, Crow published the conspiracy thriller *An Unlawful Order,* the first in a new series to feature a military heroine.

**Max "Joe" Dalton** served a little more than two years in the Navy. He was stationed in several places: Jacksonville, Florida, and San Diego, Monterey, and San Pedro, California. While in San Pedro, he went aboard the aircraft carrier uss *Bennington,* assigned to squadron vc 11. His first port was Honolulu before heading out to sea. Prior to being discharged, he went through the Panama Canal and up to Norfolk. Shortly thereafter, the USS *Bennington* was decommissioned. After his military duty Dalton was hired at Hill Air Force Base and went to mechanic training school at Utah State University in Logan. He continued working at Hill Air Force Base in many different areas before he retired after thirty-three years. Dalton studied accounting at Weber State University while working at Hill and opened Dalton Bookkeeping along with his wife, Bev, after retirement. For twenty-five years he prepared taxes for Ogden and Coalville, Utah, senior citizens on a pro bono basis. Max "Joe" Dalton and Bev were married for sixty-one years and nine months.

**Dario DiBattista** served in the U.S. Marine Corps Reserve from 2001 to 2007. A distinguished graduate of the Johns Hopkins University Masters in Writing Program, his work has been featured in the *Washingtonian, New York Times, Washington Post, Connecticut Review,* and many other places. Additionally, he has been profiled in the *New York Times* and other places and has been a commentator on National Public Radio. His editing projects include *20 Something Magazine, O-Dark-Thirty,* and *jmww.* He lives in Towson, Maryland, and teaches as an instructor for the Veterans Writing Project and as an adjunct professor for the Community College of Baltimore County. He is seeking publication of his book manuscripts, "Go Now, You Are Forgiven: A Memoir of Love, War, and Coming Home" and "The Contagion: A Novel."

University of Virginia undergraduate **Matt Farwell** is an accomplished writer whose account of being a twenty-seven-year-old homeless veteran was published by the *New York Times* in October 2011. An independent journalist, he has published his work in the *New York Times* and *Rolling Stone.* Farwell was a soldier in the U.S. Army from 2005 to 2010. After infantry and airborne training at Fort Benning, Georgia, he was assigned to the Tenth Mountain Division's Second Battalion, 87th Infantry Regiment, and deployed to Afghanistan for sixteen months. Before enlisting he studied government and history at the University of Virginia as an Echols Scholar and graduated from the United World College of the American West as a Davis Scholar.

**Leah Hampton** is the 2012 recipient of the Doris Betts Prize for Short Fiction. She is a former technical writer and English teacher, and her work has appeared in the *North Carolina Literary Review, Wallace Stevens Journal,* and elsewhere. She currently teaches at A-B Tech College in Asheville, North Carolina, and plans to pursue an MFA in creative writing.

**Jeffery Hess** is the editor of the award-winning anthology *Home of the Brave: Stories in Uniform* and the recently released follow-up, *Home of the Brave: Somewhere in the Sand.* He holds an MFA in creative writing from Queens University of Charlotte, and his writing has appeared in *Midway Journal, O-Dark-Thirty, r.k.v.r.y.,* and *Prime Number,* among others. He served aboard the Navy's oldest and newest ships and has held writing positions at a daily newspaper, a Fortune 500 company, and a university-based research center. He currently lives in Florida, where he leads the DD-214 Writers' Workshop for military veterans and is completing a novel.

**Beverly A. Jackson** writes memoir, fiction, and poetry and currently lives in Naples, Florida. Her work has appeared in more than seventy venues in both online and print literary journals. Her poetry chapbook *Every Burning Thing* was published in 2008. She is the founder and former editor in chief of Lit Pot Press and the online journal *Ink Pot* from 1999 to 2006. Her flash fiction "The Dead" was nominated for a BASS (Best American Short Story) award. She also paints and trades stock options in her free time. For more information, visit her website at http://www.beverlyajackson.com.

Durham, North Carolina, native **Ronald Jackson** has been writing professionally for twenty-seven years. His career includes stints as a sports feature writer for a Philadelphia weekly, marketing writer, science writer, ghostwriter for trade journal articles, web copywriter, executive speechwriter, and ghost blogger for executives, high-tech companies, and psychotherapy practices. In 1996 a trade article of his won a Bell South annual award for journal placements. He served in the U.S. Air Force from 1966 to 1970, working in radio transmission and radar. He was based in the Philippines, with two lengthy temporary tours in Thailand. Jackson earned a BA in English literature from Temple University and studied English literature and the teaching of college composition at the graduate level for four years at Temple. He also taught composition and literature as an adjunct instructor. In 2009 he turned his full attention to his lifetime love—creative writing—and is now writing fiction, nonfiction, and poetry. His first published story, "The Shower," appeared in the *North Carolina Literary Review* (2013 online edition). "Letter to a Drowning Sailor" is his first nonfiction publication. Jackson reads his poetry regularly at open mics in the Research Triangle area of North Carolina. His first published poem is scheduled for inclusion in the *Iodine Poetry Journal* (Spring 2014). He is currently working on a crime novel set in his hometown of Philadelphia and a collection of stories, all military related and North Carolina based, spanning the period from the Revolutionary War to the present. He has three children and four grandchildren spread across the country, whom he would love to see much more often. After twenty-one years of residence, Jackson has claimed North Carolina as his home state and plans to always return home to Durham at the end of his travels.

**Amber Jensen**'s essays and poetry have appeared in print in *North Dakota Quarterly* and *Ellipsis* and online in the *Fertile Source, Gently Read Literature, Assisi,* and *Terrain.org.*

**Alan Jones** grew up in Lawrence, Kansas. Under the threat of being drafted, he joined the Air Force in December 1951 and eight months later applied for aviation cadets. That training took him to Arizona, Texas, and Nevada, and in 1954 he was assigned to the 388th Fighter Bomber Wing at Clovis, New Mexico. The wing was preparing to fly its aircraft to Europe to become part of the NATO deterrent. Flying the great-circle route in autumn and midwinter took the wing three months to complete the move and cost it two aircraft and one pilot. Over the next two years, the pilots requalified in air-to-air gunnery, air-to-ground gunnery and bombing, and toss-bombing with tactical nuclear weapons. The mission, according to Jones, had it come to that, was to obliterate Eastern European rail yards, bridges, factories, and choke points of all sorts to stem the Soviet tide. Since leaving the Air Force, Jones earned a degree in journalism and worked for a number of daily papers in Kansas and California. He married in 1966 and had two children (Kevin Jones is a contributor here). Jones became an information officer for the state of California, retiring after twenty years with the Department of Water Resources. He has also worked as an external affairs officer for the Federal Emergency Management Agency, doing postdisaster work in fifteen to twenty states, following hurricanes, floods, ice storms, earthquakes, and the like. He and his wife, Kati, live in Pioneer, California, in a place he calls "not quite a town strung out along California Highway 88 in the Sierra at about 3,500 feet elevation—too high for foothills, but not quite the mountains."

**Kevin C. Jones** is a Marine Corps and Army National Guard veteran who served as an infantry noncommissioned officer for eleven years, including service in Operation Desert Storm. His work has been featured in the *New York Times, Ink Pot, r.k.v.r.y, Prime Number, Monkeybicycle,* the *Cobalt Review, Atticus Review, O-Dark-Thirty,* and the anthologies *Home of the Brave: Stories in Uniform, Home of the Brave: Somewhere in the Sand,* and *Boomtown: Explosive Writing from Ten Years of the Queens University of Charlotte MFA Program.* Jones is a father to four daughters and lives on Florida's Gulf Coast, where he teaches writing and literature.

**Jon Kerstetter** practiced as an emergency doctor and U.S. Army flight surgeon. He obtained his MD degree from the Mayo Medical School in Rochester, Minnesota. He also holds an MS in business from the University of Utah and an MFA in creative nonfiction at Ashland University in Ashland, Ohio. Dr. Kerstetter was the in-country director of the Johns Hopkins Program in Emergency Medicine in Kosovo. He provided humanitarian medical care in the conflicts in Rwanda, Bosnia, and Kosovo and in the hurricane disaster in Honduras. He joined the Iowa Army National Guard in 1994. During his military service he completed three tours of duty in Iraq as a combat physician. He retired from the military in 2009. "Triage" was first published in *River Teeth: A Journal of Nonfiction Narrative* (2012). It was also selected for reprint in *Best American Essays, 2013.*

**Tracy Kidder** graduated from Harvard and studied at the University of Iowa. He has won the Pulitzer Prize, the National Book Award, the Robert F. Kennedy Award, and many other literary prizes. Kidder is the author of *Mountains beyond Mountains, Strength in What Remains, My Detachment, Home Town, Old Friends, Among Schoolchildren, House,* and *The Soul of a New Machine.* His most recent published work is

*Good Prose: The Art of Nonfiction*, which he coauthored with his long-time editor, Richard Todd.

**Brooke King** served in the U.S. Army, deploying to Iraq in 2006 as a wheel vehicle mechanic, machine gunner, and recovery specialist. As a wife to a fellow veteran and mother to twin boys who were conceived in Iraq, King began writing down her unique experience as a way to cope with PTSD, but found that her writing ability, along with her combat experience, gave her a distinct voice within the war genre. Since obtaining her bachelor's degree from Saint Leo University, King has refocused her writing, bringing perspective and insight into the involvement of female soldiers in combat and war. Her work has been published in the *Sandhill Review* and the fiction war anthology *Home of the Brave: Somewhere in the Sand* and *Prairie Schooner's* winter 2013 literary magazine. Her chapbook *Love in the Shape of a War Zone* was released in 2013. Currently, King is attending Sierra Nevada College's master of fine arts program and is working on her first novel.

**Cheryl Lapp** received her MEd from the University of Mary Washington in Fredericksburg, Virginia, and her MFA in creative writing and nonfiction from Ashland University in Ohio. She currently resides in Ohio with her family, where she teaches, writes, and is a reader for *River Teeth: A Journal of Nonfiction Narrative* at Ashland University. She is currently working on her memoir about the Gulf War.

The author of the award-winning book *Gated Grief: The Daughter of a GI Concentration Camp Liberator Discovers a Legacy of Trauma*, **Leila Levinson** is an advocate for veterans and their families and an expert on transgenerational trauma. She has appeared on CNN, is a regular contributing blogger for *Huffington Post*, and has written for the *Washington Post*, the *Austin American Statesman*, the *Texas Observer*, *WWII Quarterly*, *CrossCurrents*, and *War, Literature, and Art*. As well as teaching at St. Edward's University, Levinson leads writing workshops for veterans and their families in central Texas.

**Lorrie Lykins** is a longtime correspondent with the *Tampa Bay Times* and an adjunct professor at Eckerd College in St. Petersburg, Florida. Her essay "Dive Bar" (*Prime Number Magazine*) was nominated for a Pushcart Prize in 2012.

**Rebecca McClanahan**'s tenth book is *The Tribal Knot: A Memoir of Family, Community, and a Century of Change*. She has also published five books of poetry and a suite of essays, *The Riddle Song, and Other Rememberings*, winner of the Glasgow Prize in Nonfiction. Her three books of writing instruction include *Word Painting: A Guide to Writing More Descriptively*, which is used as a text in numerous writing programs.

**Gerardo Mena** is a decorated Iraqi Freedom veteran who spent six years in special ops with the Recon Marines. Mena now writes and teaches high school English in Missouri. He has won national poetry contests, has been nominated for two Pushcarts, and was included in *Best New Poets, 2011*. His work has been published, or is forthcoming, in the *New York Times, Ninth Letter, Cream City Review*, and *Raleigh Review*, among others. For more information, you can visit his website at http://www.gerardomena.com.

**Donald Morrill** is the author of four books of nonfiction, *Impetuous Sleeper, The Untouched Minutes* (River Teeth Nonfiction Prize), *Sounding for Cool* (American Library Association/AAUP "Best of the Presses" Award), and *A Stranger's Neighborhood*. He is also the author of two volumes of poetry, *At the Bottom of the Sky* and *With Your Back to Half the Day*. Morrill is the associate dean of graduate studies at the University of Tampa in Florida and teaches in Tampa's MFA low-residency program.

**Alejandro Mujica** is a graduate of the University of Central Florida's MFA program in creative writing. He has interned for the UCF-run *Cypress Dome* literary journal and the *Florida Review*, for which he served as the assistant editor. He is the cofounder of the Student Veterans Association of Central Florida and its former director of public relations. His work can be read in *District* and *Burrow Press*. He is currently working on his memoir, which revolves around his experiences in the Marine Corps as a wartime military police officer. Alejandro and his wife are currently living in Fort Worth, Texas, and are searching for the right pair of cowboy boots.

**Anne Visser** Ney is a fourth-term MFA student (creative nonfiction and fiction) at the Vermont College of Fine Arts. She holds a BS and MS in biology from Georgia Southern University and a BA in creative writing from Eckerd College. Her essays have appeared in *Rosebud*, the *Sun*

(Readers Write), the *Eckerd Review*, and other print and electronic venues. Her writing has earned awards from the National Association of Institutions for Military Education Services, the Southeastern Writers' Association, and the Vermont College of Fine Arts. She retired from the U.S. Coast Guard Reserve as a BOSN-4 in 2010 after serving sixteen years on active duty and fifteen years as a drilling reservist. She resides with her husband, Peter, in St. Petersburg, Florida.

**Thomas Vincent Nowaczyk** was born and raised on the South Side of Chicago and dropped out of high school in his senior year to join the U.S. Marines. He served on active duty from February 1976 to December 1986 as both an infantryman and an award-winning military journalist. He is a graduate of the Basic Broadcaster Course (with honors) and the Electronic Journalism Course from the Defense Information School, Fort Harrison, Indiana. He also holds a bachelor of arts degree in humanities from Shimer College, Chicago, and studied British literature in Oxford. His work as a military journalist earned him a Department of Defense Thomas Jefferson Award for Professional Excellence, a Distinguished Performance Award from the Combat Correspondents Association, and several other honors. He currently lives in San Francisco with two Harley Davidson motorcycles and a Martin guitar.

**Elizabeth "Libby" Oberg** is a speaker, leadership trainer, life coach, and author. She works with veterans and the businesses that hire them to make the transition from military to corporate a positive one. Visit her website at http://www.maketheconnectioncoach.com. Oberg lives in Florida with her husband, Dan, and two four-legged children. Their son, daughter-in law, and granddaughter reside in Connecticut. Their daughter is still serving proudly in the U.S. Army.

**Christal Presley** received her bachelor's degree in English and her master's degree in English education from Virginia Tech. She has a PhD in education and is a former intern at Algonquin Books of Chapel Hill, North Carolina. She spent seven years teaching middle and high school English in Chatham and Danville, Virginia. Her first book, *Thirty Days with My Father: Finding Peace from Wartime PTSD*, was published in 2012.

**Kathleen M. Rodgers**'s work has appeared in *Family Circle Magazine*, *Air Force, Army and Navy Times, Family: The Magazine for Military*

*Families*, *Fort Worth Star-Telegram*, *Albuquerque Journal*, *Clovis News Journal*, and the following anthologies: *Because I Fly*, *Lessons from Our Children*, and *Home of the Brave: Somewhere in the Sand*. Her debut novel, *The Final Salute*, was released in paperback in 2008. In 2009 the Army Wife Network selected her novel as their July book-club pick, and the Military Writers Society of America awarded it a Silver Medal. In 2010 *USA Today*, the Associated Press, and *Military Times* ran stories about her sixteen-year journey to bring the novel to life. She is currently seeking a publisher for her second novel, "Johnnie Come Lately," a story about infidelity, the fallout of war, and eating disorders. Rodgers is the mother of two grown sons, Thomas (an award-winning artist) and J.P. (a first lieutenant in the Army). She lives in Colleyville, Texas, with her husband, Tom, a retired fighter pilot and commercial pilot, and the memories of their beloved chocolate lab, Bubba, who went to heaven a few days ahead of the author's dad. Please visit the author's website at http://www.kathleenmrodgers.com.

**Tonia Stacey-Gütting** is an Army wife currently stationed at Fort Drum, New York, where she and her husband are raising three Army brats. Chaplain (Major) Gütting will be with the last of the 10th Mountain Division warriors in Afghanistan. Tonia has a BA in writing from Bethel College, Minnesota. As a freelance writer she has been published by several magazines.

Having been raised as an Army brat, **Stephen Wilson** now lives with his wife, Anna, in Durham, North Carolina. They have two grown children and four nearly grown grandchildren. He holds a bachelor's degree in English from Berea College in Berea, Kentucky, and a master of forestry degree from Duke University in Durham. This essay is his first published work. He is a retired professional land surveyor, having founded and managed Freehold Land Surveys, in Carrboro, North Carolina, from February 1974 to the end of 1999, when he and Anna moved to Ho Chi Minh City, Vietnam. They spent 2000 and half of 2002 in Vietnam, teaching the English language and American history, living with the Vietnamese, and trying to learn their language. During the Vietnam War Wilson served as the executive officer on the USCGC *Port Grace*, operating on the western and southern coasts of Vietnam and in the rivers of the lower Mekong Delta. In the second half of his combat tour, he served as the communications liaison officer aboard a former American cutter now operating as part of the Navy of the Republic of Vietnam. He was the only American on board with a crew of seventeen Vietnamese officers and men. In December 1969 he returned from Vietnam and was released from active duty.

**Kim Wright** is the author of the critically acclaimed novel *Love in Mid Air* and the forthcoming novel *An Unexpected Waltz*, which will be published in June 2014. She is also the author of the best-selling historical series *City of Mystery*, which chronicles the adventures of the first forensics unit in Scotland Yard. She lives in Charlotte, North Carolina, where (somewhat like her father) she is a wine aficionado and (completely unlike her father) a competitive ballroom dancer.

# Source Acknowledgments

Chapter 1, "Welcome to Afghanistan" by Matt Farwell, originally appeared in *Fourth Genre: Explorations in Nonfiction*, 6th ed. (2011).

Chapter 3, "Remembering Forgotten Fliers, Their Survivors" by Kathleen M. Rodgers, was originally published in *Air Force Times*, March 16, 1992.

Chapter 9, "The Thirty-Day Project" by Christal Presley, is excerpted from *Thirty Days with My Father: Finding Peace from Wartime PTSD* (2012).

Chapter 12, "The Wing Shed" by Beverly A. Jackson, originally appeared in *Prime Number Magazine*.

Chapter 13, "Triage" by Jon Kerstetter, originally appeared in *River Teeth: A Journal of Nonfiction Narrative* 13, no. 2 (2012): 61–70.

Chapter 22, "War Stories" by Tracy Kidder, is excerpted from *My Detachment: A Memoir* by Tracy Kidder, copyright © 2005 by John Tracy Kidder. Used by permission of Random House, an imprint and division of Random House LLC. All rights reserved. *My Detachment: A Memoir* by Tracy Kidder, copyright © 2005 by Tracy Kidder, originally appeared in *Parade* (April 2, 2005). Reprinted by permission of Georges Borchardt, Inc., on behalf of the author.

Chapter 28, "Dependent" by Rebecca McClanahan, originally appeared in *Creative Nonfiction* (1998) and is excerpted from *The Riddle Song, and Other Rememberings* (2002).